THE
CHRISTIAN
COMBAT MANUAL

**Helps for Defending your Faith:
A Handbook for Practical Apologetics**

Mio Baptist is pleased to present this book as part of our mission to provide resources that will help people grow spiritually. Please note that Mio Baptist may not completely endorse the contents of this book. Each book we offer is carefully considered by our staff and chosen because of its overall message or impact. Though an author may utilize other versions of the Scriptures, we use the *King James Version* for all of our preaching, counseling, and teaching. We encourage every reader to read with discernment and to compare everything to the Scriptures, the only book we can depend on to be without errors.

THE
CHRISTIAN
COMBAT MANUAL

Helps for Defending your Faith:
A Handbook for Practical Apologetics

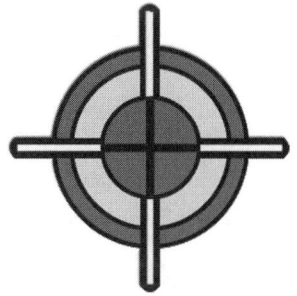

DAN STORY

God's Word to you is our highest calling.

The Christian Combat Manual: Helps for Defending Your Faith
Copyright © 2007 by Dan Story
Published by AMG Publishers
6815 Shallowford Rd.
Chattanooga, Tennessee 37421

All rights reserved. Except for brief quotations in printed reviews, no part of this publication may be reproduced, stored in a retrieval system, or transmitted in any form or by any means (printed, written, photocopied, visual electronic, audio, or otherwise) without the prior permission of the publisher.

All Scripture quotations, unless otherwise noted, are taken from the NEW AMERICAN STANDARD BIBLE,® copyright © 1960, 1962, 1963, 1968, 1971, 1972, 1973, 1975, 1977, 1995 by the Lockman Foundation. Used by permission. All rights reserved. (www.Lockman.org)

Scripture quotations marked (NIV) are taken from the HOLY BIBLE, NEW INTERNATIONAL VERSION®. NIV®. Copyright ©1973, 1978, 1984 by International Bible Society. Used by permission of Zondervan Publishing House. All rights reserved.

Scripture quotations marked (KJV) are taken from The Holy Bible, *King James Version.*

ISBN: 978-089957037-2

First printing—January 2007

Cover designed by Daryle Beam, Chattanooga, Tennessee

Interior design and typesetting by Reider Publishing Services, West Hollywood, California

Edited and Proofread by Stephen Sorenson, Dan Penwell, Georgia Varozza, and Rick Steele

Printed in Canada
13 12 11 10 09 08 07–T– 8 7 6 5 4 3 2 1

Library of Congress Cataloging-in-Publication Data

Story, Dan, 1945-
  The Christian combat manual : helps for defending your faith / by Dan Story.
      p. cm.
  Summary: "As a religious and ethical worldview, Christianity has been under siege for well over one hundred years. Today it has been shoved off center stage as the guiding moral and spiritual light in America. This book helps Christians respond positively to their faith and the criticism aimed at Christianity"--Provided by publisher.
  Includes bibliographical references.
  ISBN 978-0-89957-037-2 (pbk. : alk. paper)
 1. Apologetics. I. Title.

BT1103.S76 2007
239--dc22
                    2006039311

I dedicate this book with love and gratefulness to my son Damon. Your business acumen and commitment allows me to write and teach full time. You have played an important role in the success of my ministry.

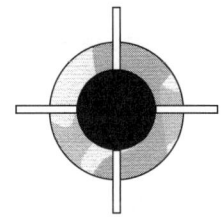

Contents

Acknowledgments — xi
Introduction — xiii

1. Apologetics: Evangelizing the Tough Minded — 1
2. Apologetics: Taking the Offense — 9

PART ONE
Establishing the Truth and Reliability of the Bible

Introduction to Part One — 21
3. The Bible's Unity and Consistency Proves Supernatural Authorship — 24
4. Eyewitness Testimony: Legal Evidence — 27
5. Textual Reliability: A Nearly Perfect Manuscript — 30
6. Historical Accuracy: Built on Archaeological Testimony — 42
7. Scientific Accuracy: No Myths or Inaccuracies — 48
8. Prophetic Accuracy: Incredible Odds — 50
9. Subjective Confirmation: Christianity "Works!" — 57

PART TWO
Creation or Evolution? Let the Scientific Evidence Speak for Itself

Introduction to Part Two	63
10. Preliminary Observations: Facts that Crack the Evolutionary Wall	65
11. How Can Something Come from Nothing?	75
12. How Can Order Evolve from Disorder?	83
13. How Can Life Emerge from Non-Life?	95
14. Where Are the Transitional Fossils?	98
15. Fakes, Frauds, and Other Phonies	114

PART THREE
We Can Demonstrate to Atheists That God Exists

Introduction to Part Three	129
16. God Has Placed Eternity in Our Hearts	131
17. Nature Demands a Creator	137
18. Moral Law Demands a Creator	140
19. The Cosmos Demands a Creator	148
20. Why Do Bad Things Happen to Good People? (The Problem of Evil)	156

PART FOUR
Jesus Christ: Man of History or Man of Myth?

Introduction to Part Four	169
21. Jesus: Historical, Fabrication, or Myth?	172
22. The Trinity: Fingerprint of Jesus Christ	182
23. Did Jesus Claim to be God?	188
24. Resurrection: Fraud, Fantasy, or Fact	198
25. Do People Go to Hell Who Never Heard of Jesus?	214

PART FIVE
Modern Issues: The World Beyond the Church

Introduction to Part Five	227
26. Naturalism: The Collapse of Christian Dominance	230
27. Postmodernism: Moral Relativism, Religious Pluralism, and the New Tolerance	243
28. Postmodern Police: Multiculturalism and Political Correctness	257
29. Apologetics to Postmodernism: Refuting Secular Beliefs and Morals	263
Appendix: Practice Socratic Responses	283

Previous titles by Dan Story

    Defending Your Faith, Kregel Publishing

    Christianity on the Offense, Kregel Publishing

    Engaging the Closed Minded, Kregel Publishing

    Fifteen apologetic booklets, Joy Publishing

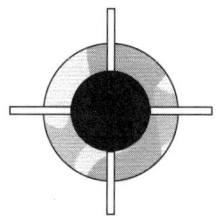

ACKNOWLEDGMENTS

DURING THE two years it took to write this book, I remarked several times to family and friends that the *Christian Combat Manual* is my apologetic magnum opus—perhaps the best apologetic book I will ever write. But it would be misleading for me to take all the credit. Any book with extensive research is a product of dozens, even hundreds, of authors. Your names are listed throughout the text and footnotes, and I thank all of you.

On the creative side, I wish to thank my editors, Dan Penwell at AMG Publishers, Stephen Sorenson, and Georgia Varozza. It has been a humbling experience working with such professionals, and what you taught me will be of immense value in future projects. Dan, your frequent emails—keeping me up to date and encouraging me along the way—have been greatly appreciated. Finally, I want to thank my wife and best friend, Lisa, for her continual support in all areas of my ministry. God bless all of you.

I am also thankful to the following companies and authors who allowed me to quote extensively from their printed books:

William D. Watkins, *The New Absolutes* (Minneapolis: Bethany House Publishers, 1996). Used by permission of Bethany House/Baker Books. All rights reserved.

Norman L. Geisler and Paul K. Hoffman, ed., *Why I Am a Christian: Leading Thinkers Explain Why They Believe* (Grand Rapids: Baker Books, 2001). Used by permission of Baker Books. All rights reserved.

Hugh Ross, *The Creator and the Cosmos; How the Greatest Scientific Discoveries of the Century Reveal God* (Colorado Springs: NavPress, 1993). Used by permission of NavPress/Pinon Press. All rights reserved.

Jonathan Wells, *Icons of Evolution: Science or Myth.* Copyright © 2000. Published by Regnery Publishing, Inc. All rights reserved. Reprinted by special permission of Regnery Publishing Inc., Washington, D.C.

Philip Johnson, *The Wedge of Truth.* Used by permission of InterVarsity Press. Zondervan Publishing House.

Nancy Pearcey, *Total Truth: Liberating Christianity From It's Cultural Captivity* (Wheaton: Crossway Books, 2004). Used by permission of Crossway Books, a publishing ministry of Good News Publishers, Wheaton, IL 60187.

William Lane Craig, *Reasonable Faith: Christian Truth and Apologetics* (Wheaton: Crossway Books, 1994). Used by permission of Crossway Books, a publishing Ministry of Good News Publishers, Wheaton, IL 60187.

Lee P. Strobel, *The Case for a Creator: A Journalist Investigates Scientific Evidence That Points Toward God.* Used by permission of Zondervan.

Mere Christianity by C. S. Lewis, copyright © C. S. Lewis Pte. Ltd. 1942, 1943, 1944. Extract reprinted by permission.

God in the Dock by C. S. Lewis, copyright © C. S. Lewis Pte. Ltd. 1970. Extract reprinted by permission.

Josh McDowell, *Evidence That Demands a Verdict: Historical Evidences for the Christian Faith* (San Bernardino, CA: Here's Life Publishers, Inc., 1979). Used by permission of Thomas Nelson, Inc.

Gary R. Habermas, *The Historical Jesus: Ancient Evidence for the Life of Christ* (Joplin, Missouri: College Press, 1996). Used by permission of Gary R. Habermas, copyright © 1996.

"The Unselfish Green Gene" by Dr. David Demick, *Impact* article # 325, July 2000. Used by permission of the Institute for Creation research.

"Discovering God Through Stories" by Gretchen Passantino, copyright © 1996. Used by permission of Gretchen Passantino, Answers in Action.

Permission granted to print portions of the interview with "The Biologist" given by George Caylor.

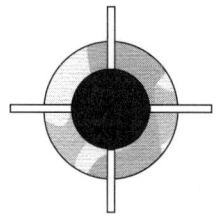

INTRODUCTION

AMERICA IS at war. I'm not referring to the war on terrorism being fought on many fronts around the world. I'm referring to a cultural war being fought among Americans over ideas, beliefs, and behaviors. I'm referring to a great moral struggle that can destroy this powerful country as quickly and completely as any conventional war.

It has happened before.

Historian David Wells observes that the fall of Rome has always perplexed historians. On the surface, it shouldn't have happened. How could wild barbarians defeat the most powerful civilization the world had ever known up to that time? Many historians believe that, ultimately, Rome fell because of the unscrupulous, depraved character of its citizens. Rome was not defeated by outsiders but by its own moral decline.

The following excerpt from Wells' book, *Losing Our Virtue*, draws a parallel between the fall of Rome and the precarious moral state of America today:

> If this surmise has any validity at all, should we not view our own deep destructive social pathologies and the rotting of our national character with some alarm? America seems so strong, so invincible as it bestrides the world, its technology unmatched, its economic

system robust . . . its government stable. . . . Rome, however, once occupied a comparable position in the ancient world, and against every human calculation and expectation, it fell. Indeed, when the barbarians arrived outside the gates of Rome, their hair dressed down in rancid butter, their breath heavy with garlic, and their tongues clattering away with primitive sounds, they found no one at home. They simply walked into the city and began their conquest. A fate as improbable as this is not beyond the repetition, even for America, if this nation cannot address its own disintegrating life, for no civilization will endure forever.[1]

This grim indictment of America appears to be coming true.

Until recent times, the Christian worldview dominated American culture. To a large degree, Christian principles and values underlaid governmental policies and the standards for judicial, educational, ethical, and social behavior in this country. This is not true today. People have become apathetic, even indifferent, to immoral behavior that a few decades ago was universally recognized as evil and condemned. Vulgarity and violence flood our entertainment. Cheating is commonplace in our universities, as is corruption and greed in our great corporations. Our judicial system has legalized abortion, most forms of pornography, and sodomy. Harold O. J. Brown wrote:

> Two [Supreme Court] decisions—*Roe v. Wade* and *Lawrence v. Texas*—are catastrophic symbols of what has been happening to the country at large. Much of the nation outside the government, and especially all that pertains to the elite or the establishment, has been or has recently become in essence anti-Christian, anti-Jewish, anti-natural law, and implicitly or explicitly pagan. All the nation's great secular universities, private and public, have turned pagan, with the exception of occasional faculty members, department heads, and other officials who have remained true to Christianity or observant Judaism.[2]

As a religious and ethical worldview, Christianity has been under siege for more than one hundred years. It has been effectively shoved off center stage as the guiding moral and spiritual light in America. In its place, the reigning worldview is godless, human-centered, naturalistic, and largely immoral secular humanism.[3]

Throughout the past hundred-plus years, as this cultural war escalated and Christian losses mounted, the church has responded in three ways.

During the late nineteenth and early twentieth centuries, many seminaries attempted to accommodate the prevailing intellectual climate that favored naturalistic science and biblical criticism. They *responded* by recasting the church into the image of the secular culture—and their efforts failed tragically. Theological liberalism infiltrated most, if not all, mainline denominations, destroying the fundamental beliefs that formerly identified Christians. The late Harold Lindsell, a church historian, put it plainly:

> It is not unfair to allege that among denominations like Episcopal, United Methodist, United Presbyterian, United Church of Christ, the Lutheran Church in America, and the Presbyterian Church U.S. there is not a single theological seminary that takes a stand in favor of biblical infallibility.[4]

As a result, many churches today are little more than social clubs. The Bible is no longer considered to be divine revelation. Jesus has been demoted to being a nice guy who offers good advice on how to live a happy, quasi-spiritual life. He is no longer God incarnate, the loving, yet judging, Lord and Savior.

During the early twentieth century, this liberalization of American churches led to a spiritual civil war. A large segment of Christendom responded by isolating and separating themselves, not only from the liberal churches but also from secular society as a whole.[5]

Many Christians still advocate this *response*. They claim that Christians have already lost the cultural war. The only thing we can do now, they say, is "dig in," put up the razor wire, and withdraw from contact with the "world" in order to protect ourselves from being seduced by pagan values.

This response also failed. It marginalized conservative Christians into becoming a distinct subculture within the broader secular society and ushered in the birth of radical fundamentalism. Many churches became anti-intellectual.[6] They became dogmatic and legalistic in doctrinal beliefs. Christianity came to be identified with strict prohibitions, and the mark of a true Christian was adherence to rigid codes of conduct.

Unfortunately, the fallout from the fundamentalist movement led to conservative Christianity losing its voice and influence in American culture. Christians became viewed as an anti-intellectual, ideologically exclusive, radical fringe group that was out of touch with mainstream America—an image that persists to this day.[7]

The third *response* to the cultural war is the most prevalent today. Increasing numbers of Christians, including evangelicals, sanction a dualistic approach to life. They maintain well-defined boundaries between the spiritual and the secular components of their lives, and function within each compartment according to the activities in which they engage.

For example, during church-related functions they maintain strict biblical values. In discussing such prominent moral issues of our times as abortion and homosexuality, they endorse biblical values. They support missionaries, encourage evangelism, and give generously to Christian causes. However, at school and work or while enjoying entertainment, these same Christians behave according to *secular* values. They compartmentalize the religious and secular aspects of their lives into separate, independent categories. The religious side is privatized and confined to church. The secular side governs everything else. It's not uncommon for Christians to go to church on Sunday morning and stop on the way home to rent videos that are full of gratuitous sex, vulgarity, and graphic violence—and yet, fail to see any inconsistencies with their biblical values.

The sad fact is, none of these three approaches to secularism—accommodation, isolation, or dualism—will win (or have won) any battles in the cultural war. The early church did not use these strategies as it fought its own culture war with the Romans. These early Christians did not accommodate, did not isolate, and did not promote living dualistic lives. They *engaged the culture* and through God's power successfully transformed most of the pagan Roman world into a Christianized world.

Engaging the Culture

We're now about two thousand years removed from the first-century Christian church. We live in an entirely different and vastly more sophisticated culture. In terms of competing worldviews, we face even more challenges to Christianity than first-century Christians faced. Consequently, we must successfully engage in today's culture war in the same way Christians did during the first centuries of the church. We must put on our spiritual armor (Eph. 6:10–17), share the Gospel, live holy lives, and challenge the prevailing intellectual beliefs of our times—just as the apostle Paul did with the Greek philosophers in Athens about two thousand years ago (Acts 17).

The Christian Combat Manual is written to help you fulfill this latter task. The following chapters are constructed to train Christians how to confront and respond to major intellectual and cultural challenges.

Chapter one introduces the subject of apologetics: what it is and why it is crucial to evangelism.

Chapter two describes what I call the Socratic method. It's an effective apologetic technique of asking "counter questions" that puts the burden of proof on the unbeliever, forcing him (or her) to defend his (or her) beliefs. This technique will surface constantly throughout this book.

The remaining chapters are divided into five parts, each of which concentrates on a specific area of apologetics and is divided into concise, focused chapters. Each chapter deals with a particular issue within the broader topic under discussion. This arrangement enhances clarity and facilitates study.

Part one focuses on the most important apologetic issue with which Christians must contend—the truth and reliability of the Bible. I provide convincing evidence why Christians can know that the Bible is a historically accurate account of divine revelation.

Part two tackles the raging controversy of evolution. Does modern science support evolution or creation? What *scientific* data can creationists muster to challenge the myth of evolution? Chapters in this section clearly lay out the philosophical and scientific case for creation as well as an effective way for you to apply this information when conversing with an evolutionist.

Part three demonstrates the existence of God. It explains not only why God *must* exist, but also why much about life and the cosmos would not make sense if He didn't. A step-by-step method for challenging atheism is presented. The concluding chapter in part three answers atheism's most powerful challenge to the existence of God—the problem of evil. Specifically, if God exists, loves us, and is all-powerful, why is there so much pain and suffering in our world?

Part four centers on Jesus Christ—His historicity, His deity, and His resurrection. It answers the question: "What happens to people who die but never heard the message of Jesus Christ?"

Part five focuses on modern issues that often challenge Christians, especially in universities and colleges, the media, and the entertainment industry—moral relativism, religious pluralism, multiculturalism, political correctness, and the "new" tolerance. I have developed six specific apologetic tactics to counter these secular "postmodern" doctrines.

My hope and prayer is that this book will not only inform and encourage you in your faith, but will motivate you to go out into the world and "contend earnestly for the faith which was once for all delivered to the saints" (Jude 3).

Endnotes

1. David Wells, *Losing Our Virtue; Why the Church Must Recover Its Moral Vision* (Grand Rapids: William B. Eerdmans Publishing Co., 1998), 7–8.

2. Harold O.J. Brown, "The Christian Future of America: Two Views; A Decisive Turn to Paganism," *Christianity Today,* August, 2004, 42.

3. See my chapter, "Secular Humanism: Man Is God," in Dan Story, *Christianity on the Offense; Responding to the Beliefs and Assumptions of Spiritual Seekers* (Grand Rapids: Kregel Publications, 1998).

4. Harold Lindsell, *The Battle for the Bible* (Grand Rapids: Zondervan Publishing House, 1981), 145.

5. See Mark A. Noll, *The Scandal of the Evangelical Mind* (Grand Rapids: William B. Eerdmans Publishing Co., 1994).

6. J. P. Moreland provides a good summary of the loss of intellectualism among evangelicals in his book, *Love Your God with All Your Mind; The Role of Reason in the Life of the Soul* (Colorado Springs: NavPress, 1997), chapter one.

7. Other historical events contributed to the demise of Christianity in terms of its relevance in modern culture. Perhaps the most significant were the revivalist's movements during the eighteenth and nineteenth centuries that deemphasized vigorous intellectualism and emphasized a more subjective, experiential form of evangelicalism. This resulted in evangelicals becoming largely anti-intellectual to the point that theology and doctrine were seen as impediments to religious experiences. This in turn left evangelicals unprepared to respond apologetically to scientific naturalism and higher biblical criticism that arose during the late nineteenth century and to the later moral challenges of contemporary postmodernism. Evangelicals should not be judged by their love for God and passion for lost souls. Rather, our poverty lies in the fact that our anti-intellectual mentality has resulted in popular culture perceiving Christianity as being merely a religion of faith as opposed to a religion of both faith and knowledge. The fallout is that evangelicals have lost their status as intellectual leaders and moral guardians (which the Church was for centuries). Our ability to curtail anti-Christian moral and philosophical ideologies (e.g. moral relativism and naturalistic evolution) is virtually nil—regardless of the fact that nearly half of all Americans (according to George Barna) claim to be either evangelicals or born-again believers. The purpose of this book is to contribute to the solution to this problem through sound and effective apologetic training. To pursue this, see Alister McGrath, *Evangelicalism & the Future of Christianity* (Downers Grove: InterVarsity Press, 1996); Mark A. Noll, *The Scandal of the Evangelical Mind* (Grand Rapids: William B. Eerdmans Publishing Company, 1994); Nancy R. Pearcey, *Total Truth: Liberating Christianity from Its Cultural Captivity*, chs.9 & 10 (Wheaton: Crossway Books, 2004). On a more popular level, see Os Guinness, *Fit Bodies Fat Minds: Why Evangelicals Don't Think and What to Do About It* (Grand Rapids: Baker Books, 1994).

APOLOGETICS
Evangelizing the Tough Minded

What Is Apologetics?

There are two kinds of people Christians will encounter while doing evangelism—those who respond to the Gospel and those who don't. The former people listen willingly, acknowledge their sins, and accept Jesus Christ as Lord and Savior. The latter, after hearing the Gospel, reject it. Most of the time those who reject offer a reason for their decision.

- They may identify with another religion.
- They may be apathetic and content with their unbelief.
- Or they may raise some kind of "intellectual" objection as to why they believe Christianity is illegitimate.

Whatever the reason, these people are frequently "tough-minded" and are in need of additional proof that goes beyond a gospel presentation and personal testimony. This is where apologetics comes into play.

The funny-sounding word "apologetics" is a derivative of the Greek word, *apologia*. The closest English equivalent is the word "defense," as translated in 1 Peter 3:15: "but sanctify Christ as Lord in your hearts, always being ready to make a defense [*apologia*] to everyone who asks you to give an account for the hope that is in you, yet with gentleness and reverence."

In spite of how the word apologetics sounds, it doesn't mean apologizing for something. In the above passage, the apostle Peter was not telling Christians to apologize for the hope that was in them. That wouldn't make sense. Rather, he was telling them to be prepared to defend their faith.

When used in the New Testament, *apologia* generally describes a *public* defense of the gospel. In Acts 22:1, for example, the apostle Paul exclaimed, "Brethren and fathers, hear my defense [*apologia*] which I now offer to you." Likewise in 2 Timothy 4:16, Paul used the same Greek word: "At my first defense [*apologia*] no one supported me, but all deserted me."[1]

Christian apologetics, then, is a study in the defense of the Christian faith. Its goal is to demonstrate that Christian truth claims are true. The Bible is historically reliable. We can trust it to be divine revelation. Jesus Christ is fully God and fully man. Jesus' resurrection really happened. Creation occurred by divine decree, and so on. All such claims, declare Christian apologists, rest on a firm foundation of objective facts and evidences that are open to ordinary investigation.

What kinds of evidences do Christian apologists use? Virtually any area of study can be applied in apologetics: logic and philosophy (sound reasoning), law (legal reasoning), medicine (such as confirmation that the crucifixion would have killed Jesus), history, archaeology, fulfilled prophecy, science, manuscript studies, and additional data from many areas of knowledge.

The Christian apologist also seeks to demonstrate that non-Christian religions and secular philosophies are false by critiquing and challenging their basic beliefs and assumptions. So the apologist points out that the same evidences that confirm Christianity falsify non-Christian religions. For instance, archaeology and fulfilled prophecy verify Christianity but repudiate Mormonism (see chapter eight). Good apologetics defend Christianity and challenge unbelievers to justify (defend) their beliefs.

Why Do We Need Apologetics?

Why is apologetics necessary? I believe there are at least three good reasons.

1. Apologetics is crucial in evangelism

In our culture, which is increasingly antagonistic to Christians, it's not surprising that a common reason a Christian gives for not sharing his (or her) faith is the fear that he will be asked questions he can't answer. Sadly, the average Christian is unable to intelligently disagree with unbelievers and provide objective support for that disagreement. Apologetics helps to remove that fear and provides convincing evidence to support Christian truth claims.

Apologetics has been a key ingredient of evangelism since the beginning of the Christian church. Many church fathers were theologians *and* apologists.[2] Moreover, the importance of apologetics in evangelism has not diminished with the passing of centuries. This includes our present generation. Philosopher J.P. Moreland wrote:

> It is no accident that the flourishing of evangelistic activity in the 1960s and 1970s was woven around the writings of C.S. Lewis, Josh McDowell, and Francis Schaeffer [apologists who wrote for ordinary Christians]. Today we need a revival of evangelistic fervor and spiritual power. And an absolutely crucial element that must take place before we will see this revival is a renaissance of apologetics and intellectual activity in the evangelical church.[3]

Christian apologetics is sometimes referred to as *pre-evangelism*. This is a good description. The goal of apologetics is to identify and remove *intellectual* obstacles that prevent people from seriously considering the Gospel.

Apologists recognize that salvation is always the work of the Holy Spirit. God is the agent of conviction, convincing, and converting; and apologetics is merely one way in which the Holy Spirit can open people's hearts and minds to the gospel. As William Lane Craig put it, "We *know* Christianity is true primarily by the self-authenticating witness of God's Spirit. We *show* Christianity is true by demonstrating that it is systematically consistent (emphasis Craig)."[4] Elsewhere Craig explained:

> Showing that Christianity is true involves the presentation of sound and persuasive arguments for Christian truth claims.... The role of the Holy Spirit is to use our arguments to convince the unbeliever of the truth of Christianity.... [The Holy Spirit] can work through rational argumentation, too.[5]

In today's largely anti-Christian world, apologetics is often a key ingredient in evangelism because many people are completely ignorant of what Christians believe and practice, and what they think they know is often erroneous. Most people from my "baby boomer" generation are familiar with fundamental Christian beliefs. Their parents probably took them to church, at least occasionally. Perhaps they attended Sunday school or vacation Bible school. Certainly, they watched the *Ten Commandments* (1956), *Ben-Hur* (1959), *The Greatest Story Ever Told* (1965), or other movies popular during that era that narrated biblical stories. In fact, prior to the 1960s, most Americans had direct contact with the Christian worldview. Most Americans knew that Jesus Christ was the Son of God—even if they didn't know exactly what that meant. They had heard of Jesus' resurrection, Adam and Eve, Moses crossing the Red Sea, David and Goliath, and Daniel in the lion's den. They were familiar with the Ten Commandments and could name some of them. They knew that Christmas and Easter celebrated Christian events.

In contrast, today's generation of people have been reared in a thoroughly *secular* environment. They don't even have a rudimentary understanding of Christianity. Many in America's younger generation have been indoctrinated by secular culture to *assume* that the Bible is religious myth; to *assume* that Jesus is no more unique than Mohammed or Buddha; to *assume* that naturalistic evolution explains the origin of life; and to *assume* that if God exists He is going to judge people according to how good they are and not according to their relationship with Jesus Christ.

As a result, our culture has largely rejected the Christian worldview. Countless people today no longer view religious truth or judge moral behavior from a traditional Christian perspective. Even people who claim to be Christians, think and behave more according to secular beliefs and values than according to biblical ones. Christianity has all but lost its voice and influence in popular culture. America today is largely "post-Christian" (Christianity is no longer the dominant worldview), relativistic (absolute truths are rejected), and pluralistic (every culture and religion are equally legitimate). Ideological clashes between Christians and non-Christians are no longer carried out in the philosopher's ivory tower. Secular sentiments and values are widely promulgated through popular culture. In today's public square—high school and college classrooms, media and entertainment industries, and the halls of government—anti-Christian values and ideas are formed and disseminated to "the man on the street." Today's non-Christians are frequently hostile to virtually everything Christians stand for, including God's moral absolutes; and view Christians as intolerant, narrow-minded people who have nothing relevant to say to modern culture.

How can Christians respond to this? How do we open the closed minds of many contemporary Americans? How do we reach people hardened to the Gospel?

I believe Spirit-empowered apologetics—combined with sharing the love of God—hold the key. Apologetics demonstrates that Christianity is true and that we *do* have something relevant to say to today's culture. We hold solutions to the problems the secular world has created: spiritual, moral, and social decay. In order to take a stand for Jesus Christ and "contend earnestly for the faith" (Jude 3) in a largely secular culture, all of us must be properly trained in apologetics (1 Peter 3:15). This is especially important for young Christians entering America's secular universities.

2. *Apologetics prepares students for secular college*

It is widely acknowledged that up to 80 percent of children reared in Christian homes fall away from the faith when they enter secular colleges and universities.[6] A recent study in *USA TODAY* supports this:

"Experts say one of students' biggest changes during college years is a decline in church attendance." According to the Higher Education Research Institute at UCLA, more than 80 percent of college freshman in the year 2000 said that they attended church services frequently or occasionally during their last years of high school. By their freshmen year in college, the number of churchgoers had dropped to 52 percent. By their junior year (2003), only 29 percent surveyed still attended church services.[7] This should not be surprising because 75 percent of American college seniors testify that their "professors teach that there is no such thing as right and wrong in a universal or objective sense."[8]

Apparently a good foundation in the Bible is not enough to keep Christian students committed to their faith. Apologetics is needed. Nancy Pearcey explained:

> Today basic apologetics has become a crucial skill for sheer survival. Without the tools of apologetics, young people can be solidly trained in Bible study and doctrine, yet still flounder helplessly when they leave home and face the secular world on their own....
>
> We need to make sure our own children leave home with [the] conviction burned deeply into their minds—that Christianity is capable of holding its own when challenged in the marketplace of ideas. . . . Before they leave home, they should be well acquainted with all the "isms" they will encounter, from Marxism to Darwinism to postmodernism. It is best for young believers to hear about these ideas first from trusted parents, pastors, and youth leaders, who can train them in strategies for analyzing competing ideologies.[9]

I agree with Pearcey's solution to this:

> To be effective in equipping young people and professionals to face the challenges of a highly educated secular society, the church needs to redefine the mission of pastors and youth leaders to include training in apologetics and worldview.... Pastors must once again provide intellectual leadership for their congregations, teaching apologetics from the pulpit. Every time a minister intro-

duces a biblical teaching, he should also instruct the congregation in ways to defend it against the major objections they are likely to encounter. A religion that avoids the intellectual task and retreats to the therapeutic realm of personal relationships and feelings will not survive in today's spiritual battlefield.[10]

Whether the church engages in training their own people or seeks out parachurch ministries that specialize in apologetics, one truth is certain—apologetic training is crucial if the church is to prepare itself to defend the faith and share the gospel effectively in today's secular world, particularly in a university environment.

3. Apologetics is affirming to our faith

Studying apologetics can highly affirm the intellectual aspect of one's faith. Such study especially helps new believers who seek to rationally justify and understand their recent commitment to Jesus Christ. When I became a Christian as an adult, there was no one in my immediate family who were practicing Christians, nor were any of my oldest friends. After my conversion, people close to me asked questions (or made derogatory remarks) about my faith. And of course, I had many questions that needed to be answered.

As one might imagine, this inspired me to investigate apologetics. Almost immediately after my conversion, I began reading apologetic books by Josh McDowell, Paul Little, and C. S. Lewis. I can't begin to describe how their writings strengthened my faith. God used apologetics to remove my doubts. It assured me that Christianity rested on a solid foundation of facts. It even increased my zeal to study the Bible. But most importantly, apologetics gave me greater confidence in sharing my faith.

Endnotes

1. Other biblical passages where the word *apologia* occurs are:

Acts 25:16: "an opportunity to make his *defense* against the chargers."
1 Corinthians 9:3: "My *defense* to those who examine me is this."

2 Corinthians 7:11: "what *vindication* of yourselves."
Philippians 1:7: "since both in my imprisonment and in the *defense* and confirmation of the gospel."
Philippians 1:16: "knowing that I am appointed for the *defense* of the gospel."

2. A good study of the early Christian apologists is *Classical Readings in Christian Apologetics: A.D. 100–1800*, L. Russ Bush, editor (Grand Rapids: Academie Books, 1983).

3. J.P Moreland, *Love Your God with All Your Mind: The Role of Reason in the Life of the Soul*, Dallas Willard, gen. ed. (Colorado Springs: NP, 1997), 54.

4. William Lane Craig, *Reasonable Faith: Christian Truth and Apologetics* (Wheaton; Crossway Books, 1994), 48.

5. Ibid., 38, 46.

6. Rick Cornish, *5 Minute Apologist: Maximum Truth in Minimum Time* (Colorado Springs: NavPress, 2005), p. 17. Several years ago I attended a seminar hosted by the Institute of Creation Research. Dr. John Morris, president of ICR, made the observation that seventy-five percent of children reared in Christian homes fall away from the faith after entering secular college.

7. Joseph Popiolkowsky and Adrienne Lewis, "Losing Their Religion," *USA TODAY*, March 9, 2004.

8. Nancy R. Pearcey, *Total Truth: Liberating Christianity from Its Cultural Captivity* (Wheaton: Crossway Books), p. 113. Pearcey is referring to a recent Zogby poll. See footnote 34, page 406 for details.

9. Ibid., 125–126

10. Ibid., 127.

Apologetics
Taking the Offense

BEGINNING IN part one, we will study common challenges skeptics and other critics raise in their attempt to disprove Christianity. We will also formulate an apologetic response to each one. But first, I want to share two apologetic tactics, the second of which I consider to be the most useful apologetic tactic you can learn.

Apologetics Tactics

Most of us trained in apologetics rely on *defensive* tactics when we encounter a witnessing opportunity. We confront challenges raised by unbelievers with logical counterarguments supported by extrabiblical facts and other evidences.

If a skeptic declares that the Bible is a religious myth or has been corrupted by later editors, a trained apologist can muster a huge amount of evidences to prove the doubter wrong. Similarly, if an unbeliever argues that pain and suffering disprove the existence of a loving, all-powerful God, an apologist can challenge that view with compelling philosophical and theological arguments (see chapter 20). He can apply this same kind of defensive tactic to virtually every apologetic issue, including the existence of God, the deity of Jesus Christ, the resurrection, and the creation.

Defensive apologetics is the most natural apologetic response. It's normal for us to want to defend our beliefs when they come under attack. Moreover, the premise of defensive apologetics is sound. Pushed far enough, the weight of supporting evidence combined with the coherence and strength of our arguments will always support Christianity and refute non-Christian beliefs.

However, there is a second apologetic approach worth noting. I call it the "Socratic method" because it uses a technique similar to that used by the ancient Greek philosopher, Socrates.

The Socratic Method

The fundamental strategy of the Socratic Method is to become the adversary during religious and ethical discussions. Rather than presenting evidences designed primarily to *defend* the Christian position on an issue, we can lovingly and sensitively challenge unbelievers to defend what *they believe*, analyze and justify *their* positions, and face the logical conclusions of their assumptions. This approach takes the burden of proof off our shoulders and places it squarely on the one who is challenging us.

Too often in religious discussions, we find ourselves pushed into a corner, with our arms folded, defending what we believe. But it shouldn't be this way. We have God's truth. Unbelievers should be the ones who defend what they believe—not us. The Socratic method challenges the critic to defend their *disbeliefs* about Christianity as well as to defend their particular worldview assumptions.

Let's say a skeptic claims that early Christians manufactured the resurrection myth (see chapter 24). We challenge him (or her) to provide objective, historical evidence (not hearsay or opinions) to back up that allegation. If an evolutionist asserts that scientific evidence disproves creation, we challenge him to account for the tremendous amount of *scientific* evidence that refutes evolution and confirms creation (see Part Two).

Putting the Socratic Method to Work

Frequently, the best defense is a good offense. This strategy encourages unbelievers to see that their opinions about Christianity are false and to consider the biblical perspective on an issue. We can challenge them to think through and defend their assumptions and their mistaken beliefs.

A wonderful passage in Proverbs describes the Socratic method in simple terms: "The first to present his case seems right, till another comes forward and questions him" (Prov. 18:17 NIV).

People's views and arguments concerning ethics and religion can sound convincing and compelling to us until we stop and analyze them, and then ask questions. When this happens frequently their arguments begin to crumble because they don't have an objective leg on which to stand. They can't justify what they believe. They have no supporting evidence. Their beliefs are merely personal opinions and hearsay manufactured by popular culture.

As we follow the principle governing Proverbs 18:17, we ask questions, particularly those that challenge skeptics and other critics to justify their beliefs. Our questions place the burden of proof on the unbelievers and challenge them to explain and justify:

- What they believe.
- Why they believe it.
- What difference it makes.

In other words, we can ask the same kind of questions that skeptics expect us to answer!

Some sample questions

I first introduced this version of the Socratic method in my book, *Engaging the Closed Minded*.[1] There I listed examples of the kind of questions that Christians can ask unbelievers in order to encourage them to evaluate their particular beliefs about any issue. Rather than repeat that list, I've selected key questions that will fit almost any apologetic issue that a Christian might encounter.

1. What do you mean by that?

This question forces critics to clarify and elaborate their views. If people are merely parroting something they heard, it quickly becomes obvious because they won't be able to explain what they mean. For instance:

- "What do you mean Christians are intolerant? Aren't you being a bit intolerant when you say I can't share my faith? Why is it intolerant to explain the Christian plan of salvation which has changed my life?"
- "What do you mean the Bible is full of contradictions? Here's my Bible. Please show me some examples."

2. How do you know that's true?

When appropriate, we can challenge skeptics to give proof or evidence for their anti-Christian assertions.

- "How do you know that Jesus, who claimed to be God and demonstrated divinity, isn't God?"
- "How do you know Jesus' resurrection is a myth? Eyewitnesses saw Jesus alive after His publicly certified death and burial."

3. Why should I believe that?

Encourage skeptics in a loving way to give the same kinds of evidence to support their views that they want from us to support ours. We want skeptics to realize that they can offer no compelling reason for why we should accept what they say.

- "Why should I believe that *The Book of Mormon* is divine revelation when (unlike the Bible) there is no historical confirmation?"
- "Why should I believe in evolution when the fossil evidence doesn't support it?"
- "Why should I believe that Joseph Smith is a prophet of God when he made numerous false prophecies?"

- "Why should I believe the Qur'an when it gives distorted information about Jesus and contradicts eyewitness testimonies in the Bible and elsewhere?"
  (Note: be prepared to point out erroneous statements about Jesus in the Qur'an.)

4. Where did you learn that?

Challenge the skeptics' sources of information. Are their sources reliable? Will these people document their beliefs outside of their personal opinions? If applicable, point out that their misinformation about Christianity is actually a byproduct of secular culture, not thoughtful analysis of the evidences:

- "Where did you learn that evolution is a scientific fact? Have you examined the data supporting creation? Is your view of evolution based on high school or college science classes?"
- "Where did you learn that Jesus' resurrection is mythical? I encourage you to get your opinion on the historicity of the resurrection by reading eyewitness testimony in the Bible rather than someone's opinion in *Newsweek* or *Time* written two thousand years after the event."
- "Where did you learn that Jesus was married? Should you believe a fiction novel or the biographical data of eyewitnesses" (i.e. the Bible)?

5. What is your solution to. . . ?

The idea here is to encourage non-Christians to see that apart from God their worldviews can't solve life's problems or answer the tough questions all people face.

- "What is your solution to human suffering if God does not exist?"
- "What is your solution to the moral depravity so widespread in our culture if there is no God to tell us how to behave and hold us accountable?"

6. What difference does that make?

How do the beliefs of non-Christians affect the Christian worldview? Do they really invalidate Christianity?

- "What difference does it make whether God created life on earth in six days or over billions of years?" (See chapter 11.)
- "Even if the Bible does contain a few minor errors (and I'm not saying it does), what difference do they make? Please show me an alleged error affecting the Bible's overall historical reliability and essential doctrine, such as the deity and resurrection of Jesus Christ."

7. If . . . is true, can you explain . . . ?

The last category of questions is designed to raise issues that a skeptic's position or worldview *cannot* explain.

- "If evolution is true, can you explain the absence of transitional fossils in the fossil record? In fact, why are there no transitional fossil parts, such as a half scale/half feather or a half leg/half wing?" (See chapter 14.)
- "If the universe suddenly exploded into existence out of nothing, can you explain how something can come from nothing?" (See chapter 11.)
- "If life emerged from non-life, can you explain how non-living chemicals can evolve into living anything?" (See chapter 13.)
- "If Jesus' resurrection never occurred, can you explain the eyewitness documentation that hundreds of people saw Jesus after His certified death on the cross?" (See chapter 24.)

Why the Socratic Method Is Effective

Most skeptics of Christianity are parroting what they learn in popular culture, in secular schools, and in books, magazines, journals, radio, and movies. These skeptics rarely have any objective evidence to support their beliefs and seldom wonder if their criticisms are true. Most non-Christians just assume that what they learn through popular culture is reliable.

An illuminating example of this occurred in the year 2000 when the late Peter Jennings hosted a two-hour special on ABC called "The Search for Jesus." Jennings interviewed several liberal theologians who stated that the Bible is full of contradictions, that editors (years later) added most of Jesus' sayings to the Bible, that Jesus was not the divine Son of God, and that He did not rise from the dead. In fact, they said scavenger dogs probably ate His body.

In April, 2004, Jennings hosted "Jesus and Paul: Word and Witness" on ABC. Again, bias in favor of a skeptic's view of Christ was evident just as it was in the show "The Search for Jesus." Most participants were liberal scholars. Overall, the program denied nearly any level of biblical authority and reinforced the claim that the Jesus of history had little resemblance to the biblical Jesus. He was, the show taught, a "social activist" and "superstitious conjurer" who was not (nor did He think He was) the Messiah or ever referred to himself as the Son of God. There is "no reliable evidence that he rose from the dead or performed any other miracles."[2]

Unfortunately, millions of uninformed viewers watching these shows *assumed* that what the liberal scholars said was factual because they *assumed* these scholars were spokesmen of Christianity.

The truth is, liberal scholars are not spokesmen of Christianity, nor do they represent objective biblical scholarship. Virtually all of their radical claims are merely speculations and opinions that flow out of a naturalistic (anti-supernatural) view of the Bible. Their claims are not based on unbiased historical and textual analysis.

As Christians, we need to challenge these erroneous and biased conclusions. Indeed, we need to challenge any secular source that disseminates distorted and unsubstantiated information about Christianity—including the Bible's account of creation. Most high school and college textbooks, as well as magazines such as *National Geographic*, promote evolution as scientific fact while ignoring the vast amount of evidence that supports creation by design. We need to challenge these claims socratically and, when skeptics are unable to substantiate them, be prepared to provide evidence supporting a creationist model of origins. (See part two.) Half-truths, distorted information, and speculations never reveal truth—they hide truth. Part of our apologetic task as we engage popular culture for Jesus Christ is to point out that personal opinions, misinformation, and speculation prove nothing. As I heard Christian apologist Craig Hawkins say more than once, "One can sincerely believe in something and be sincerely wrong."

The Socratic method is successful because it brings to light speculation and hearsay by encouraging critics to justify their arguments and opinions. Combined with our sincere love for them, this method encourages critics of Christianity to think through and evaluate their own beliefs. When non-Christians conclude for themselves that there is no objective evidence for their faultfinding assumptions about Christianity, a small victory is won in the larger spiritual battle.

Obviously, some non-Christians will intelligently respond to our Socratic questions. But when they do, we've still achieved three important goals. First, we've begun to build a sincere relationship with the skeptics through which the light of Jesus can shine. Second, we've encouraged the skeptics to evaluate their own positions on the issues at hand. They are forced to confront and mend weaknesses—if they can. Third, if they conclude for themselves that their views lack objective support, they may become willing listeners to Christian perspectives.

Try applying the Socratic method, at least initially, in apologetic situations. It will greatly increase your effectiveness in apologetics and hinder or even stop the wrong thinking and unsubstantiated arguments on which many non-Christians rely in their attacks against Christianity.

In the Appendix, I will voice challenges that tough-minded unbelievers typically raise during witnessing opportunities. Each section of the book will have its own set of challenges. Rather than apply "defensive" apologetics, try to respond socratically to each challenge. Ask counter questions that either encourage the critic to justify and defend his or her argument or that raise an issue the critic's position can't resolve. I'll suggest Socratic responses that correspond to each challenge I raise. However, before you read my responses, try to come up with your own Socratic responses.

Endnotes

1. Dan Story, *Engaging the Closed Minded* (Grand Rapids: Kregel Publications, 1999), chapter 4.

2. Gretchen Passantino, "What Does Peter Jennings Tell Us about Jesus and Paul?", Answers In Action, 2004, 1. Gretchen Passantino is director of the apologetic ministry, Answers in Actions. She provides a good critique of *Jesus and Paul: Word and Witness*. Answers In Action's web site is www.answers.org.

PART ONE

ESTABLISHING THE TRUTH AND RELIABILITY OF THE BIBLE

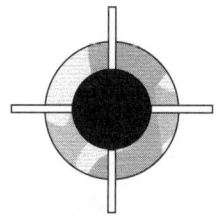

Introduction to Part One

ONE OF THE first challenges to my faith as a new believer (twenty-five years ago) is still one of the most common challenges that Christians face. It's packaged in a variety of ways, but I remember one of my best friends stating it like this: "You don't take the Bible literally, do you?"

This question reflects a typical skeptic's view of Scripture. To my friend, the Bible was not an accurate record of divine revelation. It was myth and allegory mixed with historically unsubstantiated, scientifically erroneous, and often fraudulent claims. However, if he were to ask it today, I would respond with a challenging Socratic question, such as, "Why wouldn't God say what He intended to mean?" I'd challenge my friend to explain why he thought God wouldn't communicate literally, especially since the Bible purports to be divine revelation. If God wishes to speak to us through the Bible, why would He give us incorrect and confusing information?

Let's examine the kinds of compelling evidences that we can use to document the Bible's truthfulness and reliability.

The Foundational Apologetic Issue

According to pollster George Barna, despite evangelicals' huge efforts to show non-Christians that the Bible is divine revelation, "A majority of non-Christians reject the authority and truth-basis of scripture from the start."[1] Clearly, the continental divide that separates Christians and non-Christians is whether or not the Bible is true.

To us the Bible is divine revelation from God and about God, which we can obtain from no other source. Without it, all supposed knowledge about God is merely human speculation. If the Bible does not contain divinely inspired factual (literal) information, we have no objective truth basis for any Christian belief. All biblical doctrines and principles we hold dear become questionable if the Bible's veracity is in doubt.

If the Bible is true, then it contains the very words of God. What it says about Jesus, salvation, the Holy Spirit, creation, heaven, hell, and every other subject it addresses *has to be true*. So, the foundational issue of all apologetics is providing a compelling defense for the Bible's truth and reliability.

I want to start this section by stating the governing apologetic principle I'll employ, and then examine seven apologetic evidences that together provide an airtight defense of Scripture. Here's the principle:

> If we can demonstrate that the Bible is truthful, always reliable, and can be validated by objective, non-biblical evidences, we are justified in concluding that it will be equally truthful and reliable in its non-testable, spiritual truth claims. This conclusion is confirmed subjectively when the Bible's spiritual truth claims are accepted and applied. Through the power of God, they transform people's lives. We can legitimately conclude from objective and subjective evidences that the Bible is the authoritative Word of God.

In application, this principle states that eyewitness testimony, archaeological discoveries, fulfilled prophecies, and the other evidences that we'll examine in this section demonstrate that the Bible is truthful in its historical, scientific, geographical, cultural, and other testable data. Since these verifiable facts are true, we can legitimately conclude that the Bible is equally true in its non-testable, more subjective spiritual claims such as salvation through Jesus Christ, the sanctifying work of the Holy Spirit, divine judgment, the existence of angels and demons, and so on.

This is not to imply, however, that we can only trust the Bible so far as we can prove it's true. Christians are justified in accepting the Bible's truth and authority *on its own merits*. Moreover, it's always the work of the Holy Spirit when an individual ultimately accepts the authority of Holy Scripture and Jesus Christ as Lord and Savior. (See Acts 16:14, Romans 8:16, 1 Corinthians 2:10–14.). As we read earlier, apologetics *demonstrates* the truth of Scriptures; the Holy Spirit *confirms* it.

Whenever I lead an apologetic workshop, I'm invariably asked, "How do we know that the books in the Bible are the only ones that belong there?" I have answered this question in great length elsewhere by providing five tests for canonicity based on Geisler's and Nix's book, *A General Introduction to the Bible*.[2] But the quick response (and the most important test) is that all the New Testament books were written by an apostle or someone approved by an apostle.[3] This rules out any book written after the death of the apostles. Since most rejected books are dated after the first century, we can safely assume that only the books now in the Bible actually belong there.

Endnotes

1. George Barna, *The State of the Church 2000* (Ventura, CA: Issachar Resources, 2002), 74.

2. Norman L Geisler and William E. Nix, *A General Introduction to the Bible* (Chicago: Moody Press, 1968). Also see Dan Story, *Defending Your Faith: Reliable Answers for a New Generation of Seekers and Skeptics*, (Grand Rapids: Kregel Publications, 1997), chapter five.

3. An apostle had to have been a follower of Jesus from the time of his baptism and witnessed His postresurrection appearances. (See Acts 1:21–22.)

THE BIBLE'S UNITY AND CONSISTENCY PROVES SUPERNATURAL AUTHORSHIP

THE FIRST evidence demonstrating the Bible's truth and reliability is its unparalleled unity and consistency in the face of its great diversity of content and authorship. This clearly points to the Bible's divine origin.

Josh McDowell, in his landmark book, *Evidence That Demands a Verdict*, provides the follow data that illustrates the amazing construction of the Bible:

1. Written over a 1,500 year span.
2. Written over 40 generations.
3. Written by over 40 authors from every walk of life including kings, peasants, philosophers, fishermen, poets, statesmen, scholars, etc.:

    Moses, a political leader, trained in the universities of Egypt
    Peter, a fisherman
    Amos, a herdsman
    Joshua, a military general

Nehemiah, a cupbearer
Daniel, a prime minister
Luke, a doctor
Solomon, a king
Matthew, a tax collector
Paul, a rabbi

4. Written in different places:

   Moses in the wilderness
   Jeremiah in a dungeon
   Daniel on a hillside and in a palace
   Paul inside prison walls
   Luke while traveling
   John on the isle of Patmos
   Others in the rigors of a military campaign

5. Written at different times:

   David in times of war
   Solomon in times of peace

6. Written during different moods:
   Some writing from the heights of joy and others writing from the depths of sorrow and despair

7. Written on three continents:

   Asia, Africa and Europe

8. Written in three languages:

   Hebrew: The language of the Old Testament.
   In II Kings 18:26–28 called "the language of Judah."
   In Isaiah 19:18 called "the language of Canaan."

   Aramaic: The "common language" of the Near East until the time of Alexander the Great (6th century B.C.– 4th century B.C.)

   Greek: The New Testament language and the international language at the time of Christ [similar to English today].

9. Biblical authors spoke on hundreds of controversial subjects with harmony and continuity from Genesis to Revelation. There is one unfolding story; "God's redemption of man." [1]

To appreciate the significance of this data, in terms of evidence for the divine inspiration of the Bible, consider the follow illustration.

I tell ten of my students to write a short essay on a controversial subject such as the death penalty, women in the pastorate, or whether the military invasion of Iraq was a "just" war. When the students complete this assignment, will I be able to take all ten essays, combine them into a single coherent treatise, and discover that all contributors support and complement each other? Will the viewpoints of the essayists totally agree? Will there be any contradictions? Certainly, there will be contradictions—although all ten students speak the same language, live in the same culture and same period in history, and practice the same religion.

In contrast, the Bible covers *hundreds* of topics. Forty authors on three continents wrote it during a 1500-year period, using three languages. Yet all sixty-six books of the Bible perfectly agree. There is complete harmony and unity—no conflicting accounts, no differences of opinion over controversial subjects.

What can we conclude from this? The Bible's amazing unity and consistency, given such diversity of its topics and authorship, can only be accounted for through divine guidance. The Bible is God's inspired Word.

Endnotes

1. Josh McDowell, *Evidence That Demands a Verdict* (San Bernardino: Here's Life Publishers, Inc., 1979),16.

EYEWITNESS TESTIMONY
Legal Evidence

THE SECOND apologetic evidence supporting the truth and reliability of the Bible—particularly the New Testament Gospels—is eyewitness testimony authenticating major events. This is called "primary-source" evidence. It means that the events described in the New Testament—including the life, ministry, death, and post-resurrection appearances of Jesus Christ—were recorded by people who actually witnessed them (Matthew and John) or by men who were directly associated with eyewitnesses (such as Mark and Luke).

Eyewitness testimony is also found in the Old Testament. Some of its books may have been compiled from earlier documents after the events occurred (such as Genesis), but others certainly relied on eyewitness testimony. The Exodus narratives written by Moses, as well as Joshua and Judges, "seem to rely on some of the main participants for an eyewitness account."[1]

The value of eyewitness testimony cannot be overstated. Consider a jury trial. The most compelling (and damning) evidence in any trial comes from the testimony of eyewitnesses—people who actually observed the crime. Defendants are set free, imprisoned, or even executed on the testimony of eyewitnesses. This illustrates the crucial value of eyewitness testimony.

The New Testament authors knew the value of eyewitness testimony and repeatedly appealed to it for verification of their writings. The apostle John wrote:

> What was from the beginning, what we have heard, what we have seen with our eyes, what we have looked at and touched with our hands, handled, concerning the Word of Life—and the life was manifested, and we have seen and testify and proclaim to you . . . what we have seen and heard (1 John 1:1–3).

Likewise, the apostle Peter wrote:

> For we did not follow cleverly devised tales when we made known to you the power and coming of our Lord Jesus Christ, but we were eyewitnesses of His majesty (2 Peter 1:16).

Other passages highlighting eyewitness testimony include: Luke 1:1–3; John 19:35, 20:30–31; Acts 1:1–3, 2:22, 10:39–42; 1 Corinthians 9:1, 15:5–8; 1 Peter 5:1.

The apostles appealed to eyewitness testimony because many people who had listened to Jesus' teachings and observed His miracles were still alive when the New Testament was written. Hundreds had even seen Christ after His resurrection (1 Corinthians 15:6). Legitimate testimonials to the Gospel accounts, these eyewitnesses confirmed the apostles' writings among their countrymen.

There is another important category of eyewitnesses to consider. These are the "hostile" witnesses unfriendly to Christianity (Acts 2:22–23; 26:24–28), who would have used any opportunity to publicly refute the apostles' accounts. New Testament scholar F. F. Bruce explained:

> It was not only friendly eyewitnesses that the early preachers had to reckon with; there were others less well disposed who were also conversant with the main facts of the ministry and death of Jesus. The disciples could not afford to risk inaccuracies (not to speak of willful manipulation of the facts), which would at once be exposed by those who would be only too glad to do so. On the

contrary, one of the strong points in the original apostolic preaching is the confident appeal to the knowledge of the hearers; they not only said, "We are witnesses of these things," but also "As you yourself also know" (Acts ii.22). Had there been any tendency to depart from the facts in any material respect, the possible presence of hostile witness in the audience would have served as a further corrective.[2]

In light of the potential for cross-examination by hostile witnesses, it's noteworthy that not a single piece of contrary historical evidence concerning the birth, ministry, death, and postresurrection appearances of Jesus has surfaced from the first century that claims any of these events were false. The enemies of Christianity could not refute the apostles' eyewitness accounts. This eyewitness testimony is further convincing attestation that the Gospel accounts are true and historically reliable.

Endnotes

1. Walter C. Kaiser Jr., *The Old Testament Documents; Are They Reliable & Relevant?* (Downers Grove: InterVarsity Press, 2001), 176.

2. F.F. Bruce, *The New Testament Documents: Are They Reliable? (Downers Grove: InterVarsity, 1984),* 46.

TEXTUAL RELIABILITY
A Nearly Perfect Manuscript

THE THIRD apologetic evidence supporting the truth and reliability of Scripture is the accuracy of its transmission. I want to spend more time on this evidence because it's probably the major area where the Bible comes under attack. Despite the process of recopying and translating the Bible down through the centuries, the copies we have today accurately reflect the original manuscripts inspired by God and recorded by the biblical authors.

Virtually all skeptics claim that the Bible has been so corrupted that today's copies are far different than the original manuscripts. The argument goes: The Bible is full of errors, contradictions, and historical inaccuracies. Old Testament miracles are mythical. Although Jesus may have been a miracle worker of sorts, these critics believe many of His miracles and most of His sayings were not included in the original Bible manuscripts. Later editors added them.

An article in *Newsweek*, anticipating Mel Gibson's controversial movie, *The Passion of the Christ,* illustrates this. After acknowledging that Gibson's "movie is a literal-minded rendering of the most dramatic passages scattered through the four Gospels," the author proceeds to claim that "the Bible can be a problematic source ... [It] is not always a faithful record of historical events. . . . To take the film's account of the

Passion literally will give most audiences a misleading picture of what probably happened in those epochal hours so long ago."[1]

Since the Bible is the primary source of information concerning the Passion of Jesus Christ (His suffering and crucifixion) and the only account recorded by eyewitnesses, one must wonder by what criteria the author concludes that the biblical record is misleading. There is no other historical eyewitness narrative to compare. If the author is correct, today's Bible is a corrupted version of the original writings, and the biblical narrative of the Passion and other events in Christ's life are false testimony.

Transmission of the Old Testament

How do we know that today's Old Testament is an accurate translation of the original manuscripts penned between 1450–400 BC? The most compelling evidence for the accurate transmission of the Old Testament is the discovery of the Dead Sea scrolls in 1947. Prior to this discovery, the oldest existing Old Testament manuscript is dated around AD 980.[2] However, with the discovery of the Dead Sea scrolls, portions of almost every book in the Old Testament have been found. Many of them date around 150 BC—more than a thousand years earlier than previously existing Old Testament manuscripts.

The most important Dead Sea scroll discovery was, perhaps, two *complete* copies of the book of Isaiah. They are the oldest discovered copies of any complete book of the Bible. When scholars compared the Dead Sea scroll texts of Isaiah (150 BC) to existing texts dated more than a thousand years later, the Dead Sea scrolls of Isaiah were found to be 95 percent identical with today's standard Hebrew Bible. "The 5 percent of variation consisted chiefly of obvious slips of the pen and variations in spelling."[3]

Does this same integrity apply to other Old Testament books? Absolutely. Old Testament scholar Walter Kaiser, Jr. wrote:

> It is possible to say ... that over 90 percent of the Old Testament is textually sound and uniformly witnessed to by major exemplars. Of the remaining 10 percent of the text that exhibits any type of

variation, extremely few are of such significance that they would involve any major doctrinal issue."[4]

This means that more than a thousand years of recopying Old Testament books resulted in nearly perfect transmission with no significant corruption. How do scholars account for such accuracy? The copyists knew they were copying God's Word. As such they went to incredible lengths to prevent error from creeping into their work. The entire process of recopying the Bible was controlled by strict religious rituals, and the scribes carefully counted every line, word, syllable, and letter to ensure accuracy. Beyond any doubt, the Old Testament in our Bibles today is virtually identical to the Hebrew canon completed more than twenty centuries ago.

Transmission of the New Testament

In the case of the New Testament, the evidence for accurate transmission is even greater. Two primary areas of documentation demonstrate that our present New Testament documents are nearly identical to their original, ancient writings.

Number of Manuscripts

The first confirming evidence has to do with the number of extant (still existing) manuscripts available for study. There are more copies of the New Testament than any other document from antiquity. More than 24,000 partial and complete ancient manuscripts exist. This includes more than 5,300 Greek manuscripts—the language in which most of the New Testament was written.[5] This number is extremely high compared to other ancient documents, most of which have fewer than a dozen surviving copies.[6]

Why is this huge number of extant manuscripts so important in terms of confirming the accurate transmission of the New Testament? The more copies there are to compare, the more accurate scholars can be in discovering what the original manuscripts actually said. Here's an anecdote to illustrate this.[7]

Let's say that my great, great, great-grandmother developed a recipe for chocolate chip cookies. After she died, one of her six children found the recipe, copied it down, and gave a copy to each of her brothers and sisters. Each of these six children likewise had six children and gave a copy of the recipe to each of them. And this continued during the next three generations until the total number of recipes was 9,331:

great, great, great-grandmother – 1 (the original recipe)
great-great-grandmother – 1 × 6 = 6
great-grandmother – 6 × 6 = 36
grandmother – 6 × 36 = 216
mother – 6 × 216 = 1,296
my generation – 6 × 1,296 = 7,776
Total recipes: 9,331

Let's also say that the original recipe my great, great, great-grandmother wrote was lost, as were all the copies given to her six children and those from the third, fourth, and fifth generations. The only copies left are from my generation: 7,776 (somewhat more recipes than the number of existing Greek New Testament manuscripts).

Now, suppose that all the descendants in my generation got together for a family reunion to try to determine what the original recipe actually said. When they compared recipes, they discovered that fifteen recipes said to use one-half cup of chocolate chips, twenty-five more said to use three quarters of a cup, and the remaining 7,736 said to use one cup. What do you think was the likely amount of chocolate chips used in the original recipe? Common sense says one cup.

This yarn illustrates the methodology scholars use to determine the actual texts of the original, inspired biblical documents (the autographs). Although other factors are important, such as the age of the manuscripts, the key data that scholars use is the thousands of manuscripts, which they can compare. Even though the original manuscripts are lost, there are still enough ancient copies to make an intelligent estimate of what the original writings actually said. This in turn allows Bible scholars to establish the most accurate, modern translations possible.

This procedure is important in terms of defending the authenticity of the Bible. One frequent challenge to its integrity is the existence of textual variants in the Old and New Testaments. Of course, variant readings shouldn't be surprising. They should be expected when thousands of manuscripts exist. Nevertheless, critics claim that these minor differences amount to corruption. The above illustration proves just the opposite. Variant readings among different biblical texts do not mean a loss of the original writings, but rather that the original writings are preserved within the various manuscript traditions.

Through their investigations, scholars have concluded that only one half of one percent (0.5%) of the New Testament is in doubt (about 400 words). And of this half percent, no doctrinal or historical truth is in question. No other ancient manuscript can match the Bible in terms of accuracy of transmission down through the centuries.[8]

Time Spans

The second convincing evidence that supports the accurate transmission of the New Testament concerns the short time spans between when its recorded events occurred and were first written down, on the one hand, and how close to the original writings today's copies of the Bible are. Both are important in establishing the New Testament's reliability.

Bible critics repeatedly claim that the Gospels are unreliable because they were written long after the events occurred, perhaps as late as AD 90. As a result, plenty of time elapsed which allowed for corruption or even legends to develop. The fact is, the time span between when the events in the Gospels actually occurred and when they were first recorded is amazingly short. Moreover, the period of "oral tradition" preserved the integrity of the Gospel accounts even before they were written down. A good example of this is found in the early church creeds.

Before the New Testament was compiled, the early church memorized and passed around verbal statements of faith called "creeds" which generally focus on "the death and resurrection of Jesus and his resulting deity."[9] Many of these early creeds were later recorded in the New Testament and date to within a few years of Christ's resurrection.

The most well-known oral creed, later recorded in the New Testament, is 1 Corinthians 15:3–4:

> For I delivered to you as of first importance what I also received, that Christ died for our sins according to the Scriptures, and that He was buried, and that He was raised on the third day according to the Scriptures.

Almost all scholars agree that Paul was quoting an ancient creed passed along orally from eyewitnesses to the death, burial, and resurrection of Jesus Christ. Many theologians believe that this creed dates from *three to eight years* after the resurrection![10]

We'll explore the veracity of oral tradition later. The point for now is that, thanks to the early church creeds, we have eyewitness testimonies recorded in the New Testament dating to as close as three to eight years of the resurrection. This means there is virtually no time gap between Christ's burial and resurrection and recorded historical testimony. The likelihood of corruption or fabrication is essentially nonexistent when historical testimony surfaces so quickly after an event.

There are New Testament manuscript fragments dating from between twenty-five and fifty years of the original autographs. Numerous larger New Testament manuscripts, some including complete books, date to within 100 to 150 years of the inspired manuscripts. And scholars have *complete* New Testaments dating as early as AD 325—a gap of only 225 years from the original autographs.[11]

By comparison, other ancient documents have much larger gaps between when they were originally written and existing copies. The writings of the Greek philosophers, Plato and Aristotle, the Roman historian, Tacitus, and most other ancient manuscripts have a time span of more than a thousand years between when they were originally written and existing copies. Furthermore, rather than thousands of copies, as in the case of the New Testament, most other ancient works are preserved by fewer than a dozen.[12]

With this established, let's look at the approximate dates the Gospels were written. We'll focus on the Gospels because they contain most historical data on Jesus Christ.

There is strong textual and historical evidence that the Gospels of Matthew, Mark, and Luke were written within thirty years of Jesus' death and that the Gospel of John was written by the end of the first century. Scholars determine this primarily by the contents of the New Testament.

Several major historical events occurred during the last half of the first century that directly impacted both Christians and Jews. These events would certainly have been included in the New Testament if they had occurred prior to its completion. Jerusalem and the temple were destroyed in AD 70. Fire destroyed much of Rome in AD 64; and Christians underwent tremendous persecution and martyrdom under the reign of Nero prior to his death in AD 68.

Such earth-shaking events most certainly would be included in the New Testament—if they had occurred before it was written. This is especially true for the Book of Acts that describes major events during the first thirty years of the Christian church. In fact, Jesus even prophesied the destruction of the temple and Jerusalem some forty years before they occurred (Matthew 24:1–2; Luke 19:41–44). Since these prophecies are in the Gospels, it is unimaginable for their fulfillment not to have been recorded in Acts if they occurred prior to its writing. Yet no single New Testament book mentions any of these events.

How do scholars use these facts to date the Gospels? They "argue backward from the book of Acts."[13] Here's how it's done.

As most Christians know, Luke wrote the Gospel of Luke and the Book of Acts for someone called Theophilus. Luke's Gospel gives historical and even biographical data about Jesus Christ. The Book of Acts focuses primarily on the ministries of Peter and Paul and the events surrounding the spread of Christianity from the ascension of Jesus to Paul's arrival in Rome, the capital of the Roman Empire.

Bible teachers frequently refer to Luke as a physician: Dr. Luke. More importantly, Luke was also a first-rate historian who traveled with the apostle Paul and carefully documented their travels. According to the introduction to Acts, Luke wrote his Gospel before he wrote Acts, which begins by referring to the Gospel of Luke.

It's clear from reading Acts that Luke was interested in significant historical events in the early church. He included in Acts the martyrdom of Stephen and James, the names of many gentile and Jewish leaders, a detailed account of Paul's missionary journeys including the names of cities, churches, officials, and so on. It's inconceivable that Luke would omit momentous historical events such as the Jewish War with Rome that began in AD 66 and resulted in the destruction of Jerusalem and the Temple in AD 70, if these events occurred before Acts was completed. Nor is it likely he would have failed to report the burning of Rome and martyrdom of Christians under Nero between AD 64–68. Likewise, as their biographer, Luke would never have omitted Paul's and Peter's death in the mid-AD 60s, especially since he recorded Stephen's and James's death. Instead, Acts ends suddenly with Paul under house arrest in Rome, expecting to be released—which he likely was and later imprisoned a second time and martyred.[14]

What do scholars conclude from this? First, it's strong evidence that Luke completed the book of Acts by the mid-AD 60s. It's the best explanation for the absence of certain significant historical data. Second, it's compelling evidence that the Gospels of Matthew and Mark as well as Luke were written before Acts. Let's consider this further.

Acts was written after the Gospel of Luke, which means that Luke was also written prior to the mid-AD 60s. Conservative scholars date Luke between AD 59–63. But what about the Gospels of Matthew and Mark? Today, most New Testament scholars agree that Luke and Matthew were written after Mark because both Matthew and Luke apparently used Mark as primary source material. Obviously, Mark is the oldest of the three Gospels. Most scholars agree that Mark was probably written during the mid to late AD 50s[15]—easily within the lifetimes of eyewitnesses of the resurrection. Matthew was likely written a little before Luke.

All three of the Synoptic Gospels (Matthew, Mark, and Luke) were almost certainly written within thirty years after Jesus' death. This is far too short a time for translators to add to or change their contents. Too many eyewitnesses were still alive to point out and refute any tampering.

In terms of apologetics, the case for the accurate transmission of the New Testament is airtight. Unlike other ancient works, not enough time elapsed between the occurrence of biblical events—such as the birth, crucifixion, burial, and postresurrection appearances of Jesus

Christ—and when these events were recorded to allow for incidental tampering, transmission errors, legends, or purposeful corruption.

Suppose someone today attempted to rewrite history by claiming that a hit-and-run driver killed President John F. Kennedy on November 22, 1963, in Phoenix, Arizona. Scarcely anyone would believe it. Why? Because people my age can recount exactly where they were and what they were doing the moment Kennedy was murdered. (I was ditching school with three friends and escaping to the mountains.) No one who lived through those days will ever forget the smallest details. In like manner, forty years from now people will be able to describe in detail the tragic attack on America on September 11, 2001.

The scenario is no different in the case of the resurrection and other major events recorded in the New Testament. Many thousands of people witnessed these events. In one instance, Jesus miraculously fed five thousand men plus women and children (Matthew 14:21). When these events were later recorded in the New Testament, many people still alive could easily refute corrupted accounts. Yet not a contrary piece of historical evidence from the first century contradicts New Testament history—including Jesus' miracles and His resurrection.

Oral Tradition

Finally, let's explore a fairly common challenge to the reliability of the New Testament Gospels. Although this minor allegation may be packaged in several ways, it's usually expressed like this:

> "How do you know that the events recorded in the Gospels weren't distorted or invented *before* they were written down?"

This question brings us back to the time of oral tradition when historical facts surrounding Jesus were memorized and passed on verbally before being written down.

At least three lines of evidence illustrate how precise verbal communication was during this period.

First, the oral period lasted no longer than twenty or twenty-five years, from the time of Jesus' resurrection to the writing of the Gospel of Mark.[16] This is far too short a time span for corruption or fabrication to intrude. Hundreds, maybe thousands, of people who personally witnessed events surrounding Jesus Christ would have preserved the integrity and accuracy of oral tradition.

Second, our world depends on the printed word. Once out of high school or college, many of us don't have to remember complicated things; we can look them up on the Internet or in a book. This wasn't the case during first century Jewish culture. People had to rely on oral information in practically every area of life, including religion. Some Jewish rabbis memorized the entire Old Testament![17] Philosopher and theologian, William Lane Craig, wrote, "Studying the oral pre-history of the gospel forms actually reinforces the likelihood that many of the traditions were quite carefully preserved ... The ancient Mediterranean cultures, particularly Judaism, relied heavily on memorization of sacred traditions."[18]

This same reliance on memorization and oral communication became part of early Christian tradition, as early church creeds illustrate. What amazes us today was ordinary for people of the first century. People who were dependent on oral communication weren't likely to make mistakes. These people were used to preserving and passing on oral information accurately. Their culture depended on it.

Third, as mentioned previously, essential Christian beliefs such as the resurrection and deity of Jesus Christ, were originally canonized in oral creeds or statements of faith. The earliest Christians memorized them years before the New Testament was written, and they were later incorporated into many of the Epistles.[19]

What's important for us to realize is that these early creeds became part of the essential teachings of the church almost immediately after Jesus' resurrection, in some cases within three to eight years. They reflect a belief in the heart of the Gospel long before the written New Testament canon. If these early Christian creeds, focusing as they do on Jesus' deity and resurrection, were later recorded almost verbatim in the Epistles, how did any theological corruption enter during the period of oral tradition? The early Christian creeds and New Testament writings are virtually identical.

How do scholars identify these early creeds in the Epistles? Sometimes, as in 1 Corinthians 15, the author told us that he was passing along teachings or traditions. In other places, differences in style, syntax, and vocabulary from what an author normally used, indicated early creedal statements incorporated into the text of the Epistles.[20]

Endnotes

1. Jon Meacham, "Who Killed Jesus?, *Newsweek*, Feb. 16, 2004, 46–48.

2. Randal Price, *The Stones Cry Out* (Eugene: Harvest House Publishers, 1997), 280.

3. Gleason L. Archer, Jr., *A Survey of Old Testament Introduction* (Chicago: The Moody Press, 1974), 25.

4. Walter C. Kaiser Jr., *The Old Testament Documents; Are they Reliable & Relevant?* (Downers Grove: InterVarsity Press, 2001), 49.

5. Josh McDowell, *Evidence That Demands a Verdict* (San Bernardino, CA: Here's Life Publishers, 1979), 39.

6. Ibid., 41–43.

7. I got the idea for this illustration from apologist Greg Koukl in his ministry (Stand to Reason) newsletter. Unfortunately, I don't recall how he actually described it, but I appreciate its clarity and sought to represent it here.

8. Normal L. Geisler and William E. Nix, A *General Introduction to the Bible* (Chicago: Moody Press, 1983), 367. This book provides a good study of the process of textual transmission of the Bible.

9. Gary R. Habermas, *The Historical Jesus; Ancient Evidence for the Life of Christ* (Joplin, Missouri: College Press Publishing Company, 1999), 144.

10. Ibid., 154.

11. Norman L. Geisler and William E. Nix, G*eneral Introduction to the Bible, Revised and Expanded* (Chicago: Moody Press, 1986), 408.

12. Josh McDowell, *Evidence That Demands a Verdict*, 42.

13. Gary R. Habermas, "Why I Believe the New Testament Is Historically Reliable," in *Why I Am A Christian*, ed. Norman L. Geisler and Paul K. Hoffman (Grand Rapids: Baker Books, 2991), 149.

14. Ibid., 149–159.

15. William Lane Craig, *Reasonable Faith; Christian Truth and Apologetics* (Wheaton: Crossway Books, 1994), 206.

16. Oral tradition is not unique to Christianity. It's just that the oral period of the church is remarkably short compared to other religions. The sayings of Buddha as well as Mahavira (founder of Jainism) were passed on orally for several hundred years.

17. Lee Strobel, *The Case for Christ; A Journalist's Personal Investigation of the Evidence for Jesus* (Grand Rapids: Zondervan Publishing House, 1998), 43.

18. William Lane Craig, *Reasonable Faith*, 209.

19. Gary R. Habermas, *The Historical Jesus*, 143.

20. Gary R. Habermas, "Why I Believe the New Testament Is Historically Reliable," in 159.

HISTORICAL ACCURACY
Built on Archaeological Testimony

THE FOURTH evidence confirming the Bible's truth and reliability is its historical accuracy. Since the late nineteenth century, Bible critics have claimed that large portions of the Bible are fantasy. Its historical information, they say, is false, and its miraculous claims are the creation of later editors attempting to supernaturalize the Bible. Again, the *Newsweek* article quoted in the last chapter illustrates this:

> The Bible is a product of human authors who were writing in particular times and places with particular points to make and visions to advance. . . .The Gospels were composed to present Jesus in the best possible light to potential converts in the Roman Empire—and to put the Temple leadership in the worst possible light. . . . It was as the church's theology took shape, culminating in the Council of Nicaea in 325, that Jesus became the doctrinal Christ, the Son of God.[1]

One reason this challenge to Scripture has been successful, at least historically, is because for years there was little confirmation of biblical facts by non-biblical sources. Many of the Bible's significant events, as well as nations, cities, peoples, and battles mentioned in its text, are recorded only in the Bible. Hence, critics who rejected the Bible's historicity assumed that this information was imaginary.

However, for more than a hundred years, archaeological investigation has demonstrated time and again the Bible's historical reliability by confirming literally hundreds of Old and New Testament accounts. Let's look at a few examples:

- Early Bible critics assumed that Moses could not have written the Pentateuch (the first five books of the Old Testament) because writing had not yet been invented (the Documentary Hypothesis). However, the discovery of the Elba Tablets in northern Syria has proven that a written language existed a thousand years before Moses.
- The Hittites were considered mythical because there was no record of their existence anywhere except in the Bible. Today, archaeology has documented 1,200 years of Hittite history.
- Archaeologists have confirmed the existence of Sodom and Gomorrah,[2] Jericho, Ur (Abraham's hometown), Dan, Beersheba, and other ancient cities thriving during the time of the Patriarchs. (Interestingly, it was discovered that the walls of Jericho "fell down flat"—outward—as reported in Joshua 6:20. "This explains how it was possible that 'every man charged straight in[to the city]' (Joshua 6.20), for the debris had formed a sort of natural bridge or ramp to scale what was left of the walls.")[3]
- Archaeology has confirmed many of the Bible's social customs, names, nationalities, religious practices, places, and trade routes. The Nuzi Tablets (c. 1500 BC) "include treaties, marriage arrangements, rules regarding inheritance [and] adoption" that are consistent with the patriarchal times described in Genesis.[4]
- Chuck Colson and Nancy Pearcey report that "archaeologists have found cuneiform tablets containing references to people such as Abraham and his brothers, Nahor and Haran."[5]
- In 1993, archaeologists uncovered a rock fragment in northern Israel bearing an ancient inscription referring to "the house of David."[6]

- There is compelling evidence for the great worldwide flood. (See Genesis 7.) Ancient Mesopotamians, Egyptians, and Greeks (as well as less advanced cultures such as the native American Indians) all possess flood stories dating from primordial times. In particular, the *Gilgamesh Epic* "describes a great flood sent as punishment by the gods, with humanity saved only when the pious Utnapishtim (AKA 'the Mesopotamian Noah') builds a ship and saves the animal world hereon."[7]
- Archaeology has confirmed many New Testament accounts and people, such as Herod and Pontius Pilate. Many of Luke's historical references, including ancient cities he mentioned in Acts, have been confirmed by archaeologists. Altogether, Luke named thirty-two countries, fifty-four cities, and nine islands without making a single error.[8] Sir William Ramsay, one of the greatest archaeologists who ever lived, wrote, "Luke's historical accuracy, supported by archaeological evidence, provides credibility to his depiction of Jesus Christ and the accuracy of his writings. . . . The book of Luke is unsurpassed in respect of its trustworthiness."[9]

Old Testament scholar Walter Kaiser, Jr. summed up the value of archaeology when he explained:

> The study of archaeology has helped illuminate the Bible by casting light on its historical and cultural location. With increasing clarity, the setting of the Bible appears more vividly within the framework of general history. . . . Archaeology has demonstrated the validity of many biblical references and data. It has continued to cast light, whether implicitly or explicitly, on many of the Bible's customs, cultures, and settings during various periods of history.[10]

Do other religions have this kind of historical verification? "No," says Paul Maier, professor of Ancient History. "No religion or culture on earth has. . . . *more specificity* [detailed information] in its earliest historical records than the Torah [Old Testament]."[11]

Consider Mormonism. Like Christianity, Mormons claim that their religion rests on a foundation of historical facts. However, unlike Christianity, the Mormon religion *lacks any confirming archaeological evidence*. Here's one example.

Mormons claim that the Nephite and Lamanite nations, each with huge populations, lived in large, fortified cities in what is now upstate New York. These nations waged large-scale wars with each other for hundreds of years, culminating in a conflict, supposedly around AD 385, in which the Nephites were destroyed. The victorious Lamanites became the ancestors of the American Indians.[12]

Guess what? Not a shred of archaeological evidence supports this—not a pot, not a weapon, not a ruin!

When I was in graduate school, I took a course titled "Witnessing to Jehovah's Witnesses and Mormons" taught by Professor Joe Gudel. During his own research for historical verification of Mormonism, Gudel consulted the National Geographic Society. The following is a portion of the letter he received back from the Society:

> We appreciate the interest that prompted your letter of August 31st [1984].
>
> Neither the Society nor any other institution of equal prestige has ever used the Book of Mormon in locating archaeological sites. Although many Mormon sources claim that the Book of Mormon has been substantiated by archaeological findings, this claim has not been verified scientifically.

In contrast, archaeology has verified hundreds of biblical claims. Not one archaeological discovery has ever contradicted one historical fact in Scripture. Says renowned archaeologist Nelson Glueck, "It may be stated categorically that no archaeological discovery has ever controverted a biblical reference. Scores of archaeological findings have been made which confirm in clear outline or exact detail historical statements in the Bible."[13]

No other religion in the world can make that claim.

Here's the point. Much of the data in the Bible is a matter of historical record *independent* of the Bible. If skeptics examine the Bible the same way historians examine other ancient documents, they must accept its historical reliability. This is especially true of the New Testament

Gospels—historical data of Jesus Christ. As one scholar put it, "One must either reject all the historical works of classical antiquity or else admit the gospel accounts along with them."[14] Why can he make such an outrageous claim? Dr. John Warwick Montgomery wrote, "To be skeptical of the resultant text of the New Testament books is to allow all of classical antiquity to slip into obscurity, *for no documents of the ancient period are as well attested bibliographically as the New Testament* [emphasis added].[15] So, when skeptics reject the Bible, they do so on *philosophical and moral grounds*, not on historical grounds. They simply do not want to believe it. They don't want to be held accountable to the moral and spiritual claims that are intrinsically bound to the historical data in Scripture.

Endnotes

1. Jon Meacham, "Who Killed Jesus?, *Newsweek*, Feb. 16, 2004, 46, 50, 51.

2. Randall Price, *The Stones Cry Out* (Eugene, OR: Harvest House Publishers, 1997), chapter 6.

3. Walter C. Kaiser Jr., *The Old Testament Documents; Are They Reliable?* (Downers Grove: InterVarsity Press, 2001, 112.

4. Paul L. Maier, "Archaeology; Biblical Ally or Adversary?" *Christian Research Journal*, Vol. 27, No.02, 19.

5. Charles Colson and Nancy Pearcey, *How Now Shall We Live?* (Wheaton: Tyndale House Publishers, 1999), 278. See Genesis 11:26–29.

6. Price, *The Stones Cry Out*, 167. Examples of "House of David" are found in 2 Samuel 3:1, 1 Kings 12:19–20, 26, and 2 Kinds 7:21.

7. Maier, "Archaeology; Biblical Ally or Adversary?" 19.

8. Norman Geisler and Ron Brooks, *When Skeptics Ask: A Handbook of Christian Evidences* (Wheaton: Victor Books, 1990), 201.

9. Sir William Ramsay, *The Bearing of Recent Discovery on the Trustworthiness of the New Testament* (Grand Rapids: Baker Book House, 1953). Quoted in *Evidence for the Resurrection* (Torrance, CA: Rose Publishing, 2004).

10. Kaiser Jr., *The Old Testament Documents; Are They Reliable?*, 98.

11. Maier, "Archaeology; Biblical Ally or Adversary?", 19.

12. For an excellent study of Mormonism, see Ron Rhodes & Marian Bodine's book, *Reasoning from the Scriptures with the Mormons* (Eugene, OR: Harvest House Publishers, 1995).

13. Quoted in Norman L. Geisler and Abdul Saleeb, *Answering Islam; the Crescent in the Light of the Cross* (Grand Rapids: Baker Books, 2001), 241.

14. William Lane Craig, *Reasonable Faith; Christian Truth and Apologetics* (Wheaton: Crossway Books, 1994), 165.

15. John Warwick Montgomery, *History and Christianity* (San Bernardino, CA: Here's Life Publishers, 1983), 29.

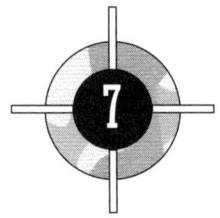

SCIENTIFIC ACCURACY
No Myths or Inaccuracies

ANOTHER COMMON misconception among skeptics and other non-Christians is that the Bible contains scientific fallacies and inaccuracies. In fact, the scientific accuracy of Scripture represents a fifth evidence for the truth and reliability of the Bible.[1]

The Bible does not claim to be—nor is it—a science textbook. If it were, it would have quickly become outdated long ago because science is always in a state of change. The central purpose of the Bible is not to teach science but to show people how to become reconciled with God and achieve eternal life through Jesus Christ. This does not mean, however, that the Bible is inaccurate when it refers to natural phenomena or other scientific data. The Bible does not contain anything scientifically false. Whenever the authors of Scripture touch on a scientific matter, they present truth, not error.

The Bible, which makes numerous scientific references that were far advanced for the science of its day, contains none of the absurdities found in the sacred writings of the contemporaries of biblical authors. A few examples will demonstrate this.[2]

- Greek mythology taught that the world rested on the shoulders of Atlas. Job 26:7 correctly reveals that God "hangs the earth on

nothing"—the earth rests in space without any visible means of support.
- Ancient astronomers estimated that the heavens contained about five thousand stars. The prophet Jeremiah wrote in 33:22 that "the host of heaven [stars] cannot be counted."
- Isaiah 40:22 refers to the earth as a "circle."
- The Bible accurately describes natural phenomena whose processes were unknown at the time biblical texts were written. Ecclesiastes 1:6 states, "Blowing toward the south, then turning toward the north, the wind continues swirling along; and on its circular courses the wind returns." In the following verse, the author added, "All the rivers flow into the sea, yet the sea is not full. To the place where the rivers flow, there they flow again" (vs. 7).

Together, these passages clearly describe the circular movement of the earth's winds as well as the earth's hydraulic system, where water evaporates from the oceans, rains on the earth, and returns again to the sea via rivers to repeat the cycle. It's doubtful that the author of Ecclesiastes was trying to write a scientific treatise here. Regardless of what Solomon was trying to communicate, these descriptions do not violate known scientific facts and were recorded in the Bible centuries before modern science. This stands in stark contrast to the contemporaries of biblical authors whose writings were full of scientific fallacies.

Of course the most controversial subject pitting the Bible and science against one another is naturalistic evolution. We'll consider it in Part Two.

Endnotes

1. The following is a partial restatement of a portion of chapter 11 in my book, *Defending Your Faith; Reliable Answers for a New Generation of Seekers and Skeptics* (Grand Rapids: Kregel Publications, 1997), 132–134.

2. A good study comparing scientific data as viewed by ancient peoples with the biblical writers is Kenny Barfield's, *Why the Bible Is Number 1; The World's Sacred Writings in the Light of Science* (Grand Rapids: Baker Book House, 1988).

PROPHETIC ACCURACY
Incredible Odds

FULFILLED PROPHECY is the sixth evidence confirming the Bible's truth and reliability. Many apologists believe this is the strongest single evidence that the Bible is divine revelation.[1] It perhaps best answers the question, "How do Christians know the Bible is true and reliable?"

No other book in existence (religious or otherwise) offers the vast number of accurate and detailed predictions as the Bible. According to the *Encyclopedia of Biblical Prophecies*, there are 1,817 predictions in the Bible: 1,239 in the Old Testament and 578 in the New Testament.[2]

Professor John Bloom suggests that specific criteria be used before any alleged prophecy can be considered authentic. To qualify as bona fide prophecy, a prediction,

1. "must be clear enough to be recognized when it has occurred,"
2. "must be known to have been made before it is fulfilled,"
3. "must not be influenced [e.g. fulfilled] by the prophet himself, or by his zealous band of followers;"

4. "must be more than a good guess," that is, the prophet must refer to events far in the future, be specific in detail, and not accompanied by false prophecies.[3]

Thus, Jeanne Dixon would be disqualified as a prophet (even though she supposedly predicted President Kennedy's assassination) because most of her prophecies never came true. (This latter qualification is clearly endorsed Deuteronomy 18:20–22.) Unarguably, only biblical prophecies pass this test of authenticity.

Old Testament prophecies encompass a variety of events and circumstances. In particular, they focus on the Jewish nation (her apostasy, dispersal, and return to the land of Israel), the rise and fall of other nations and cities surrounding Israel (such as Egypt, Babylon, and Nineveh), and the events and circumstances surrounding the predicted Jewish Messiah (Jesus Christ). Here's a small sample:

- Daniel accurately predicted the succession of the great world kingdoms: the Medes and Persians followed by Greece and Rome (Daniel 2:37–42).
- Cyrus, king of Persia, was mentioned by name (Isaiah 44:28 and 45:1) 150 years before he was born.
- The prophet Ezekiel described in detail the destruction of the ancient cities of Tyre and Sidon (Ezekiel 26 and 28).
- The dispersal of the Israelites to Assyria (722–721 BC) and Babylon (586 BC), and the eventual return of the Babylonian exiles to their historic homeland, was prophesied nearly seven centuries before these events occurred (Deuteronomy 28:64–65, 30:1–5). A second dispersal occurred after the destruction of Jerusalem and the temple in AD 70. Some believe the prophecy in Isaiah 11:11 was fulfilled more than twenty-five centuries later when Israel again became an independent nation in 1948.
- According to the *Encyclopedia of Biblical Prophecies,* there are "191 prophecies concerning the anticipated Jewish Messiah and Savior. Each was literally fulfilled in the birth, life, death, resurrection, and ascension of Jesus of Nazareth."[4] A few examples are included in the following chart:[5]

Important Old Testament Prophecies About Jesus

OT Prophecy	NT Fulfillment
Born a virgin (Isaiah 7:14)	Matthew 1:22, 23
Born in Bethlehem (Micah 5:2)	Luke 2:4–7
Preceded by a forerunner (Malachi 3:1)	Matthew 11:10
Entered Jerusalem on a donkey (Zechariah 9:9)	Matthew 21:4, 5
Betrayed for 30 pieces of silver (Zechariah 11:12)	Matthew 26:14, 15
Spat on and struck (Isaiah 50:6)	Matthew 26:67
Crucified with other prisoners (Isaiah 53:12)	Luke 22:37
Pierced through hands and feet (Psalms 22:16)	John 20:25–27
Pierced through His side (Zechariah 12:10)	John 19:34–37
Soldiers gambled for clothing (Psalms 22:18)	Matthew 27:35
Buried in a rich man's tomb (Isaiah 53:9)	Matthew 27:57–60
Would be resurrected (Psalms 16:10)	Matthew 28:5–7
Would return a second time (Daniel 7:13, 14)	Revelation 19

In terms of messianic prophesy, Isaiah 53:2–12 is probably the most astounding biblical passage. It precisely described twelve aspects of Jesus' suffering and death that were literally fulfilled in Jesus Christ.

1. He was rejected;
2. He was a man of sorrows;
3. He lived a life of suffering;
4. He was despised by others;
5. He carried our sorrow;
6. He was smitten and afflicted by God;
7. He was pierced for our transgressions;
8. He was wounded for our sins;
9. He suffered like a lamb;
10. He died with the wicked;
11. He was sinless; and
12. He prayed for others.[6]

Why is fulfilled prophecy such an important evidence for the Bible's truth and reliability? Among the many hundreds of prophecies found in Scripture, not a single God-ordained prophet made a single error. Every biblical prophecy up to the present day has been fulfilled exactly as predicted. What incredible accuracy!

Skeptics have claimed that predictions concerning Jesus could have been fulfilled accidentally or even deliberately. If so, biblical prophecy is fraudulent and the Bible loses its primary apologetic verification. However, such allegations are preposterous. Apart from divine revelation, how could anyone predict the place and time of Jesus' birth, being pierced in the side, betrayed for thirty pieces of silver, soldiers casting lots for His garments, or being buried in a rich man's tomb? Moreover, the statistical impossibility of even a few of these prophecies coming true as predicted destroys any illusion that biblical prophecies are accidental.

Peter Stoner and Robert Newman, in their book, *Science Speaks*, demonstrated the statistical impossibility of any one man, from the time the prophecies were spoken down to the present day, accidentally or deliberately fulfilling *just eight* of the (at least) 191 prophecies Jesus fulfilled. Their analysis reveals that the chance of this happening is one in 10^{17} power. Stoner and Newman give an illustration that helps to visualize the magnitude of such odds:

> Suppose that we take 10^{17} silver dollars and lay them on the face of Texas. They will cover all of the state two feet deep. Now mark one of these silver dollars and stir the whole mass thoroughly, all over the state. Blindfold a man and tell him that he can travel as far as he wishes, but he must pick up one silver dollar and say that this is the right one. What chance would he have of getting the right one? Just the same chance that the prophets would have had of writing these eight prophecies and having them all come true in any one man, from their day to the present time, providing they wrote using their own wisdom.[7]

In contrast, other religions that claim prophecy have a dismal track record, which may explain why few religions tout prophecy. The *Qur'an*, for example, is one of many religious books that avoid making any predictions (except for the Last Judgment, which of course can't be checked out). As Bloom observed, "Few 'gods' will permit their authority to be challenged by any tangible evidence which we can test today."[8]

Examples of False Prophecy

Here are a few examples of false prophecy from religions that claim prophetic authority. "Prophets" of the Jehovah's Witnesses have made significant predictions that have never come true.

In 1909, an official publication of the Jehovah's Witnesses, *Studies in the Scriptures*, Series 11, "The Time Is at Hand," predicted:

- "[W]ithin the coming twenty-six years all present governments will be overthrown and dissolved" (pg. 98).
- "In view of the strong Bible evidence concerning the Times of the Gentiles, we consider it an established truth that the final end of the kingdoms of this world, and the full establishment of the Kingdom of God, will be accomplished at the end of A.D. 1914" (pg. 99). But the Battle of Armageddon did not occur in 1914.
- A publication titled *Millions Now Living Will Never Die* predicted, "Scriptures definitely fix the fact that there will be a resurrection of Abraham, Isaac, Jacob and other faithful ones of old ... we may expect 1925 to witness the return of these faithful men of Israel from the condition of death, being resurrected and fully restored to perfect humanity" (pg. 88).

Mormon prophecy fares no better. In fact, it's even more bizarre. Consider these examples:

In *Journal of Discourses* 13:271 (July 24, 1870), Brigham Young claimed that the moon was inhabited.

In *Journal of Discourses*, 1856, it was predicted that "Brigham Young will become President of the United States."

In 1868, *Journal of Discourses*, Elder Orson Pratt predicted that New York City would "in a few years become a mass of ruins."

In *Doctrines and Covenants*, 84:1–5, 31 (September 1832), Founder Joseph Smith, Jr., predicted, "Mount Zion, which shall be the city of New Jerusalem ... shall be built ... in the western boundaries of the

State of Missouri, and dedicated by the hand of Joseph Smith.... For verily this generation shall not all pass away until a house shall be built unto the Lord... upon the consecrated spot as I have appointed." [9]

Smith stated in *History of the Church* that "unless the United States redress the wrongs committed upon the Saints in the state of Missouri and punish the crimes committed by her officers that in a few years the government will be utterly overthrown and wasted, and there will not be so much as a potsherd left."[10]

Secular prophets fare no better. A 1976 study by the *People's Almanac* of twenty-five "top psychics" resulted in a 92 percent failure rate. The remaining 8 percent "could easily be explained by chance and general knowledge of circumstances."[11]

The favored soothsayer for unbelievers who wish to point out successful non-Christian prophets is Nostradamus, the French astrologer and physician. Nostradamus began making prophecies in 1547, which were later published in a book titled *Centuries*. Supposedly, he predicted the French Revolution, World War 1, and other notable events. However, like modern psychics, Nostradamus' predictions were often "enigmatic, ambiguous, and inaccurate."[12] Read a few of them, and you'll quickly see how vague and unintelligible they are.

Commenting on Nostradamus, Christian apologist Norman Geisler pointed out that his "predictions are very ambiguous and could fit a great variety of events. His followers are inconsistent in how they interpret what he said. And some of his prophecies have been shown to be false. In fact, not a single prediction of Nostradamus has ever been proven genuine."[13]

Biblical predictions, on the other hand, are detailed, given far in advance, clear and explicit, and beyond any possibility of human forecast. In terms of apologetics, the strength of biblical prophecy is that only an omniscient God who knows the future could make and fulfill such predictions.

Endnotes

1. For a good study of the value of fulfilled prophecy in terms of apologetics, see John Warwick Montgomery, ed., *Evidence for Faith: Deciding the God Question* (Dallas: Prove Books, 1991), Part 4.

2. Quoted in Norman L. Geisler, *Baker Encyclopedia of Christian Apologetics* (Grand Rapids: Baker Book House, 1999), 609.

3. John A. Bloom, "Truth Via Prophecy," in John Warwick Montgomery's, *Evidence for Faith*, 176–177.

4. Geisler, *Baker Encyclopedia of Christian Apologetics*, 610.

5. Dan Story, *Defending Your Faith; Reliable Answers for a New Generation of Seekers and Skeptics* (Grand Rapids: Kregel Publications, 1997), 79.

6. Geisler, *Baker Encyclopedia of Christian Apologetics*, 611.

7. Robert C. Newman and Peter W. Stoner, *Science Speaks; Scientific Proof of the Accuracy of Prophecy and the Bible* (Chicago: Moody Press, 1976), 106–107.

8. Bloom, "Truth Via prophecy," *Evidence For Faith*, 178.

9. Walter Martin, *The Maze of Mormonism* (Ventura, CA: Regal Books, 1978), 353.

10. Ibid., 356.

11. Geisler, *Baker Encyclopedia of Christian Apologetics*, 615.

12. Quoted from an interview with Norman Geisler in Lee Strobel's, *The Case for Faith; A Journalist Investigates the Toughest Objections to Christianity* (Grand Rapids: Zondervan, 2000), 133.

13. Ibid.

SUBJECTIVE CONFIRMATION
Christianity "Works!"

IF THE INFORMATION in this section doesn't convince skeptics (at least intellectually) that the Bible is divine revelation, I don't know what else will.

God has chosen to reveal information about Himself in the Bible, as well as the nature of people, the reality of sin, and the way to be reconciled with Him. No other contender exists that even remotely compares with the Bible in confirming evidences. As Norman Geisler stated during an interview with Lee Strobel, "The Bible claims to be the Word of God and the Bible proves to be the Word of God."[1]

We can express this conclusion in the form of a second apologetic principle. Like the first principle (see introduction to Part One), it will also guide our apologetic methodology throughout this book:

> No one can make a faith decision to receive Jesus Christ unaided by the Holy Spirit. Nevertheless, if a person were to make a decision to choose a religion based solely on the evidence and if he were intellectually honest, he would be forced to choose Christianity and to reject all other religions.

Unfortunately, demonstrating the truth of Scriptures and the divine nature of Jesus Christ (see Part Four) does not automatically result in an unbeliever becoming a Christian. People can choose to make a willful decision to reject Jesus in spite of the best evidence. People can and do make emotional and moral commitments to unbelief. But these are not *rational* reasons. They are "don't-bother-me-with-the-facts" kind of responses. When we bring a skeptic to the point where he or she sees that the real basis for disbelief is not intellectual, we've done our job as apologists.

So far we have looked at *objective* evidences—non-biblical evidences that support the Bible from outside the Bible. However, these are not the only evidences confirming Christianity and in many witnessing opportunities, not even the best. This brings us to the seventh variety of evidence for the Bible's authority and reliability—*subjective* confirmation.

Subjective confirmation does not depend on anything outside of Scripture, but rather has to do with the divine power of the Bible on its own. I'm not referring to the inner, spiritual confirmation all true Christians experience (Romans 8:16), although that is certainly powerful evidence for the truth of Christianity.

For many non-Christians, God has prepared their hearts and minds for the gospel. They do not have the intellectual obstacles that apologetics address. These people just need to witness our faith in action while hearing about the love and forgiveness of Jesus Christ. They need to see that Jesus Christ can change their lives just as He has changed the lives of millions of Christians.

When we apply biblical principles to our everyday lives, Christianity fulfills its promises. It achieves what it claims it will achieve. It transforms us, heals our wounds, removes our guilt, and changes our view of life. We once rejected God, now we crave to live close to Him. We once depended on alcohol or drugs to get through life, now we have the power of God. We were once anxious and fearful, now we have "the peace of God, which surpasses all comprehension" (Philippians 4:7). As Os Guinness put it, "The Christian faith is not true because it works; it works because it is true. It is not true because we experience it; we experience it—deeply and gloriously—because it is true." [2] The Bible is not only confirmed by the kinds of objective and empirical evidences we have investigated, but also by our religious experiences. This is the "subjective" message non-Christians need to hear.

Endnotes

1. Lee Strobel, *The Case for Faith; A Journalist Investigates the Toughest Objections to Christianity* (Grand Rapids: Zondervan, 2000), 137.

2. Os Guinness, *Time for Truth*, quoted in Hank Hanegraaff, *The Covering; God's Plan to Protect You from Evil* (Nashville: W publishing Group, 2002), 43.

PART TWO

CREATION OR EVOLUTION? LET THE SCIENTIFIC EVIDENCE SPEAK FOR ITSELF

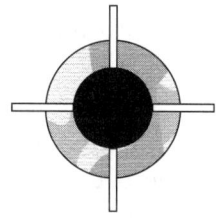

INTRODUCTION TO PART TWO

SINCE THE 1925 Scopes Trial, the debate between evolution and creation has probably received more media coverage and raised the ire of more educators and scientists than any other apologetic issue. The power of law has sided mostly with evolution, mandating that evolution is science and creation religion. Many believe evolution should be taught in public schools while creation can be preached to the credulous from the pulpit.

However, law does not make evolution true anymore than it would make creation true. The issue is one of scientific evidence, not law. Which model of origins does the scientific evidence support: creation or evolution? Hundreds of books and articles have been written on this topic from a Christian perspective and on a popular level. Let's explore, using a three-step strategy, what I believe are the key scientific evidences that falsify evolution and verify creation.

1. Evaluate three preliminary observations that reveal the theory of evolution is not the scientific stronghold defenders claim.
2. Challenge and refute four bedrock assumptions that form the infrastructure of naturalistic evolution (Darwinism). If these four

assumptions are indefensible, the theory of evolution obviously rests on a foundation of sand.
3. Examine several examples of evolutionary "fakes, frauds, and phonies."

Note that the following chapters rely on the facts of science, not on theological arguments. This approach is vital to effective apologetics, and it works. Sincere and fair critics who shun creation because it's "religion" and not science, must consider creation if we can demonstrate the scientific evidence leads in that direction. Our job as Christian apologists is to do this, and the facts are on our side. As William Dembski pointed out, "The very sorts of arguments that Darwinists had been using to try to discredit intelligent design and relegate it to the sphere of religion rather than science ended up discrediting Darwinian evolution itself and exposing its unscientific presuppositions."[1]

Endnotes

1. William Dembski, "The New Age of Information," *World*, April 3, 2004, 45.

PRELIMINARY OBSERVATIONS
Facts that Crack the Evolutionary Wall

Fact One: Most People Reject Atheistic Evolution

From the birth of modern science, several hundred years ago until the late nineteenth century, science and Christianity were mutually compatible. Most scientists were Christians, and their amazing discoveries into the complex interworkings of nature only fueled their conviction that God designed life and the cosmos. "Copernicus, Kepler, Newton, and Galileo . . . were inspired in their scientific discoveries by the conviction that they were revealing the intricate plan of a Divine Artisan."[1]

Not so today. The majority of scientists accept a naturalistic explanation for the origin of life and the universe that precludes a creator God. However, even though secular science teaches that evolution through natural processes is fact, most Americans do not believe in this kind of atheistic evolution. According to a Gallup poll, "45 percent of Americans believe man did not evolve, but was created by God in the last 10,000 years. Just 12 percent thought humans developed over millions of years without God, while another 37 percent agreed with the statement that man evolved in a process guided by God."[2]

Why do most Americans reject atheistic evolution? Most people aren't atheists. As the above statistics reveal, only 12 percent of Americans actually believe that humans (and other living things) evolved by natural processes in which God played no part. Evidently, 88 percent of Americans are theist. This raises an interesting question. If most Americans believe in a creator God, why do so many readily accept evolution as a fact of life rather than strongly rejecting it? Sadly, naturalistic evolution has become an essential doctrine of secular culture. It's what students are taught in secular schools; it's what we see on television shows such as *Discovery;* it's what we read in *National Geographic.* We don't really believe it, but sometimes unthinkingly embrace it just as we do other worldview presuppositions that are ingrained in our culture.

This mental programming isn't surprising considering that the pacesetters in the scientific community are predominantly atheists. A 1998 survey of "elite scientists . . . those who have been elected to membership in the National Academy of Sciences. . . . [shows that] disbelief in supernatural theism among Academy members was over 90 percent, for biologists it was 95 percent."[3]

From an apologetics perspective, it may be helpful when engaging evolutionists to point out that nearly 90 percent of Americans reject atheistic evolution and accept some form of divine creation. Statistically, the person to whom you are talking to is probably not an atheist—even though he or she may inadvertently endorse evolution. If you get an evolutionist to admit belief in a supernatural being, divine activity in creation logically follows. You have established a fertile point of contact that may open the door for introducing evidences that support creation by design.

Fact Two: Evolutionists Can't Agree with Each Other

There is no standard evolutionary theory to which all evolutionists agree. Even well-known evolutionists differ on how evolution works.

Consider the fact that three eminent and outspoken evolutionists each entertain a different hypothesis regarding evolutionary theory.

British evolutionist Richard Dawkins of Cambridge University, England, is the best-known advocate of neo-Darwinism. This view postulates that evolution is a gradual process propelled by natural selection and random mutational changes in DNA. Its proponents believe that chance alterations (mutations) in DNA are beneficial to an organism, aiding its survival. Accumulations of these beneficial mutations eventually develop into useful traits that are passed on to succeeding generations. After millions of years and millions of tiny genetic changes, eventually, a totally new animal evolves whose genetic makeup and physical appearance is different from its ancestors—who by now have become extinct. Most people are familiar with this evolutionary view.

The late American paleontologist and evolutionist, Steven Jay Gould of Harvard, promoted "punctuated equilibrium." He vigorously (and correctly) argued that the fossil record does not support gradual evolution over millions of years. The lack of transitional fossils makes this clear. Gould hypothesized that evolution takes place rapidly among isolated populations, resulting in the sudden appearance ("punctuated") of new plants or animals followed by long periods when no evolutionary changes occur ("equilibrium").

Nobel Prize winner Frances Crick, now deceased, endorsed yet another theory called "directed panspermia." Recognizing the impossibility of life arising from inanimate matter (abiogenesis), he suggested that space aliens (or something from outer space) seeded planet earth with life—possibly bacteria. Once this initial impregnation occurred, other evolutionary processes carried on from there. (If this sounds familiar, maybe it was because the movie, *Mission to Mars*, contained a similar scenario.)

Of course, all three of these evolutionists built their theories on the foundation of philosophical naturalism. (See chapter twenty-six.) So whatever means evolution used to develop life, no God existed to help it along—let alone create it. Nevertheless, they all *disagreed* on how the process works. Dr. Henry M. Morris, founder of the Institute for Creation Research (ICR) wrote, "Although . . . [evolutionists] close ranks when doing battle with creationists, they wrangle bitterly among themselves."[4]

In terms of tactical apologetics, we can use this lack of unity among evolutionists to point out that the theory is not as homogeneous and invincible as they would like people to believe. Evolution is a theory, not a fact. Ironically, the opposing pillars of evolution inadvertently lend credence to creation by design. Creationists agree—all of these three theories mentioned are wrong.

Fact Three: The Underlying Premise of Evolution Is Philosophy Not Science

People who reject creation in favor of evolution are unwittingly making a philosophical decision—not a scientific one. Phillip Johnson, who has written extensively on this subject, observed that "the doctrine that some known process of evolution turned a protozoan into a human is a philosophical assumption, not something that can be confirmed by experiment or by historical studies of the fossil record."[5]

This point is crucial to understand as we seek to confront and defeat evolution in the public arena. You see, many professional evolutionists are committed to a philosophical worldview called naturalism. Naturalistic evolution endorses the premise that the origin and development of life and the cosmos can be accounted for by purely natural processes at work in a wholly material universe. Nature is a closed system that cannot be affected by any nonmaterial entity such as God. Of course, there is no observable or testable evidence for this worldview. Hence, the core issue that separates creationists and evolutionists is philosophy. Johnson explained:

> Darwinists know that the mutation-selection mechanism can produce wings, eyes, and brains not because the mechanism can be observed to do anything of the kind, but because their guiding philosophy assures them that no other power is available to do the job. The absence from the cosmos of any Creator is therefore the essential starting point for Darwinism.... As an explanation

for how complex organism came into existence in the first place, it is pure philosophy.[6]

Elsewhere Johnson illustrated this point with a quote from Harvard Genetics Professor Richard Lewontin.

> We take the side of science *in spite of* the patent absurdity of some of its constructs, *in spite of* its failure to fulfill many of its extravagant promises of health and life, *in spite* of the tolerance of the scientific community for unsubstantiated just-so stories, because we have a prior commitment, a commitment to materialism. It is not that the methods and institutions of science somehow compel us to accept a material explanation of the phenomenal world, but, on the contrary, that we are forced by our *a priori* adherence to material causes to create an apparatus of investigation and a set of concepts that produce material explanations, no matter how counter intuitive, no matter how mystifying to the uninitiated. Moreover, that materialism is absolute, for we cannot allow a Divine Foot in the door (Emphasis in quote).[7]

Why are some devout evolutionists blatant dogmatists? Because they are terrified to connect the supernatural world to science. They are convinced that creationists have a hidden agenda to bring religious beliefs into public schools.

A long-time friend of mine is a confirmed evolutionist who taught high school biology and chemistry in public schools. As I wrote this book, I asked him to read chapters in which I laid out the case for creation and the problems with naturalistic evolution. My friend had virtually no rebuttals to my arguments against evolution; the evidence was too strong. Nevertheless, he wrote, "I am ... of the opinion that creationism should be explored in social studies classes as part of the curriculum on religions of the world." He continued, "Creationists believe that they need to 'defeat evolution in the public arena' and have [an] agenda that would result in their religious belief included in all public school science text material."

Nothing can be further from the truth. Most Americans—including Christians—reject the notion that only the theory of creation origins can be taught in public schools. According to a recent poll, 64 percent of Americans favor teaching creationism along with evolution in public schools. This concept was endorsed not only by "conservative Christians, but also by majorities of secular respondents, liberal Democrats and those who accept the theory of natural selection."[8] This shouldn't be surprising. Johnson observed, "In a country where the vast majority of citizens believe in God, it is controversial to require that public schools teach as fact (or as implicit in the very definition of 'science') that God played no discernible part in the creation of plants, animals, and human beings."[9] Creationists are not afraid of evolution. In fact, most creationists prefer that students also be taught evolution because when the two models are compared, it becomes clear that creation better accounts for the scientific data.

It's rare to find this sentiment among evolutionists. Almost without exception, Darwinists vigorously oppose teaching the creation model of origins in public schools. Consider the following excerpt from a lengthy article in the *Los Angeles Times*: "In science, scientists as well as educators have concluded that evolution—and only evolution—should be taught in science classes because it is the only scientific explanation for why the universe is the way it is today."[10]

Darwinists are committed to philosophical naturalism. They're committed to a philosophical worldview more than they're committed to science. They know that if the two models of origins are given equal treatment, evolution will come up short. This is evident when creationists and evolutionists debate. Most observers agree that evolutionists nearly always (if not always) lose![11] As Phillip Johnson put it, "Science educators are not confident that their cherished theory can survive the kind of teaching that encourages critical thinking."[12]

Perhaps this is the real reason why the National Academy of Sciences released a 140-page booklet entitled, *Teaching Evolution and the Nature of Science*. The booklet clearly attacks creation science and suggests teaching guidelines for public schools that urged educators *not* to teach creationism but rather to present the theory of evolution as the "most important concept in modern biology."[13]

If belief in Darwinian evolution was grounded in science rather than philosophy, there would not be such paranoia. Darwinists would willingly examine and debate the scientific data and go with the facts, regardless of where they lead. If the evidence leads to creation, honest scientists would endorse creation. If it leads to evolution, they would endorse evolution. This is what happened in 2004 to the 81-year old British philosopher, Anthony Flew. An atheist since the age of fifteen (he once debated C. S. Lewis over the existence of God), Flew was willing to "go where the evidence leads." He concluded that naturalistic processes were inadequate to explain the origin of life. In a recent article in the *Christian Research Journal*, Flew was quoted as saying, "It is simply out of the question that the first living matter evolved out of dead matter and developed into an extraordinary, complicated creature of which we have no examples. There must have been some intelligence."[14]

The creationists' challenge to evolutionists is to let the facts speak for themselves. Johnson expressed this well:

> A real science does not employ propaganda and legal barriers to prevent relevant questions from being asked, nor does it rely on enforcing rules of reasoning that allow no alternative to the official story. If the Darwinists had a good case to make, they would welcome the critics to an academic forum for open debate, and they would want to confront the best critical arguments rather than to caricature them as straw men. Instead they have chosen to rely on the dishonorable methods of power politics.[15]

Unfortunately, the majority of today's leading evolutionary scientists refuse to acknowledge scientific data supporting creation, let alone give creationists a public voice—as the following interview illustrates. Columnist George Caylor interviewed a molecular biologist for an article entitled, "The Biologist," that ran on February 17, 2000 in *The Ledger* (Lynchburg, Virginia). Permission was granted by Mr. Caylor to reprint part of the interview.[16] The biologist requested anonymity, so the interview was between "G" (George Caylor) and "J" (the molecular biologist).

G: "Do you believe that the information int he human DNA code evolved?"

J: "George, nobody I know in my profession believes it evolved. It was engineered by 'genius beyond genius,' and such information could not have been written any other way. The paper and ink did not write the book! Knowing what we know, it is ridiculous to think otherwise."

G: "Have you ever stated that in a public lecture, or in any public writing?"

J: "No. I just say it evolved. To be a molecular biologist requires some to hold on to two insanities at all times. One, it would be insane to believe in evolution when you can see the truth for yourself. Two, it would be insane to say you don't believe in evolution. All government work, research grants, papers, big college lecturers—everything would stop. I'd be out of a job, or relegated to the outer fringes where I couldn't earn a decent living."

G: "I hate to say it, but that sounds intellectually dishonest."

J: "The work I do in genetic research is honorable. We will find the cures to many of mankind's worst diseases. But in the meantime, we have to live with the 'elephant in the living room.'"

G: "What elephant?"

J: "Creation design. It's like an elephant in the living room. It moves around, takes up an enormous amount of space, loudly trumpets, bumps into us, knocks things over, eats a ton of hay, and smells like an elephant. And yet we have to swear it isn't there!"

Many geneticists, molecular biologist, and other scientists recognize the evidence for creation. Unfortunately, career considerations, peer pressure, the need to maintain funding, and academia's overall commitment to philosophical naturalism prevents them from publicly expressing their true beliefs.

With these three facts about evolution and evolutionists established, we can now examine the scientific data that refutes evolution. We'll look at four challenging questions that naturalistic evolution must explain if evolution is true:

- "How can something come from nothing?"
- "How can order evolve from disorder?"
- "How can life emerge from non-life?"
- "Where are the transitional fossils?"

Let's see how well the facts of science and the laws of physics uphold the evolutionary position on these issues in comparison to the scientific evidence that supports creation by divine design.

Endnotes

1. Nancy Pearcey, *Total Truth: Liberating Christianity from Its Cultural Captivity* (Wheaton: Crossway Books, 2004), 180.

2. Quoted in "Coral Ridge Ministries Launches Creation Outreach, *Impact*, May 2004, p. 5. A similar statistic from an earlier Gallup poll reports that "about fifty percent of Americans believe in creationism, forty percent in theistic evolution [God guided or, at least, initiated evolution], and ten percent in materialistic or Darwinian evolution." Tony Carnes, *Christianity Today*, Nov. 15, 1999, 27.

3. Phillip E. Johnson, *The Wedge of Truth; Splitting the Foundations of Naturalism* (Downers Grove: InterVarsity Press, 2000), 86.

4. Henry M. Morris, "A House Divided," *Back to Genesis* (Institute for Creation Research, February 2000), a.

5. Phillip E. Johnson, *Defeating Darwinism* (Downers Grove: InterVarsity Press, 1997), 34–35.

6. Phillip E. Johnson, *Darwin on Trial* (Downers Grove: InterVarsity Press, 1991), 115.

7. Quoted in Phillip E. Johnson, *First Things*, "The Unraveling of Scientific Materialism," Nov. 1997, (in firstthings.com.), 3.

8. Laurie Goodstein, "Broad support found for teaching both creationism, evolution," The San Diego Union-Tribune, August 31, 2005. The poll was con-

ducted in July 7–17, 2005, by the Pew Forum on Religion and Public Life and the Pew Research Center for the People and the Press.

9. Johnson, *The Wedge of Truth*, 66.

10. "Evolution 101," *Los Angeles Times*, April 15, 1998.

11. A good documentation of the consistent failure of evolutionists to win debates with creationists in the early days of the debate, is Marvin L. Lubenow, *"From Fish to Gish"* (San Diego: CLP Publishers, 1983).

12. Johnson, *The Wedge of Truth*, 83.

13. Cited in Janet & Craig Parshall, *Tough Faith* (Eugene OR: Harvest House Publishers, 1999), 23. The Parshalls are quoting *The Washingtion Times*, April 10, 1998, A9.

14. Douglas LeBlanc, "Atheists and Theists Analyze Anthony Flew's Newfound Deism, *Christian Research Journal*, Vol. 28, no. 3 (2005), 42.

15. Phillip E. Johnson, *The Wedge of Truth*, 141.

16. George Caylor, email correspondence, 10–24-06.

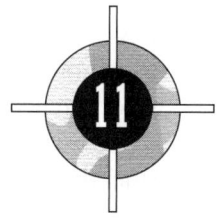

How Can Something Come from Nothing?

MOST EVOLUTIONISTS believe that the universe suddenly exploded into existence some fifteen billion years ago through a phenomenon referred to as the "Big Bang." According to Big Bang cosmology:

> The entire physical universe—all the matter and energy, and even the four dimensions of space and time—burst forth from a state of infinite, or near infinite, density, temperature, and pressure. The universe expanded from a volume very much smaller than the period at the end of this sentence, and it continues to expand.[1]

This "Big Bang" is the first principal assumption on which naturalistic evolution depends. Without a blink, popular scientists and their media pulpit preach this view as established fact. A recent article in the science section of the *San Diego Union-Tribune* states: "Well, for one thing, everything arose from nothing. Before there was a universe, there was no time, space, matter or energy. Nothing existed but nothing. Then the Big Bang happened—a sudden, inexplicable expansion of space that carried matter and energy along with it."[2]

The key issue is not so much *whether* a Big Bang occurred, but *how* it occurred. Although most young earthers (people who accept a literal six-day creation as described in Genesis 1) categorically deny a Big Bang, the origin of the universe is not explained even if such an event happened. Darwinists must still answer this question: "Who lit the fuse?" Where did the matter and energy behind the Big Bang come from? No known laws of physics explain how matter or energy can arise spontaneously out of nothing. In fact, this assumption violates the laws of physics. Henry Morris explained that the First Law of Thermodynamics (Law of Energy Conservation) "states that nothing is now being either 'created' or destroyed. It therefore teaches quite conclusively that the universe did not create itself; there is nothing in the present structure of natural law that could possibly account for its own origin."[3]

He further pointed out that the First and Second Laws of Thermodynamics are "*proven* scientific laws, if there is such a thing. They have been experimentally tested, measured, and confirmed, thousands of times, on systems both extremely large and extremely small, and no scientist today doubts their full applicability in the space-time coordinates assessable to us. For that reason, the cosmic implications of the two Laws are profound."[4]

In short, the laws of physics only prove that nothing comes out of nothing. Nothing only "creates" nothing. This totally agrees with the biblical doctrine of creation, which teaches that God spoke the cosmos into existence out of nothing. (See Psalm 33:6, Hebrews 11:3, 2 Peter 3:5.) If the Big Bang theory is true, as one person put it, "God spoke and bang, it happened."

Of course, to avoid the anathema of divine creation, many secular cosmologists disclaim any model of origins that requires the supernatural. Some cosmologists insist that there are unknown laws of physics yet to be discovered, and that science will one day explain how matter can suddenly pop into existence out of nothing. My evolutionist friend sanctions such a view when he suggested, "Astrophysicists live in a theoretical world beyond their touch . . . As new information becomes available, the model is refined."

Other Darwinists contend that quantum physics allow for uncaused events to occur at the subatomic level.[5] They claim that subatomic particles can suddenly materialize spontaneously out of vacuum fluctuations. William Lane Craig commented on this:

> These subatomic particles... are called "virtual particles." They are theoretical entities, and it's not even clear that they actually exist as being opposed to being merely theoretical constructs.
>
> However, there's a much more important point to be made about this.... These particles, if they are real, do *not* come out of nothing. The quantum vacuum is not what most people envision when they think of a vacuum—that is, absolutely nothing. On the contrary, it's a sea of fluctuating energy, an arena of violent activity that has a rich physical structure and can be described by physical laws. These particles are thought to originate by fluctuations of energy in the vacuum.
>
> So it's not an example of something coming into being out of nothing, or something coming into being without a cause. The quantum vacuum and the energy locked up in the vacuum are the cause of these particles.... We have to ask, well, what is the origin of the whole quantum vacuum itself. Where does *it* come from?
>
> You've simply pushed back the issue of creation. Now you've got to account for how this very active ocean of fluctuating energy came into being....If quantum physical laws operate within the domain described by quantum physics, you can't legitimately use quantum physics to explain the origin of that domain itself. You need something transcendent that's beyond that domain in order to explain how the entire domain came into being. Suddenly, we're back to the origins question.[6]

Grasping the flimsy metaphysical straw of quantum theory, other evangelists for Darwinism place their faith in "the multiple-universe theory of Andre Lind[e], which imagines an unending series of stacked-up quantum waves that generate new big bangs and expanding universes cascading one after another on top of each other."[7] In other words, if an infinite number of unseen universes exist, sooner or later one was bound to show up, by pure *chance*, that is "finely tuned for life."[8] Our universe just happens to be that one!

Is there any evidence for other universes? "There is none," explained Nancy Pearcey, of the Discovery Institute. "By definition, they cannot be observed. Nor has anyone offered a plausible scientific explanation for how they arise....[T]he idea of...unknowable universes sprouting like mushrooms, goes beyond science and into philosophy."[9]

Or as philosopher Robin Collins pointed out in an interview with Lee Strobel:

> Even if [Andre] Linde's theory could account for the existence of many universes, this would not destroy the case for design. It would just kick the issue up another level. In fact, I believe it would point *toward* design.
>
> Regardless of which multiple-universe theory you use, in every case you'd need a 'many-universe generator'—and it would require the right structure, the right mechanism, and the right ingredients to churn out new universes.
>
> It's highly unlikely that such a universe-generating system would have all the right components and ingredients in place by random chance.... If a many-universe-generating system exists, it would be best explained by design.
>
> Theists have nothing to fear from the idea that there may be multiple universes. There would still need to be an intelligent designer to make the finely tuned universe-generating process work.[10]

At best, highly imaginative quantum theories are wild-eyed speculations. They are metaphysical guesses, the fanciful visions of secular astrophysicists and cosmologists that move far beyond known laws of physics. They are unobservable and unprovable, more science fiction than science. As Craig and Collins pointed out above, such theories only push the dilemma back a notch. They still don't account for how the matter and energy behind the Big Bang, the quantum vacuums, or multiple universes came into existence in the first place. Who made the laws of physics that allowed something to come from nothing? Who lit the fuse for the Big Bang?

Granted, no model of origins—creation or evolution—is subject to absolute, mathematical proof. Nevertheless, the creationist model is consistent with the known laws of physics, in particular the First and Second Laws of thermodynamics. If the Big Bang occurred, it only confirms that the universe had a beginning. To put it somewhat differently, since no effect can be greater than its cause, something more powerful than the universe caused the universe to be. (See chapter nineteen.)

Should Creationists Debate the Age of the Earth?

Some creationists reject Big Bang cosmology as a useful apologetic point of contact when engaging Darwinists because it implies an old earth. I disagree. I believe the Big Bang theory can be used in defense of creation in spite of one's position on the age of the earth.

In the evolution/creation debate, many Christians assume that all evolutionists are atheists. In fact, there are very few true atheists in America. Most evolutionists do not rule out the existence of God. They just believe in evolution. The real issue for many non-Christians, in the terms of why they reject biblical creation, is their skepticism that God created the cosmos and life on earth in six literal days. Many unbelievers throw out the entire creation account (and hence Christianity) because they think the idea of a six-day creation week is unscientific and biblical fantasy.

Many conservative Christians, including well-known theologians and scholars, accept an old-earth view of creation. They love the Lord dearly and believe in the truth, authority, and reliability of the Bible. Their old-earth view of creation does not interfere with their acceptance of Jesus Christ and following Him.

When engaging evolutionists, though, it's best for us not to make the validity of creation depend on the age of the earth. The truth is, an old earth is not an obstacle to creationism, and one can believe in an old earth and still be a creationist. Old earth creationists simply accept a model of origins that allows for an old earth, such as progressive creation or the gap theory.[11] All creationists agree that the God of Scripture is the Creator and Sustainer of all that is (Colossians 1:16–17).

Because the earth's age is the heart of the matter for many skeptics, acknowledging that it is not crucial to creationism is an apologetic strategy that may diffuse or even eliminate the stumbling block of evolution. Non-Christians are less likely to argue against creation when we point out that an old-earth model of origins does not necessarily violate biblical creation.

It's okay for young-earth creationists to use Big Bang cosmology to demonstrate the existence of a Creator, even if they don't accept the old-earth position. We desire to guide the skeptic closer to the God of the Gospels. Once an evolutionist becomes a Christian, he or she can examine the evidence and decide how old the earth is. Many of today's young earth creationists were once old-earth Darwinists.

I am not endorsing "theistic" evolution, which most creationists dismiss. Theistic evolution attempts to harmonize naturalistic evolution (Darwinism) with belief in the God of the Bible and hold hands with whatever prevailing evolutionary theory is in vogue. Explained Nancy Pearcey:

> Theistic evolutionists generally accept exactly the same scientific theories as atheists or naturalists; the only thing they ask is that they be allowed to propose a theological meaning behind it all—known only by faith, and not detectable by scientific means. In essence, they allow atheists to define scientific knowledge, so long as theology is allowed to put a religious spin on whatever science comes up with.[12]

The end result of this watered-down view of origins is a God who has nothing to do with creation other than turning on the timer. As Phillip Johnson pointed out, "What good is God if he never does anything we can detect?"[13]

The goal of apologetics is to defend the essentials of our faith. The fact that conservative Christians are divided over the age of the earth implies that it is not an essential doctrine. Dr. Duane Gish, at the Institute of Creation Research in Santee, California, uncompromisingly believes in a young earth. He has participated in more than three hundred debates, defending creation against many prominent evolutionists. Yet in a recent seminar I attended, even Dr. Gish encouraged his audience not to debate the age of the earth.[14]

Nancy Pearcey gives this much-needed warning:

> Instead of joining together to oppose the hegemony of the naturalistic world, Christians often get caught up in fighting each other.

The bitterest debates were often not with atheistic evolutionists but among believers with conflicting scientific views: young-earth creationists, old-earth creationists, flood geologists, progressive creationists, "gap" theorists, and theistic evolutionists. There were endless arguments over theological questions like the length of the creation "days" and the extent of the Genesis flood.

Meanwhile, secularists were happy to fan the flames. As Phillip Johnson once put it, "They all but said, 'Let us hold your coats while you fight.'" For if Christians were going to endlessly divide, then it was clear that secularists would conquer.[15]

As Christians we can agree that God created life and the cosmos and is active in its continual existence. At least in apologetics, let's consider the age of the earth to be an "in-house" issue that the Christian family can debate with charity and friendliness.

Endnotes

1. Hugh Ross, *The Creator and the Cosmos; How the Greatest Scientific Discoveries of the Century Reveal God* (Colorado Springs: NavPress, 1993), 20.

2. Scott LaFee, "Why Does it Matter What Lies Between Matter?", *The San Diego Union-Tribune*, March 5, 2003, E4.

3. Henry M. Morris, *Scientific Creationism* (El Cajon, CA: Master Books, 1991), 25.

4. Ibid.

5. William Lane Craig, "Why I Believe God Exists," in *Why I Am a Christian; Leading Thinkers Explain Why They Believe*, ed. By Norman L. Geisler and Paul K. Hoffman (Grand Rapids: Baker Books, 2001), 64.

6. Quoted from an interview with William Lane Craig, "The Evidence of Cosmology: Beginning with a Bang," in, Lee Strobel, *The Case for a Creator; a Journalist Investigates Scientific Evidence That Points Toward God* (Grand Rapids: Zondervan, 2004), 101.

7. Henry M. Morris, "The Cosmic Bubbleland," *Back to Genesis* (Institute of Creation Research, June 2001, b.

8. Craig, "Why I believe God Exists," in *Why I Am a Christian*, 71–72.

9. Nancy Pearcey, *World*, September 2, 2000, 17. Quoted in Summit Ministries, *The Journal*, December 2000.

10. Quoted in a interview with Robin Collins, Lee Strobel, *The Case for a Creator*, 141–142, 144.

11. Many Christians subscribe to "Progressive Creation." Like six-day creationists, they acknowledge that God was personally involved in creation. Plants and animals did not evolve from common ancestors. However, these Christians believe that the age of the earth conforms to conventional science. Rather than creating all of life in six literal days, God periodically introduced new groups of plants and animals into the earth along traditional geological time frames. Some view each of the Genesis days as initiating these creative periods.

12. Nancy Pearcey, *Total Truth: Liberating Christianity from Its Cultural Captivity* (Wheaton: Crossway Books, 2004), 203.

13. Phillip E. Johnson, *The Right Questions; Truth, Meaning & Public Debate* (Downers Grove: InerVArsity Press, 2002), 82.

14. "Debate Workshop; Darwin Vs. Gish," Institute for Creation Research, Santee, CA, January 19, 2002.

15. Pearcey, *Total Truth*, 173.

How Can Order Evolve from Disorder?

THE SECOND principal assumption on which naturalistic evolution depends is that the origin and subsequent evolution of the universe and life were random and accidental. Evolutionists include in this scenario much more than such physical things as the perfect placement of planets in our solar system or the wondrous and intricate structure (design) of plants and animals. They also include such things as moral values, an appreciation of beauty and music, love and other emotions, and even religious beliefs. All of these, according to naturalistic evolutionists, arose from chaos and developed through the purposeless, random power of natural selection. Even abstract thoughts (our minds) and consciousness are said to be products of evolution. Consider the following excerpt from an article by a staff writer with a large San Diego newspaper. He refers to Nobel Prize winner, Francis Crick.

> [Crick] believes that all of the brain's behaviors, including consciousness, result from the brain's physical processes.... Human self-awareness is essentially the consequence of countless neurons, sensory cells and other physiological systems interacting with the environment to created the intangible entity we know as our

minds.... Everything we think, say and do, contend[s] Crick... can be explained biologically.[1]

This is a large pill to swallow, observationally as well as scientifically. Everywhere, nature virtually screams out for order and design. From the simplest one-celled organism to the human brain (the most complex matter in the known universe), from the laws of physics to the interrelatedness of biotic systems, from the life-sustaining chemistry of the air to the placement of the stars in our galaxy, intelligence and purpose are clearly at work and in evidence.

As we've already seen, evolutionists who claim that the universe and nature are products of chance are engaging in conjecture and naturalistic philosophy. Overwhelming scientific evidence supports the creationist's thesis that life and the cosmos are products of an intelligent, cosmic Designer—the God of Scripture. This brings us to a relatively new but extremely compelling and persuasive argument for creation—*Intelligent Design*.

Intelligent Design

The Intelligent Design movement began in earnest in the early 1990s. It differs primarily from "scientific creationism" (usually represented by young-earth creationists) by accepting the conventional view of an old earth. More than any other avenue of scientific apologetics, Intelligent Design has been the most successful in gaining peer review and recognition. It is a formidable challenge to naturalistic evolution and the voice most often heard when challenging educators to allow alternate models of origin to be critically examined in public schools and colleges.[2]

There are three primary areas of evidence utilized by Intelligent Design, and young-earth creationists can apply all three in the defense of biblical creation.

1. *The Anthropic Principle*

Not long ago, someone asked if I believe that life exists on other planets. I told him I have no idea, but that since God is the God of the universe, if life does exist on other plants, He created it. However, I added, I believe it is unlikely that life exists anywhere but on planet earth. I explained that my opinion is supported by the *anthropic principle*, one of the most compelling evidences supporting creation by design.

The anthropic principle "states that the universe was fitted from the very first moment of its existence for the emergence of life in general and human life in particular."[3] William Lane Craig put it even more precisely: "The entire universe and its history are fine-tuned from its inception with incredible precision to produce man on earth"[4]

The strength of the anthropic principle, as affirmation of design (and hence the existence of God), lies in its observation that life can exist only within very narrow margins. Necessary "fundamental constants" are in place, not only on earth but also throughout the entire universe, which are essential for life. In particular, if the physics of the universe itself differed even minutely, life on earth would be impossible. For example:

- If the structure of an atom differed in terms of the ratio of proton to electron mass, molecules could not form.
- If the average distance between stars in our galaxy were slightly different, their orbits would become erratic, resulting in extreme temperature variation on earth.[5]
- If the force of gravity slowed the expansion of the universe even slightly (or if expansion was faster), it would have been impossible for galaxies and the solar system to have formed. The margin of error in the expansion of the universe is only 1 part in 10^{60}.[6]
- If the speed of light were slightly faster or slower, other constants in the universe would be altered, making any kind of life impossible.
- If the centrifugal force of planets rotating around the sun did not balance exactly with gravitational forces, the plants would not remain in orbit.
- If Jupiter were not in its present orbit, the earth would be bombarded with asteroids and comets that are now drawn to Jupiter by its gravitational field. (This happened in July, 1994, when Comet Shoemaker-Levy 9 slammed into Jupiter.)

- If the sun were much larger or closer, water would boil away, and the earth would be too hot to support life. On the other hand, if the sun were more distant, all water would freeze and, again, life on earth could not exist.
- If gravitational forces were altered even minutely (1 part in 10^{40}), "the sun would not exist, and the moon would crash into the earth or sheer off into space."[7]
- Here on earth still other factors must be "just right" for life on earth to exist:
- The thickness and movement of the earth's crust must be perfectly balanced. A thicker crust would lead to no oxygen; a thinner crust would increase volcanic and tectonic activity, destabilizing the earth's greenhouse gases that regulate the earth temperature. Either could preclude life on earth.
- If the chemical composition of the atmosphere were different, the atmosphere would be poisonous.
- If the sea-to-land-mass ratio, depth of the oceans, and the earth's cloud cover were different, the earth's ability to store and release heat would change dramatically.
- If the earth's orbit took longer than twenty-four hours (or was not in a nearly perfect circle), temperature variations between night and day would change dramatically. If its orbit were shorter than twenty-four hours, wind velocities would greatly accelerate.
- If the axial tilt of the earth differed, surface temperatures would become too great.

How do we account for such a fine-tuned universe? There are only two answers. Since there is no physical cause to explain how all of these fundamental constants came to be so perfectly balanced, secular cosmologists conclude that this balance is merely a cosmic accident created by pure chance.

The only other answer explaining the existence of a universe perfectly fine-tuned for life on earth is Intelligent Design or creation. It appears infinitely more probable that the earth and universe were designed to sustain life—in particular, human life on earth. It is irrational and statistically outrageous to *assume* (as Darwinists do) that all of these fine-tuned factors are the result of random processes. Astrophysicist Hugh Ross put this into perspective:

> Technology and interdisciplinary research have enabled scientists to develop an extensive list of physical characteristics that must fall within limited ranges for a planet (or any other astronomical body) to be capable of life support. Those characteristics involve the planet's star, moon(s), planetary companions, and galaxy, as well as the planet's surface, interior, and atmospheric conditions. This list grows longer with every year. It started with two parameters in 1966, grew to eight by 1970, to twenty-three by 1980, to thirty by 1990, and to forty by 1995. Currently, the list includes more than 120 parameters and shows no signs of leveling off....
>
> The data demonstrate that the probability of finding even one planet with the capacity to support life falls short of one chance in 10^{140} (that number is 1 followed by 140 zeros).[8]

If the earth and the cosmos were designed, there must be a Designer—God. The anthropic principle has become one of the most compelling arguments for the existence of God. As Normal Geisler wrote, "The Anthropic Principle is based on the most recent astronomical evidence for the existence of a superintelligent Creator of the cosmos."[9] This leads to a second evidence for Intelligent Design.

2. Irreducible Complexity

The same indisputable design observed throughout the cosmos is also found in the smallest particles of living matter. Random, accidental processes cannot account for the incredible complexity of even a single cell. Only a Supreme Intelligence could have organized the raw materials and supplied the vast amount of information found within living cells.

In his 1993 book, *Darwin's Black Box*,[10] biochemist Michael Behe made popular the phrase—irreducible complexity. Behe drew attention to the fact that organisms, even at a molecular level, are complex, organized systems comprised of innumerable, interacting parts. If any one of these parts is not fully developed and functioning from the beginning, the organism can't survive. Hence, for an organism to evolve, each of these individual, interrelated parts must have evolved simultaneously while remaining functional throughout the entire process.

Behe illustrated this with a mousetrap. He pointed out that a mousetrap is composed of five parts (base, spring, hammer, holding bar, and trigger). Remove any of these parts, and the mousetrap doesn't work. Moreover, if any of these parts were not fully functioning at all times throughout the "evolution" of a mousetrap, the trap would be useless. In other words, remove the spring, and the trap won't work. Replace it with a partly developed spring, and the trap still won't work.

The mousetrap is "irreducibly complex." It could not have "evolved" step-by-step because it could not function until all the parts were fully formed and working together. Behe likened the mousetrap to far more sophisticated biological systems, some with hundreds of interacting parts, all of which would have had to evolve simultaneously and be fully functioning during each step of each system's development.

In an evolutionary scenario, each stage of an organism's development must have function or it will have no survival value and therefore fail to develop. The key here is *function*, as Nancy Pearcey explained:

> Natural selection is said to work on tiny, random improvements in function—which means it does not kick in until there is at least *some* function to select from. But irreducible complex systems don't have *any* function until a minimum number of parts are in place—which means those parts themselves cannot be products of natural selection. We're talking about a minimum number of interacting pieces that must be present before natural selection even begins to operate.[11]

Professor Stephen Meyer explained it like this:

> Natural selection only preserves things that perform a function—in other words, which help the organism survive to the next generation....The problem with irreducibly complex systems is that they perform no function until all the parts are present and work-

ing together in close coordination with one another. So natural selection cannot help you build such systems.[12]

Consider this illustration. Evolutionists claim that the human eye (all eyes, for that matter) evolved from a light-sensitive spot on a tiny organism in the distant past. However, in order for the alleged light-sensitive spot to develop, the interdependent parts that comprise it must all have had function. But such parts could not have had function because they would have had no survival value until the light-sensitive spot was already in place. In other words, for a light-sensitive spot to evolve, its individual parts must already be working (functioning) *before* natural selection can kick in. But that is impossible because the individual parts themselves would have required natural selection in order to evolve. This is a classic case of "catch–22"; the individual parts of the light-sensitive spot can't come into existence independent of natural selection, yet natural selection can't begin until the individual parts are already functioning.

Even a single living cell is so complex that the chance of one evolving accidentally through random natural processes is impossible. "According to most mathematical calculations, a universe even 100 billion years old is not old enough for the development of a single cell."[13] This is understandable when one realizes a cell's complexity.

Bacterial cells are probably the simplest of all living organisms. The tiniest weigh less than 10^{-12} grams. Yet each is "a veritable microminiaturized factory containing thousands of exquisitely designed pieces of intricate molecular machinery, made up altogether of one hundred thousand million atoms, far more complicated than any machine built by man."[14]

A typical cell may contain many thousands of different kind of proteins used to perform many varieties of tasks.[15] In an interview with Lee Strobel, Dr. Stephen Meyer described the odds of merely a single protein molecule developing through natural processes (let alone an entire cell):

> Even a simple protein molecule, or the gene to build that molecule, is so rich in information that the entire time since the Big Bang would not give you . . . the 'probabilistic resources' you would need to generate the molecule by chance . . . .

> The probabilities of forming a rather short functional protein at random would be one chance in a hundred thousand trillion trillion trillion trillion trillion trillion trillion trillion trillion trillion. That's a ten with 125 zeros after it!....
>
> And that would only be one protein molecule—a minimally complex cell would need between three hundred and five hundred protein molecules.[16]

Referring to Behe's book, Nancy Pearcey provided an eye-opening illustration of the elaborate structure of a living cell. It is complex far beyond the most sophisticated human technology. I'm quoting her in length because of her fascinating description of a single cell's incredible complexity.

> More than a hundred years ago, Darwin thought the living cell as extremely simple—nothing but a bubble of jelly (protoplasm). Over the past few decades, however, new technologies like the electron microscope have produced a revolution in molecular biology. We now know that the cell bristles with high-tech molecular machinery far more complex than anything devised by mere humans. Each cell is akin to a miniature factory town, humming with power plants, automated factories, and recycling centers. In the nucleus is a cellular library, housing blueprints and plans that are copied and transported to factories, each of which is filled with molecular machines that function like computerized motors. These manufacture the immense array of products needed within the cell, with the processes all regulated by enzymes that function as stopwatches to ensure that everything is perfectly timed....
>
> The outside surface of the cell is studded with sensors, gates, pumps, and identification markers to regulate traffic coming in and out. Today biologists cannot even describe the cell without resorting to the language of machines and engineering....
>
> Each cell has an automated "rapid transit system" in which certain molecules function as tiny monorail trains running along tracks to whisk cargo from one part of the cell to another. Other molecules act as loading machines, filling up the train cars and

attaching address labels. When the train reaches the right "address" in another part of the cell, it is met by other molecules that act as docking machines, opening them up and removing the supplies. To frame a mental image of the cell, picture it as a large and complex model train layout, with tracks crisscrossing everywhere, its switches and signals perfectly timed so that no trains collide and the cargo reaches its destination precisely when needed.[17]

Michael Behe focuses primarily on irreducible complexity at a molecular and cellular level. The concept can be applied on a much larger scale, which also makes it easier to understand.

Take the scenario of a reptile's forearms evolving into bird wings. Unless the reptile developed an appendage that met its survival needs at all points during its development, the appendage would have no survival value and therefore not develop. A half wing/half leg would not benefit a reptile or a bird, thus a half wing/half leg would have no survival value and not evolve.

How do creationists account for fully functioning organisms with innumerable interacting parts, none of which would have survival value during any intermediate stage of its development? The same way we account for a fully developed mousetrap. It's a product of an Intelligent Designer.

Evolutionists are fully aware of the complex nature and apparent design of living organisms. Unfortunately, their naturalistic worldview prevents them from acknowledging the Designer. Neo-Darwinist Richard Dawkins, in his book *The Blind Watchmaker*, states that "biology is the study of complicated things that give the appearance of having been designed for a purpose."[18] In other words, he believes that living things have all the appearance of design, but of course, they aren't designed because there is no such thing as a supernatural Designer. Atheist Francis Crick made a similar statement: "Biologists must constantly keep in mind that what they see was not designed, but rather evolved."[19]

This is philosophy, not science. The incredibly complex design of living cells (and entire organisms) points conclusively to a Designer—not random processes or accident. Saying there is no design is a statement of faith, not of fact based on evidence.

3. Information Theory

The third evidence refuting the illusionary theory that an orderly universe, including the tiniest bits of life, accidentally evolved out of disorder is called Information Theory. This testimony for creation looks at the vast amount of data stored in DNA and analyzes how it got there.

Living things possess a distinct, nonmaterial component called "information."[20] This information is a language or message specifically imprinted in DNA, in the genes. (The genes provide instructions to the cells so that the cells become what the genes order.) However, because the information housed in DNA is nonmaterial, it can't be identified as the actual chemical composition of the DNA. Phillip Johnson, father of the Intelligent Design movement, explained: "The important thing about DNA is not the chemicals but the information in the software, just as the important thing about a computer program or a book is the information content and not the physical medium in which that information is recorded."[21]

Creationists argue that the vast information housed in DNA—how it's coded and transmitted—requires an intelligent source. It had to have been programmed into the DNA because the information content in DNA is *information*—not matter. Just like information in this book cannot be reduced to merely paper and ink, so information encoded in DNA cannot be reduced to physical or material properties. It must be programmed into DNA just as my thoughts are imprinted as specific words in this book. This requires intelligence, not chance. Instructions imply information, and information points to intelligence. Information, instructions, and intelligence can't be reduced to mere chemicals, random physical properties, and processes. Chance produces disorder, not order; it does not organize data.

We might think of this like the letters of a Scrabble game.[22] If we randomly pulled them out of the box and placed them on the board, they would spell nothing. The letters are meaningless if not placed in a specific order ("sequence"). Only an intelligent being could arrange the letters so that they communicate information. As atheist Richard Dawkins acknowledged, the nucleus in each of the trillions of cells in the human body "contains a digitally coded database larger, in information content, than all 30 volumes of the Encyclopedia Britannica put together."[23]

In short, "the information written in DNA is not the product of DNA."[24] It isn't matter—although it's imprinted in matter. It had to originate from an Intelligence source. "Neither chance, nor chance combined with natural selection, nor self-organizational processes have the causal power to produce information."[25] An intelligent Creator (God) had to have programmed the vast amount of information into DNA.

Endnotes

1. Scott LaFee, "Undead Heads," *The San Diego Union-Tribune*, March 24, 2004, F1.

2. For an outstanding study of the history of the Intelligent Design movement, see Thomas Woodward's, *Doubts about Darwin: A History of Intelligent Design* (Grand Rapids: Baker Books), 2003.

3. Norman Geisler, *Baker Encyclopedia of Christian Apologetics* (Grand Rapids: Baker Books, 1999), 26. Pages 26–27 list "an incredibly restrictive set of demands [that] must have been present in the early universe."

4. William Lane Craig, *Reasonable Faith; Christian Truth and Apologetics* (Wheaton; Crossway Books, 1994), 91.

5. Geisler, *Baker Encyclopedia of Christian Apologetics*, 26.

6. Nancy R. Pearcey, *Total Truth: Liberating Christianity from Its Cultural Captivity* (Wheaton: Crossway Books, 2004), 188.

7. Geisler, *Baker Encyclopedia of Christian Apologetics*, 26.

8. Hugh Ross, "Exotic Life Sites; The Feasibility of Far-Out Habitats," *Facts and Faith*, Q4–2001, 22, 23.

9. Geisler, *Baker Encyclopedia of Apologetics*, 28.

10. Michael J. Behe, *Darwin's Black Box: The Biochemical Challenge to Evolution* (New York: The Free Press, 2003).

11. Pearcey, *Total Truth*, 186.

12. Quoted in an interview with Stephen C. Meyer, Lee Strobel, *The Case for a Creator* (Grand Rapids: Zondervan, 2004), 79.

13. *Answers to Evolution: 16 Reasons to Doubt Darwinism* (Torrance, CA: Rose Publishing, 2004).

14. Michael Denton, *Evolution: A Theory in Crisis* (Chevy Chase, MD: Adler & Adler, 1985), 250.

15. Behe, *Darwin's Black Box*, 52.

16. Strobel, *The Case for a Creator*, 229.

17. Pearcey, *Total Truth*, 185–186.

18. Richard Dawkins, *The Blind Watchmaker*, cited in, Phillip E. Johnson, *The Wedge of Truth; Splitting the Foundations of Naturalism* (Downers Grove: InterVarsity Press, 2000), 153.

19. Francis Crick, *What Mad Pursuit* (New York: BasicBooks, 1988), 138.

20. Phillip E. Johnson, *Defeating Darwinism by Opening Minds* (Downers Grove: InterVarsity Press, 1997), 70.

21. Johnson, *The Wedge of Truth*, 53.

22. Pearcey, *Total Truth*, 192–197. Pearcey developed this analogy between Scrabble letters and the chemical "letters" in DNA.

23. Richard Dawkins, *The Blind Watchmaker, 2–3*, cited in Johnson, *The Wedge of Truth*, 26. Other researchers say three or four complete sets of the *Britannica*. See Charles Colson and Nancy Pearcey, *How Now Shall We Live?* (Wheaton: Tyndale House Publishers, 1999), 75.

24. Ibid.

25. Quoted in an interview with Stephen C. Meyer, Strobel, *The Case for a Creator*, 237.

HOW CAN LIFE EMERGE FROM NON-LIFE?

THE FOUNDATION of naturalistic evolution depends on matter and energy somehow popping into existence out of nothing, and it also requires that life somehow (miraculously!) emerged from non-life. Evolutionists claim that at least once, inorganic chemicals in some kind of "prebiotic soup" reacted randomly with sunlight, lightning, or another energy source and allowed self-replicating cells to develop by accident. Called "abiogenesis," this process initiated the evolutionary journey of all living things.

Our next challenge to Darwinists is for them to demonstrate how life came into existence from non-life. By what remarkable process did living things emerge from nonliving chemicals to launch biological evolution?

Does the scientific evidence support abiogenesis? No. This phenomenon has never been observed in nature. Nor—in spite of numerous attempts—has life been created from non-life in a laboratory. There is no known mechanism for how living organisms could have emerged from mythical chemical soup. In fact, no physical evidence indicates that such a "soup" ever existed. Biochemist Fazale Rana explained:

> To date, origin-of-life researchers have failed to recover any geochemical remnants of prebiotic molecules—organic molecules

produced by nonbiological processes ... Perhaps most devastating of all is the absence of primordial soup on early Earth. All origin-of-life models that appeal exclusively to natural processes have as their chief requirement a primordial soup. Even if a primordial soup existed, however, the chemical processes supposedly taking place in the soup seem incapable of producing life.[1]

Today, increasing numbers of geochemists and origin-of-life researchers agree that the chemical composition of the earth's early atmosphere prevented the development of organic molecules.[2] Oxygen and other chemicals in the primitive atmosphere would have destroyed such molecules before they could evolve into living organisms. The real obstacle to life emerging out of non-life, however, is that it is statistically impossible. The earth is not old enough for even the simplest organism to spring out of a primordial soup. This is even more of a problem for Darwinists today than it was fifty years ago.

Renowned British mathematician and astronomer, the late Sir Fred Hoyle, offered illustrations to demonstrate the statistical impossibility of life emerging by chance. He described the probability as similar to giving 10^{50} blind people a Rubik's Cube and having all of them solve the puzzle at the same time.[3] Elsewhere, Hoyle calculated that the probability of life originating by random processes as one chance in $10^{40,000}$. He later described it this way: "The chance that higher life forms might have emerged in this way is comparable with the chance that a tornado sweeping through a junkyard might assemble a Boeing 747 from the materials therein."[4]

Tiny organisms emerging by chance from non-life is only half the problem. They next had to evolve into more complex, multicelled organisms and begin evolving into the myriad of living creatures inhabiting the earth. This is statistically impossible also. Astrophysicist Hugh Ross provided the necessary figures to illustrate this:

> The problems of primordial soups are big, but bigger yet is the infeasibility of generating, without supernatural input, an enormous increase in complexity ...

Years ago, molecular biophysicist Harold Morowitz calculated ... that if one were to take the simplest living cell and break every chemical bond within it, the odds that the cell would reassemble under ideal natural conditions (the best possible chemical environment) would be one chance in $10^{100,000,000,000}$. Most of us cannot even begin to picture a speck of chance so remote.

With odds as remote as 1 in $10^{100,000,000,000}$ the time scale issue becomes completely irrelevant. What does it matter if the Earth has been around for ten seconds, ten thousand years, or ten billion years? The size of the universe is of no consequence either. If all the matter in the visible universe were converted into building blocks of life, and if assembly of these building blocks were attempted once a microsecond for the entire age of the universe, then instead of the odds being 1 in $10^{100,000,000,000}$ they would be 1 in $10^{99,999,999,916}$.[5]

No scientific evidence has revealed that inorganic, non-living chemicals ever evolved into organic life.

Endnotes

1. Fazale R. Rana, "Origin-of-Life Predictions Face Off: Evolution vs. Biblical Creation," *Facts for Faith*, Q2–2001, 45–46.

2. See Jonathan Wells, *Icons of Evolution: Science or Myth? Why Much of What We Teach About Evolution Is Wrong* (Washington DC: Regnery Publishing, Inc., 2000), 9–22.

3. Fred Hoyle, *The Intelligent Universe* (New York: Holt, Rinehart, and Winston, 1983), p.11. Quoted in Charles Colson and Nancy Pearcey, *How Now Shall We Live?* (Wheaton: Tyndale House Publishers, 1999), 74.

4. "Hoyle on Evolution," *Nature*, V. 294, 12 November, 1981, p.105. Quoted in Luther D. Sunderland, *Darwin's Enigma: Fossils and Other Problems*, (Santee, CA: Master Books Publishers, 1984), 58–59.

5. Hugh Ross, *The Creator and the Cosmos: How the Greatest Scientific Discoveries of the Century Reveal God* (Colorado Springs: Navpress, 1993), 139–140.

WHERE ARE THE TRANSITIONAL FOSSILS?

IT'S ONE THING to argue that ancient events support evolution and it's quite another for Darwinists to deny empirical evidences for creation that one can examine today, such as the fossil record. As Norman Geisler observed, the case for evolution depends primarily on the fossil record: "The only real evidence for or against evolution," he wrote, "is the fossil record. Every other argument for evolution is based on what could have been. Only the fossil record records examples of what actually did happen."[1]

Darwinists claim that the fossil record reveals a gradual evolution of animal life from primitive forms to complex forms with transitional phases between major groups (fish and amphibians, amphibians and reptiles, reptiles and birds/mammals). If this is true, there should be hundreds, even thousands, of transitional specimens in the fossil record.

The fact is that there is virtually no support for evolution in the fossil record. There is no concrete evidence that shows primitive life forms evolved into complex life forms, because no credible transitional fossils have been found between any groups of animals. Honest paleontologists admit this. The late Dr. Colin Patterson, former senior paleontologist at the British Museum of Natural History and editor of its journal, was asked why he didn't include photographs of transitional fossils in his book, *Evolution*. He repled, "If I knew of any, fossils or living, I would certainly have included them."[2]

One of America's leading paleontologists and evolutionists, the late Stephen J. Gould, described "the extreme rarity of transitional forms in the fossil record" as "the trade secret of paleontology."[3]

Darwin knew there were no transitional fossils when he formulated his theory during the mid-nineteenth century. He merely assumed they existed. In chapter six of his book, *The Origin of Species*, Darwin wrote: "First, why, if species have descended from other species by fine gradations, do we not everywhere see innumerable transitional forms? Why is not all nature in confusion, instead of the species being, as we see them, well defined?"[4]

Today, after many years of research and excavations, paleontologists still haven't discovered any transitional fossils—not even any transitional parts such as a half-scale/half-feather or half-leg/half-wing. Nancy Pearcey writes about this:

> Instead of filling in the gaps, new [fossil] findings have actually made the gaps more pronounced than ever. Why? Because the fossil forms tend to fall *within* existing groups, leaving clear gaps *between* groups—just as there are clear gaps between modern animals like horses and cows, dogs and cats. Put another way, variation tends to be limited to change *within* groups, instead of leading gradually from one group to another.[5]

Microevolution versus Macroevolution

Despite the lack of fossil evidence, evolutionists insist that modern animals evolved from primitive ancestors. Many varieties of animals walking around today, they contend, are obviously related to fossil specimens: the mammoth and the modern elephant, the extinct horse and modern horse, and so on. The mistake evolutionists make in this assumption is that they confuse "microevolution" with "macroevolution." The former is testable, observable, and hence scientific. The latter is pure conjecture.

Microevolution

Microevolution focuses on limited changes that occur in organisms as they adapt to changing environmental conditions, resulting in variations within animal types.

The first time I was in Yellowstone National Park, a friend I was hiking with photographed what we believed to be a wolf. To our chagrin, we discovered later that it was only a coyote. Yellowstone coyotes are much larger and grayer than the small brown variety I often see in Southern California. The high mountains and cold temperatures of Yellowstone have resulted in a different variety of coyote. In contrast, macroevolution is said to be one kind of species evolving into another kind of species.

Creationists have long recognized microevolution, which is well established scientifically. Selective breeders have used it for centuries to produce hundreds of varieties of dogs, cats, and other domesticated animals (as well as countless varieties of orchids, apples, roses, and other plants). We must understand, however, that these variations do not represent evolution as commonly understood. In fact, selective breeding, which requires the manipulation of genes through intelligent human intervention, contradicts naturalistic evolution.

For years scientists have tried, without success, to create new species through selective breeding. As Chuck Colson and Nancy Pearcey observed:

> Centuries of experiments show that the change produced by breeding does not continue at a steady rate from generation to generation. Instead, change is rapid at first, then levels off, and eventually reaches a limit that breeders cannot cross....
>
> Breeding shuffles and selects among existing genes in the gene pool, combining and recombining them, much as you might shuffle and deal cards from a deck. But breeding does not create new genes, any more than shuffling cards creates new cards. A bird cannot be bred to grow fur. A mouse cannot be bred to grow feathers. A pig cannot grow wings.
>
> What's more, as breeders keep up the selection pressure, the organism grows weaker until it finally becomes sterile and dies

out. This is the bane of modern farming: Our highly bred cows and chickens produce more milk and eggs, but they are also much more prone to disease and sterility. There is a natural barrier that no amount of breeding is able to cross.[6]

The authors also noted that "when an organism is no longer subject to selective pressure, it tends to revert to its original type."[7] Left alone, changes bred into a species will eventually vanish; the animals will revert to their former state. "If all the dog breeds were allowed to interact sexually, they would quickly revert back to their wild dog ancestries."[8] This is what happened to finches in the Galapagos Islands. (See chapter fifteen.) Evolutionists have long claimed that changes in the size and shape of Galapagos' finches, as they adjusted to changing food supplies, supports macroevolution (one species evolving into another new and distinct species). They assume that these minor changes (beak size particularly) will eventually result in an entirely new variety of bird.

This has not been the case, however. When environmental conditions stabilize, the food supply stabilizes and the finch beaks return to their previous size. This is simply another example of microevolution—animals adapting to changing environmental conditions within the limits of their existing gene pool.

How Microevolution Works in Nature

God created (designed) living creatures "after their kind." (See Genesis 1.) In scientific terms, this means that God created the original "prototypes" of all the kinds of animals that have existed—extinct and modern. He endowed each category of animal with a specific gene pool that housed the genetic potential for diverse varieties within each created kind. In other words, God created distinct families of dogs, cats, horses, elephants, ants, spiders, daisies, ferns, and so on. There is no evidence, as is purported to occur through macroevolution, that one variety of plant or animal ever evolved into another kind. There may be huge horses and tiny horses, mastodons and modern elephants, living animals and extinct animals, but all variations fall within each creature's created genetic potential.

For example, all canines—wild dogs, domesticated dogs, wolves, coyotes, foxes, jackals, and so on—developed from the gene pool of the first dog-kind. But this is not macroevolution, which claims that modern canines evolved from a non-dog ancestor. Rather its microevolution, through which God's original created kinds utilize their full genetic potential strictly within the limits of their original created gene pool. Extinct and modern canines have never been anything but dogs. The fossil record does not reveal a half dog/half something else. Dogs have always been just dogs. As the original dog-kind dispersed and adapted to diverse environmental conditions, numerous forms of dogs developed. Breeders simply utilize this same gene pool to produce today's domestic dogs.

Evolutionists, on the other hand, claim that in the distant past all living things shared common ancestors. Over eons of time, they believe physical modifications occurred through macroevolution. Animal types developed new body parts and organs that are more complex. Eventually, these accumulated modifications resulted in entirely new varieties of animals. The ancestors became extinct, and new species arose to take their place.

We must note, though, the tremendous difference between cyclical variations within animal kinds and the evolution of an entirely new kind from a different kind. Microevolution is testable and observable, but no scientific evidence supports macroevolution. Evolutionary scientists who preach macroevolution are merely extrapolating that the "machinery" at work in microevolution works in macroevolution. In other words, the same mechanism that allows animals to change within the limits of their gene pools also allows them to evolve into entirely new kinds of animals. Given enough time and mutations, evolutionists claim, new species will evolve—like fish into amphibians or reptiles into mammals. This is groundless speculation. Nancy Pearcey also addressed this issue:

> They reach into the same grab bag and pull out the same examples of small-scale changes, things like different breeds of dogs or variation in the size of finch beaks or radiation-induced mutations in fruit flies or the development of resistance to insecticides.

Exactly what do these changes amount to? They are small-scale adaptations that allow the organisms to survive under adverse conditions—in other words, minor adjustments that allow them to *stay* dogs or finches or fruit flies or *whatever they already are*. In no case do these minor variations demonstrate that the organism is changing into something new or that it originally evolved from something else. As [Phillip] Johnson has pointed out, the only reason people find such limited change convincing is that they have already been persuaded on *other* grounds—on philosophical grounds—that naturalism is true [emphasis included].[9]

Science has *never* been able to demonstrate macroevolution. No one has witnessed the evolution of distinct varieties of animals. Laboratory experiments and observations in nature have only confirmed microevolution.[10] Species can develop no further than the limits of their existing gene pool. Thus, when cockroaches become resistant to a pesticide or a bacteria becomes resistant to antibiotics, this change does not represent the evolution of a new species of cockroaches or bacteria. No morphological changes have occurred—changes in the form and structure of the organisms.[11] Either resistance already existed in a small proportion of the population, or the changes are merely the biochemical effects of beneficial mutations (very rare in nature) that allow one variety to become dominant within a population of cockroaches or bacteria. The new breed of resistant cockroaches and bacteria are still cockroaches and bacteria—not new species.

Let's look at the "mechanism" that Darwinists believe drives evolution.

Mutations

When the structure of the DNA molecule was unraveled during the mid-twentieth century, Darwin's theory of natural selection received renewed support. Evolutionists believed they had finally discovered the fuel that powered the slow and gradual evolution of new species—mutations. Here's how this evolution supposedly worked.

Random changes (mutations) in DNA molecules, which carry hereditary information, benefit an organism. This new genetic material gives the creature a slight advantage in the struggle to survive, allowing it to propagate and pass on the trait to its descendants. Over eons of time and the occurrence of countless small, beneficial mutations, supposedly a new, genetically distinct species eventually evolves.

More often than not, in popular culture, evolutionists reduce this concept of mutations to its simplest form, grossly misleading and oversimplifying the process. Consider, for example, a recent article in my local newspaper:

> Evolutionary changes occur when a member of a species experiences a mutation in a gene that gives him a new skill, like running faster, seeing farther or thinking better. This genetic mutation increases his likelihood of survival and having more children, thereby allowing the new mutation to spread quickly through the population.[12]

Does the author *really* believe that a single mutation can result in a new skill, "like running faster, seeing farther, or thinking better?" The journalist makes it sound almost as if a new characteristic can appear in a single generation. This kind of unsophisticated reductionism should be an embarrassment even to committed evolutionists. Be that as it may, the mutation hypothesis receives little scientific support because of two insurmountable problems.

First, beneficial mutations are rare. Almost all mutations are harmful—or at best neutral—and either kill the organism or reduce its chances for survival. A deformity weakens, not increases, an animal's survival potential. If mutations were passed along to offspring, they would not necessarily result in evolution upward toward new and improved species. More likely, they would result in de-evolution leading to extinction.

Here's another way to picture this. Genes carry coded information or instructions. If this information is written incorrectly and the instructions are garbled, it's like a mistake in the recipe for grandma's cookies. If salt is accidentally written into the recipe instead of sugar, the result won't be mouth-watering cookies but something destined for the trash.

Experiments, such as those with the fruit fly (*Drosophila melanogaster*), have confirmed this. Scientists have produced all kinds of weird fruit flies in laboratories, but never a new kind of fly. Minor changes do not accumulate to create major changes. In fact, it's less than unlikely that any artificially mutated fruit fly would even survive in nature.[13] Scientists have bred a four-winged fruit fly (normal fruit flies have two wings). But instead of a faster-flying, more agile fruit fly, the creature is "seriously handicapped" because the extra wings lack flight muscles![14] This hardly endorses the theory that mutations and natural selection lead to brand new species.

The second insurmountable problem with the assumption that organisms can accumulate enough beneficial mutations to evolve into entirely new species is the time factor. The time required for a primitive animal to evolve into a higher animal through random mutations and natural selection does not exist—even on an evolutionary timetable. In fact, the universe itself—not just the planet earth—is not old enough for today's complex living organisms to have evolved from single-celled organisms through random mutational change. You see, there must be a continuous sequence of complementary mutations. Evolutionary change does not occur in a few generations, nor does a single new trait result in an entirely new species. If Darwin's finches were to evolve into a genetically distinct, new kind of bird, more than body size and beak shape must change. There is a quantum leap between different varieties of finches and an eagle. This problem is compounded exponentially when one kind of animal, such as an amphibian, is supposed to have evolved into another entirely different kind of animal, such as a reptile.

In the past, when confronted with the necessity of countless multiple and subsequent mutations, evolutionists fell back on the claim that the earth is about five billion years old. There was plenty of time, they insisted, for higher life forms to evolve from primitive ancestors. This ruse is no longer available. With the advent of "super (high-speed) computers," technicians can simulate the random, trial-and-error processes promulgated by evolutionists. "The outcome was jolting: The computers showed that the probability of evolution by chance processes is essentially zero, no matter how long the time scale."[15]

Biologist Dr. Gary Parker explained that the chances of getting three related mutations in a row is one in a billion trillion (10^{21}). To illustrate the odds of this, he stated that "the ocean isn't big enough to hold enough bacteria to make it likely for you to find a bacterium with three simultaneous or sequential related mutations." Parker continued:

> What about trying for four related mutations? 10^{28}. All of a sudden, the earth itself isn't big enough to hold enough organisms to make that very likely. And we're only talking about four mutations. It would take many more than that to change a fish into a philosopher, or even a fish into a frog. Four mutations doesn't even make a start toward real evolution. But even at this point some evolutionists have given up the classic idea of evolution, because it just plainly doesn't work.[16]

The Cambrian Explosion

We have seen that the mechanism Darwinists claim powers macroevolution (i.e. mutations) is insufficient to produce new animal types. Let's return to the issue of transitional fossils and look more closely at the fossil record. It shows virtually no evidence of transitional species.

Invertebrates: The First Supposed Stage of Evolution

We'll start with the oldest and most primitive life forms. Let's assume that by some miracle single-celled life somehow emerged out of some kind of primordial, inorganic muck (abiogenesis) and evolved into multi-celled animals. Even if this occurred, no fossil evidence supports the evolution of these more complex life forms.

According to the evolutionary timetable, multi-cellular life would have had to evolve virtually "overnight." This well-known fact is a result of the so-called "Cambrian Explosion," and it's a formidable argument against evolution because the "phenomenon would have required the sudden infusion of massive amounts of new genetic and other biological information that only could have come from an intelligent source."[17]

Evolutionists believe that for several billion years prior to the Cambrian Period, life on earth consisted almost entirely of single-celled organisms such as bacteria and algae. Suddenly, about 550 million years ago, the Cambrian Period exploded on the geological scene. During a mere five to ten million years (a very minute length of time in evolutionary history), well-preserved representative fossils of nearly every phyla of invertebrates that ever lived suddenly appeared in the fossil record. These highly complex organisms include trilobites, jellyfish, worms, corals, mollusks, as well as relatives of modern day starfish and sea urchins, and "an endless parade of arthropods, those spindly legged, hard-shelled ancient cousins of crabs and lobsters, spiders and flies.... Within a span of no more than 10 million years, creatures with teeth and tentacles and claws and jaws materialized with the suddenness of apparitions."[18]

What's difficult to explain for Darwinists is the high degree of complexity in these creatures—and how they evolved so quickly. For example, the eye of the squid is very similar to the human eye, containing a lens, pupil, and optic nerve. This kind of complexity would require a long period of evolution. Yet all the representative Cambrian invertebrates suddenly appeared in the fossil record fully formed and without ancestors. In other words, millions of species of diverse, complex, highly organized, multi-celled animals supposedly evolved from single-celled organisms without a single pre-Cambrian transitional form ever being found in the fossil record. Evolutionary scientists estimate that it would require 250 million years for insects to evolve. But where are the missing 250 million years of transitional insect fossils? I agree with Dr. Walter Bradley, who stated that "the Cambrian explosion, during which almost all the major animal phyla appeared suddenly, might be the best example of a fiat miracle."[19]

Not only do many highly complex creatures in the fossil record have no evolutionary past, they also have no evolutionary future. Those that have not become extinct have changed little or not at all from their first appearance in the fossil record to the present day. Thus, they are sometimes called "living fossils." For instance, the lungfish, many modern insects, and other arthropods (dragonflies, cockroaches, centipedes, crustaceans, spiders, etc.) showed up in the fossil record millions of years ago fully developed and looking almost exactly as they do today, except for size. (Many fossilized insects are much larger than modern specimens.)

This phenomenon is easily explained by *microevolution*, through which animals adapt to changing environmental conditions within the limits of their existing gene pools. When God created various "kinds" of animals, He created major design forms. Subsequent species are relatively minor variants of the original created designs.

Vertebrates

The next stage in evolution, according to Darwinists, is the vertebrates—animals with backbones. Is there any evidence that they evolved from the Cambrian invertebrates?

One of the "earliest" vertebrates to have supposedly evolved from invertebrates is fish. However, in spite of the hundred million years between Cambrian invertebrates and the first appearance of fish, not a single transitional fossil has been found. When fish appear in the fossil record, they are fully developed—possessing fins, scales, and gills.

Supposedly, after fifty million years, fish fins turned into legs, and amphibians crawled out of the water. Yet when amphibians appear suddenly in the fossil record, they are fully developed with no known transitional ancestors—in spite of the fifty-million-year gap.[20]

The same is true of reptiles and mammals. Although certain reptiles had skeletal features similar to some amphibians and mammals (an example of common design), "of much more significance is the fact that each of the various orders of amphibians, reptiles and mammals appear suddenly in the fossil record, without incipient forms leading up to it and without transitional forms between it and any other order."[21]

What about evolution within individual classes of animals, such as mammals? The lack of transitional specimens occurs here, too.

Imagine the modifications necessary to convert a land animal into a whale. It would require countless thousands of transitional species to change forearms into fins, move nostrils to the top of the head, and develop tail flukes. Yet none of these necessary transitional animals have been found. Like other marine mammals, whales appear suddenly in the fossil record fully formed and distinct from other mammals.

But what about all those transitional species one finds illustrated in magazines and textbooks? Aren't they replicas based on fossil evidence? No, the textbook drawings of transitional species are simply artists' conceptions of what they think such animals would look like if they did exist! Here's what America's preeminent evolutionist, the late Stephen Jay Gould, had to say concerning this issue, "The extreme rarity of transitional forms in the fossil record persists as the trade secret of paleontology. The evolutionary trees that adorn our textbooks have data only at the tips and nodes of their branches; the rest is inference, however reasonable, not the evidence of fossils."[22]

Archaeopteryx

We now come to *Archaeopteryx,* the evolutionist's fossil "ace in the hole." Evolutionists tout this one louder than any other, stating it's a bonafide transitional specimen. Many evolutionists claim that *Archaeopteryx* is clearly a transitional fossil, linking reptiles and modern birds. It had wings and fully developed feathers like a bird, but also possessed a toothed jaw like a reptile, a long lizard-like tail, and claws on its wings.

I want to make an observation before we evaluate whether or not *Archaeopteryx* is truly a transitional species or merely an extinct bird. If a transitional fossil does exist, this specimen is probably it. *Archaeopteryx* is the only fossil in existence whose physical appearance seems to offer a clear example of a transitional link between major groups of animals. (Other so-called transitional species are much easier to discredit.) Whether or not it is a missing link between reptiles and birds, the evidence of transitional fossils in the fossil record remains incredibly flimsy. If *Archaeopteryx* isn't a transitional fossil, none exists!

That said, I do not believe *Archaeopteryx* is a transitional specimen. It's merely a species of an extinct group of birds. "Paleontologists now agree that *Archaeopteryx* is not the ancestor of modern birds.... [It is merely] the earliest known bird—or at least, the earliest undisputed bird."[23] There are too many structural differences between *Archaeopteryx* and modern birds for the latter to be descendants of the former."[24] In fact, based on anatomical similarities, "the most likely candidates for the ancestors of *Archaeopteryx* lived tens of millions of years *later*."[25]

It's not just creationists who say this. *Archaeopteryx* expert, Allan Feduccia, wrote:

> I conclude that *Archaeopteryx* was arboreal and volant [can fly], considerably advanced aerodynamically, and probably capable of flapping, powered flight to at least some degree. *Archaeopteryx* probably cannot tell us much about the early origin of feathers and flight in true protobirds because *Archaeopteryx* was, in the modern sense, a bird."[26]

Archaeopteryx is an extinct species of bird that possessed a strange mixture of bird and reptile-like features. But it is not unique. Similar mixtures are found in other animals, such as the lungfish and the egg-laying mammal, the duckbilled platypus. The lungfish has fins and gills like other fish but also lungs, a heart, and a larval stage like an amphibian. The platypus lays eggs like a reptile but possesses hair, mammary glands, and other characteristics found only in mammals. Are they intermediate (transitional) species? No, for in both cases, none of their organs are transitional. In other words, lungfish organs that resemble a fish are typical of ordinary fish, and those that resemble an amphibian are like those found in amphibians. They are not "halfway" evolved organs between the two. Likewise, the reproductive system and structure of eggs in the platypus are fully reptilian but its mammary glands, hair, and so on are fully mammalian. The lungfish and platypus have a fascinating mixture of distinct, fully developed organs not normally found in one species, but in no way are they transitional in development or function, even at a molecular level.[27]

Likewise, although *Archaeopteryx* possess certain reptilian-like features such as teeth, a long tail, and claws, its wings and flight feathers are as fully developed as any modern bird. There is no fossil evidence that any series of pre-bird transitional reptiles led up to *Archaeopteryx*. In fact, the fossil evidence reveals that there is not one undisputed (even among evolutionists) transitional species of any kind anywhere in the fossil record. Animal types appear suddenly in the fossil record, not gradually, and then remain comparatively unchanged throughout their time on earth. The fossil evidence also shows that all major groups of animals are distinct from one another throughout the fossil record. Moreover, specific anatomical characteristics are already fully formed and functional when they first appear. Feathers and wings suddenly showing up in the fossil record are fully formed. No part-leg/part-wing or part-scale/part-feather fossils have ever been found. Creationist Henry Morris observed, "The evolutionary transition from invertebrates to vertebrates must have involved billions of animals, but no one has ever found a fossil of one of them."[28]

Endnotes

1. Norman L. Geisler, *Baker Encyclopedia of Christian Apologetics* (Grand Rapids: Baker Books, 1999), 226.

2. Quoted in Luther D. Sunderland, *Darwin's Enigma; Fossils and Other Problems* (Santee: Master Books, 1984), 89.

3. Quoted in Phillip E. Johnson, *Darwin on Trial* (Downers Grove: InterVarsity Press, 1991), 59.

4. Charles Darwin, *The Origin of Species by Natural Selection or the Preservation of Favored Races in the Struggle for Life* (New York: Random House), 124.

5. Nancy R. Pearcey, *Total Truth: Liberating Christianity from Its Cultural Captivity* (Wheaton: Crossway Books, 2004), 166.

6. Charles Colson and Nancy Pearcey, *How Now Shall We Live?* (Wheaton: Tyndale House Publishers, 1999), 84.

7. Ibid.

8. Hugh Ross, *The Creator and the Cosmos; How the Greatest Scientific Discoveries of the Century Reveal God* (Colorado Springs: NAVPRESS: 1993), 103.

9. Nancy Pearcey in Phillip E. Johnson, *The Right Questions; Truth, Meaning & Public Debate* (Downers Grove: InterVarsity Press, 2002), 12–13.

10. Phillip E. Johnson, *The Wedge of Truth; Splitting the Foundations of Naturalism* (Downers Grove: InterVarsity Press, 2000), 48.

11. Jonathan Wells, *Icons of Evolution; Science or Myth? Why Much of What We Teach About Evolution Is Wrong* (Washington DC: Regnery Publishing, 2000), 182.

12. Ronald Kotulak, "Study on brain-building genes could go to your head," The *San Diego Union-Tribune*, Sept. 9, 2005, A3.

13. Sunderland, *Darwin's Enigma*, 136–138.

14. Wells, *Icons of Evolution*, 178.

15. Colson and Pearcey, *How Now Shall We Live?*, 73.

16. Henry M. Morris and Gary E. Parker, *What Is Creation Science* (San Diego, Creation-Life Publishers, 1983), 63.

17. Quoted in an interview with Stephen C. Meyer, Lee Strobel, *The Case for a Creator; A Journalist Investigates Scientific Evidence That Points Toward God* (Grand Rapids: Zondervan, 2004), 238.

18. Madeleine Nash, "When Life Exploded," *Time*, December 4, 1995, 67–68.

19. Walter Bradley, "Why I Believe the Bible is Scientifically Reliable," in Norman L. Geisler and Paul K. Hoffman, ed., *Why I Am a Christian; Leading Thinkers Explain Why They Believe* (Grand Rapids: Baker Books, 2001), 170.

20. In 2004, a new fossil was discovered that was "hailed as evolution's 'missing link' between water- and land-dwelling animals." It was a species of *fish* that "had a neck, big ribs, arm bones, and a functional wrist joint." However, Ken Ham, president of Answers in Genesis, responded: "There is nothing new about it, except it's a new genus and species. . . . We already know some fish use their fins to prop themselves out of the water. Catfish do that." Casey Luskin of the Discovery Institute adds: "The whole question of how fins turned into feet is not solved by this fossil." See Sarah Eekhoff Zylstra, "Doubts About Fish Story: Anti-Darwinists downplay 'Missing Link,'" *Christianity Today*, June, 2006, 15.

21. Henry M. Morris, ed., *Scientific Creationism* (El Cajon: Master Books, 1991), 83–84.

22. Quoted in Geisler, *Baker Encyclopedia of Christian Apologetics*, 226.

23. Wells, *Icons of Evolution*, 112, 116.

24. Ibid., 116.

25. Ibid., 120.

26. Feduccia, Alan, "Evidence from Claw Geometry Indicating Arboreal Habits of *Archaeopteryx*," *Science*, vol. 259 (February 5, 1993), 792. Quoted in Henry M. Morris, *That Their Words may Be Used Against Them* (San Diego: Institute for Creation Research, 1997), 191.

27. Michael Denton, *Evolution: A Theory in Crisis* (Chevy Chase, MD: 1985), 109, 294.

28. Morris, ed., *Scientific Creationism*, 81–82.

FAKES, FRAUDS, AND OTHER PHONIES

WE HAVE SEEN that the scientific evidence does not support macroevolution. However, in their passion to prove otherwise, some Darwinists have sought less than honorable means to prove their case. This has resulted in a sinister side of evolutionary theory that Christian apologists need to expose. Although most evolutionary scientists are honest—even if deluded—some have unashamedly manipulated facts and committed outright fraud in order to gain fame and promote their naturalistic worldview.

During the past century, several fossil frauds and fakes have been exposed. Especially notable were fossils of supposed pre-human ancestors. The most notorious and well-known are the Piltdown fraud (the jaw of an orangutan attached to a human skull) and Nebraska Man (a supposed "missing link" between man and ape based on a single tooth that turned out to belong to an extinct pig). More recently, there was the "Piltdown bird," *Archaeoraptor*, touted by *National Geographic* magazine in 1999 as positive proof that birds are really dinosaurs. It turned out to be a fabrication that "consisted of a dinosaur tail glued to the body of a primitive bird."[1]

In addition to fossil frauds and fakes, there have been numerous phony "evidences" for evolution that resulted from poor research and an unwillingness to reveal truth when it came to light. Even today, many high school and college life-science textbooks continue to display false information as evidence for evolution.

A recent book that shattered many myths of evolution is Jonathan Wells's *Icons of Evolution; Science or Myth? Why Much of What We Teach About Evolution Is Wrong*. Wells examined numerous popular and long-standing evidences for evolution that are packaged in high school and college textbooks. All of them have been discredited, but few have been removed from the texts. This book, *Icons of Evolution,* is a "must read" for any student entering a secular college where evolution is standard fare in life-science classes. Here's a brief synopsis of some of Wells's examples.

Peppered Moths

Photographs in biology textbooks show peppered moths resting on tree trunks in the British Isles. Contrasting photos show the moths changing from a light to a dark color as pollution darkens the tree trunks. This has long been hailed as a "classic textbook example of natural selection in action."[2] Darwinists claim the photographs document evolution because the moths evolve new camouflage to protect themselves against bird predators.

Unfortunately (for Darwinists), it turns out "that peppered moths in the wild don't even rest on tree trunks."[3] The textbook photographs were staged. "Some are made using dead specimens that are glued or pinned to the trunk, while others used live specimens that are manually placed in desired positions."[4]

Actually, it doesn't matter whether the moths rest on trunks or even change color. Peppered moths are still peppered moths. Changes in coloration do not illustrate macroevolution. Rather they are classic examples of microevolution—of the moth's ability to adapt to changing environmental conditions within the limits of its existing gene pool. The potential to change color has always been part of their genetic makeup, which God programmed into them.

The Miller-Urey Experiment

According to the evolutionary paradigm, life emerged in the distant past from inorganic, nonliving chemicals. This is not happening today, evolutionists say, because atmospheric conditions do not allow it. Free oxygen, which is essential for life's "continuance," would destroy non-living organic molecules at a much faster rate than they could possibly form. Nevertheless, according to evolutionists, at least once in the distant past, conditions in the primitive atmosphere supposedly lacked free oxygen, allowing "complex organic (i.e. carbon based) molecules to come together," triggering organic evolution.[5]

This theory gained wide acceptance, partly due to a laboratory experiment in 1953 by graduate student, Stanley Miller, and his advisor, Harold Urey, Ph.D. They developed what they assumed was an environment similar to the earth's primitive atmosphere. By sending an electric spark into a gaseous mixture (presumably to simulate lightning), they succeeded in producing amino acids, the building blocks of protein. (Protein is a basic ingredient of life.)[6] However, they didn't create life itself, as many suppose. Their experiment "soon found its way into almost every high school and college biology textbook as evidence that scientists have demonstrated the first step in the origin of life."[7]

Today, geochemists recognize that the Miller-Urey experiment failed to simulate the actual conditions of earth's primitive atmosphere, which makes the findings meaningless in terms of origin of life studies. The evidence increasingly suggests that the earth's primal atmosphere did contain free oxygen. Explained Wells:

> If the principle ingredient of the primitive atmosphere was water vapor [released from ancient volcanoes], the atmosphere must also have contained some oxygen. Atmospheric scientists know that ultraviolet rays from sunlight cause dissociation of water vapor in the upper atmosphere. This process, called "photodissociation," splits water molecules into hydrogen and oxygen. The hydrogen escapes into space, leaving the oxygen behind in the atmosphere."[8]

The likelihood of oxygen in the earth's early atmosphere isn't the only problem with the Miller-Urey experiment. It's unlikely that the amino acids produced would ever assemble proteins:

Proteins in all living things are assembled from the same basic "alphabet" of 20 amino acids. Each different type of protein is formed from a unique arrangement of these chemical "letters." To form a protein that actually works, the amino acid letters must be arranged in precise sequences, like letters in a sentence. This precise sequence creates a certain protein that has a specific function in the cell.... [Hence] connecting amino acids to form a useful protein is a lot harder than just making an amino acid. Hooking amino acids together requires removing a molecule of water for each amino acid added to the chain, but amino acids are highly water-soluble (they dissolve in water). This means that although water is a necessary part of the Miller-Urey theory, the presence of water also keeps amino acids from forming proteins.[9]

Despite recent studies that have destroyed the illusion that Miller and Urey created life in a laboratory, many modern textbooks make no mention of the experiment's failure. Instead, they promote the Miller-Urey experiment as evidence for a naturalistic origin of life. If the experiment proved anything at all, it proved that for life to originate it must result from careful orchestration by an intelligence and purposeful Designer.

Darwin's Finches

Another icon of evolution that has been discredited concerns "Darwin's finches." When Charles Darwin visited the Galapagos Islands in 1835, there were thirteen or fourteen different species of finches. They ranged in size from a blackbird to a small sparrow. Each had distinct plumage and behavior. Some finches were almost completely black; others were light brown. Some were primarily ground dwellers; others foraged in tree branches. However, the various species differed primarily in the size and shape of their beaks. They ranged from parrot-like beaks to slender warbler-like beaks. One variety had a straight wood-boring beak.[10]

Later evolutionists calculated that these morphological differences evolved as the finches adjusted to drought conditions and less-available food supplies. Thus, they asserted, natural selection will eventually create new species of finches. In fact, evolutionists claim, "if droughts occur about once every 10 years on the islands, a new species of finch might arise in only about 200 years."[11]

This claim is simply untrue, and researchers know it. Science textbooks fail to mention that changes in beak size are cyclical and that large and small beaks are always present in finch populations. After a drought ends, their beaks return to average size. This is microevolution—adaptation within the limits of the finches' existing gene pool. Here's what other researches actually said about finches' beak size and shape: "The available evidence is clear.... Selection oscillates with climatic fluctuations, and does not exhibit long-term evolutionary change."[12] "The evolutionary change... [researchers] observed during the drought of 1977 was reversed by the heavy rains of 1983.... 'The birds took a giant step backward, after their giant step forward.'"[13]

Haeckel's Embryos

Another widely held, but mythical evidence for evolution is embryonic development. Supposedly, this was one of the best evidences for evolution. Many high school and college textbooks taught that developing embryos "recapitulate" their evolutionary history by passing through ancestral adult forms as they develop, suggesting common ancestry.[14] Once again, the truth is considerably different from what evolutionists claim:

> Biologists have known for *over a century* that Haeckel [who first proposed this theory] faked his drawings; vertebrate embryos never look as similar as he made them out to be. Furthermore, the stage Haeckel labeled the "first" is actually midway through development; the similarities he exaggerated are preceded by striking differences in earlier stages of development.[15]
>
> In some cases, Haeckel.... doctored his drawings to make the embryos appear more alike than they really were.... Even the embryos he chose are distorted to fit his theory [emphasis added].[16]

Pre-human Ancestors

The most controversial fossil evidence surrounds the supposed evolution of humans. We've already seen that two of the most famous alleged pre-human fossils—the Piltdown Man and Nebraska Man—turned out to be frauds. But what about all those drawings we see in books and magazines? Don't they represent known fossils of pre-humans?

Textbook drawings, illustrations in *National Geographic,* and documentaries on television typically show modern man evolving through a series of transitional forms from ape-like ancestors. What these drawings, illustrations, and documentaries fail to mention, however, is the wild and creative imaginations of the evolutionists who commissioned these drawings. The artistic license taken to create the mythical pre-human ancestors is beyond ludicrous. With a handful of bones, paleontologists create fanciful specimens of fully formed pre-human ancestors that in fact never existed.

Quoting Henry Gee, chief science writer for *Nature,* Wells points out that all the evidence for human evolution "between about 10 and 15 millions years ago—several thousand generations of living creatures—can be fitted into a small box." Thus the conventional picture of human evolution as lines of ancestry and descent is "a completely human invention created after the fact, shaped to accord with human prejudices."[17]

In other words, there is meager fossil evidence to support the contention that human beings evolved from ape-like ancestors. As one author stated:

> If the evidence for fossil men were presented within a court of law as proof of evolution, the case would be thrown out for a lack of objective evidence. If the fossil displays and artistic renderings of fossil people and transitional creatures were subject to "truth in advertising" standards, somebody would go to jail.[18]

There is no reliable evidence that modern Homo sapiens evolved from ape-like ancestors. Who are all those extinct fossil primates that paleontologists claim are pre-human? They are most likely extinct specimens (or variation within gene pools) of created "kinds" of non-human primates that vanished in the distant past—just like other fossils. They do not represent evolutionary "common ancestry" but rather created "common design." Richard Leakey, perhaps the world's foremost paleoanthropologist, said: "If pressed about man's ancestry, I would have to unequivocally say that all we have is a huge question mark. Today, there has been nothing found to truthfully purport as a transitional species to man.... If further pressed, I would have to state that there is more evidence to suggest an abrupt arrival of man rather than a gradual process of evolving."[19]

Features That Defy Evolution

Another convincing argument against evolution is the countless examples of plants and animals that defy evolution. The following examples are a few of the hundreds that could be examined.

Bombardier Beetle

Biologist Gary Parker discussed the bombardier beetle, which has an ingenious chemical-defense mechanism.[20] It can literally shoot a blast of noxious gases at the boiling point of water (212°F) into a predator's face. But how does the bombardier keep from killing itself? Another researcher wrote, "The slightest alteration in the chemical balance would result immediately in a race of exploded beetles."[21] Parker explained:

> Successful firing of the bombardier beetle's cannons requires two chemicals (hydrogen peroxide and hydroquinones), two enzymes and enzyme blockers, pressure tanks, and a whole series of nerve and muscle attachments for aim and control. Try to image all those parts accumulating by time, chance, and natural selection?[22]

This beetle is a classic example of irreducible complexity. The various apparatus involved in its chemical defense are products of a large number of highly complex, interactive parts. No single piece of equipment would have survival value independent of the other parts, nor would any single part (or the organ as a whole) have any function until it was fully developed and operative. The fact that evolutionists can't explain is how such complex, interrelated biochemical processes evolved step by step.

Cleaner Fish

Another example of features that defy evolution is the symbiotic behavior of the cleaner fish, which swims into the mouths of larger, predatory fish in order to feed on food debris and parasites. This behavior benefits both the predator and the cleaner fish, but this doesn't explain the origin of the relationship. What caused the predator to stop eating the little fish—and what motivated the little fish to swim into the mouth of a predator in the first place? Neither would have any survival value until after the traits were in place. It's difficult to imagine how this behavior developed through time and chance. Design seems a much more likely reason.

Metamorphosis

What mechanism stimulated the evolution of metamorphosis, the change in form from one stage to the next during the life cycle of an organism? For example, the butterfly begins as a caterpillar (in the larva stage) changes into a cocoon (the pupa stage), and finally changes into an adult butterfly. During the metamorphosis of an insect such as the butterfly, during the pupa stage all the organ systems of the larva dissolve into a "veritable soup of fragmented cells and tissues" that later assemble into a different type of organism.[23]

    This raises several question evolution can't answer. How did random evolutionary processes cause a larva to turn into a pupa or chrysalis in mere minutes? What survival value (function) stimulated the jellylike material within the chrysalis to evolve into a beautiful butterfly? Which came first, the caterpillar or the butterfly? Evolutionists have no explanation for metamorphosis.

Bird Lungs

Unlike mammals and reptiles, birds posses a unique, continuous flow-through lung system. No evolutionary pathway can account for this remarkable organ. Molecular biologist Michael Denton described this issue in detail:

> In all other vertebrates the air is drawn into the lungs through a system of branching tubes which finally terminate in tiny air sacs, or alveoli, so that during respiration the air is moved in and out through the same passage. In the case of birds, however, the major bronchi break down into tiny tubes which permeate the lung tissue.... These so-called parabronchi eventually join up together again, forming a true circulatory system so that air flows in one direction through the lungs.... No lung in any other vertebrate species is known which in any way approaches the avian system. Moreover, it is identical in all essential details in birds as diverse as humming birds, ostriches and hawks.
>
> Just how such an utterly different respiratory system could have evolved gradually from the standard vertebrate design is fantastically difficult to envisage.... Just as the feather cannot function as an organ of flight until the hooks and barbules are coadapted to fit together perfectly, so the avian lung cannot function as an organ of respiration until the parabronchi system which permeates it and the air sac system which guarantees the parabronchi their air supply are both highly developed and able to function together in a perfectly integrated manner.[24]

The challenge for evolutionists is to explain why only birds developed such a unique, one-of-a-kind organ, and how did it develop step-by-step?

Bacterial Flagellum

Features that defy evolution are not restricted to large organisms. Even tiny biochemical processes within a single cell defy evolutionary explanations. William Dembski wrote:

Bacterial flagellum, which is an acid-powered rotary motor with a whiplike tail that spins 20,000 rpm and whose rotating motion enables a bacterium to navigate through its water environment. The intricate machinery in this molecular motor—including a rotor, a stator, O-rings, bushings, and a drive shaft—requires the coordinated interaction of numerous complex proteins. Engineers marvel at this example of nanoengineering. Darwinists reflexively attribute it to natural selection, even though no plausible Darwinian pathway has ever been proposed to account for it (and that despite thousands of research articles about this one biological system).[25]

The Plant World

Systems unexplained by evolution are also evident in the plant world. "Botany offers many examples of complex adaptations which have never been explained convincingly in gradualistic terms."[26] An intriguing example has to do with plant physiology:

Plant cells have metabolic energy-producing structures and reactions similar to our own cells, but have, in addition, the complex mechanisms for photosynthesis. This would appear to give them, at the cellular level, a survival advantage, since they can use the daily presence of sunlight as a food source, and not rely on the uncertainties of a scavenger existence. Indeed, other one-celled organisms, the euglenas, have both chloroplast and eating abilities, making them both plant-like and animal-like. Why, then, have plant cells—or euglenoid organisms—not evolved to a higher level than animal cells? Why, indeed, did they ever split off from the animal kingdom at all (or vice-versa)? And, why did the "higher plants" evolve the ability to produce virtually every one of the many vitamin and mineral nutrients needed by the bodies of animals, and thus set themselves up as our main food target? In further support of creation, it is also true that plants, in addition to being our main food source, contain many chemicals that have healing and restorative properties for us. Physicians and pharmacologists have long known that the green world is the source of most of the useful medicines and balms which can bring healing and relief of suffering. Why should the plants have evolved the means of healing their evolutionary enemies?[27]

Does this sound like evolution? Not at all. I agree with the author when he reminds us:

> Fundamental biological division of the living world, mysterious from a hypothetical evolutionary viewpoint, suddenly comes into clear focus through a single Bible passage. Genesis 1:29, 30 shows us why it is that plants fulfill nearly all of our diverse nutritional needs and are absolutely essential to our good health and longevity. "And God said, Behold, I have given you every herb bearing seeds, which is upon the face of all the earth, and every tree, in which is the fruit of a tree yielding seeds; to you it shall be for meat [v. 29, KJV]."[28]

Conclusion

Most rank-and-file evolutionists whom Christians encounter and other skeptics of Christian truth-claims, derive their opinions on biblical creation from popular culture: secular magazines, documentaries, high school and college science classes, and ubiquitous and misleading national newspapers. Rarely do these mediums provide scientific data from the creationist camp. A *National Geographic* article entitled, "Was Darwin Wrong?"[29] illustrates this. Although the author answered his question with a resounding "No," he chose not to offer disputable evidence from the creationist camp. In all, this lengthy article was little more than a litany of worn-out arguments that evolutionists have used for a generation to defend macroevolution—selective breeding, bacterial and insect resistance, Darwin's finches, fruit flies, and so on. As we've clearly seen, these evidences only confirm microevolution; they give no support to macroevolution.

Charles Darwin cautioned in his book, *The Origin of Species*, "If it could be demonstrated that any complex organ existed which could not possibly have been formed by numerous, successive, slight modifications, my theory would absolutely break down."[30] We have just answered his challenge with numerous examples. There's a good reason for evolution to break down!

Throughout this chapter, I have relied heavily on the research of Michael Denton, Australian molecular biologist and medical doctor. Denton, a "self-described agnostic,"[31] has no *a priori* theological or philosophical objection to evolution. He is a good scientist who goes where the evidence leads. It seems fitting that Denton be given the last comment in this section. His words are especially compelling because he possesses no allegiance to the Christian worldview.

> The concept of the continuity of nature [uninterrupted evolution from common ancestors] has existed in the mind of man *never* in the facts of nature. In a very real sense, therefore, advocacy of the doctrine of continuity has always necessitated a retreat from pure empiricism, and contrary to what is widely assumed by evolutionary biologists today, it has always been the anti-evolutionists, not the evolutionists, in the scientific community who have stuck rigidly to the facts and adhered to a more strictly empirical approach....
>
> The idea that it was the opponents of evolution [e.g. creationists] who were blinded by the error of *a priorism* is one of the great myths of twentieth-century biology.[32]

Endnotes

1. Jonathan Wells, *Icons of Evolution; Science or Myth? Why Much of What We Teach About Evolution Is Wrong* (Washington DC: Regnery Publishing, 2000), 124.
2. Ibid., 138.
3. Ibid., 138.
4. Ibid., 150.
5. John Morris, "Hasn't Life Been Created in The Laboratory?" *Back to Genesis*, August 2001, d.
6. Wells, *Icons of Evolution*, 10.
7. Ibid.
8. Ibid., 15.
9. This summary of the problems facing the Miller-Urey experiments are found in *Answers to Evolution: 16 Reasons to Doubt Darwinism* (Torrance, CA: Rose Publishing, 2004),Q5 & Q6.

10. Michael Denton, *Evolution: A Theory in Crisis* (Chevy Chase, MD: Adler & Adler, 1985), 30–31.

11. Wells, *Icons of Evolution*, 74. This quote was from a 1999 booklet published by the National Academy.

12. Wells, *Icons of Evolution*, 173.

13. Ibid., 168–169.

14. Ibid., 87.

15. Ibid., 82–83.

16. Ibid., 91.

17. Ibid., 220–221.

18. David T. Moore, *Five Lies of the Century; How Many do You Believe?* (Wheaton: Tyndale house Publishers, 1995), 148.

19. This quote is found in *Answers to Evolution*, Rose Publishing. It is taken from a PBS documentary in 1990. The title of the documentary was not given.

20. Michael Behe provided a thorough discussion of this amazing beetle in *Darwin's Black Box: The Biochemical Challenge to Evolution* (New York, The Free Press, 1996), 31–36, 47.

21. Ibid., 33

22. Gary E. Parker, *What Is Creation Science?* (San Diego: Creation-Life Publishers, 1983), 52.

23. Denton, *Evolution: A Theory in Crisis*, 147, 220.

24. Ibid., 210–212

25. William A. Dembski, "Darwin's Predictable Defenders: A Response to Massimo Pigliucci," *Christian Research Journal*, (vol. 25. No. 01), 31.

26. Denton, *Evolution: A Theory in Crisis*, 225.

27. David Demick, M.D., "The Unselfish Green Gene" (*Impact*, July 2000), iii.

28. Ibid., iv.

29. David Quammen, "Was Darwin Wrong? No.," *National Geographic*, November, 2004.

30. Quoted in Denton, *Evolution: A Theory in Crisis*, 213.

31. Thomas Woodward, *Doubts About Darwin: A History of Intelligent Design* (Grand Rapids: Baker Books, 2003), 24.

32. Denton, *Evolution: A Theory in Crisis*, 353–355.

PART THREE

We Can Demonstrate To Atheists That God Exists

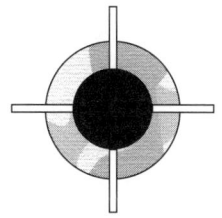

INTRODUCTION TO PART THREE

FOURTH-CENTURY theologian and Bishop of Hippo, Saint Augustine, wrote in his book, *Confessions:* "Man is one of your creatures, Lord, and his instinct is to praise you.... The thought of you stirs him so deeply that he cannot be content unless he praises you, because you made us for yourself and our hearts find no peace until they rest in you."[1] Augustine captured a profound theological truth in this famous quote: God has placed an intuitive awareness of His existence in the hearts of all people (Ecclesiastes 3:11).

This innate yearning for a relationship with the Divine is a worldwide phenomenon that has been documented countless times. Studies of ancient and recent civilizations confirm that belief in supernatural beings is an ingredient of all cultures. The same is true in America today. According to pollster George Barna, nine out of ten American adults believe in some kind of God, and "seven out of ten believe in a God who is the 'all-powerful, all-knowing, perfect creator of the universe who rules the world today.'"[2]

The fact is, few people are true atheists. Atheism is an anomaly. People are not atheists by birth; they become atheists by exposure to a secular culture. Consequently, in terms of God's existence, the issue evangelists usually encounter is not whether God exists, but what He is like. The apologetic task, most often, is not to demonstrate that God exists, but to prove that "God is the kind of God found in Scripture."[3]

This is not to say that there aren't many functioning atheists—people who profess to believe in God but think, talk, and behave as if God *doesn't* exist. More serious yet, and the primary reason why apologetics in defense of God's existence is important, the majority our culture's pacesetters—the intellectual elite who control the media and entertainment industries and run our universities—are apparent atheists. They clearly promote a human-centered, largely immoral, godless worldview that has permeated virtually all sectors of modern culture. Since the 1960s, atheists have been remarkably triumphant in promoting their ideology emphasizing that belief in God is irrational. Although few in number, these atheists wield tremendous influence in our society today.

There are many arguments for God's existence. Peter Kreeft and Ronald Tacelli, in their *Handbook of Christian Apologetics*, dedicate a chapter to twenty such arguments.[4] In the following four chapters, I have selected what I believe are the most effective, usable, and durable arguments for God's existence. They include scientific, philosophical, and subjective evidences.

Endnotes

1. Saint Augustine, *Confessions*, Translated by R.S. Pine-Coffin, (New York: Dorset Press, 1986), 21.

2. George Barna, *The State of the Church: 2002* (Ventura: Issachar Resources, 2002), 50.

3. Kenneth D. Boa and Robert M. Bowman Jr., *Faith Has Its Reasons; An Integrative Approach to Defending Christianity* (Colorado Springs: NP, 2001), 115.

4. Peter Kreeft and Ronald K. Tacelli, *Handbook of Christian Apologetics; Hundreds of Answers to Crucial Questions* (Downers Grove; InterVarsity Press, 1994), Chapter 3.

GOD HAS PLACED ETERNITY IN OUR HEARTS

MOST CHRISTIAN theologians acknowledge that God has placed an instinctive awareness of His existence into the human soul. This knowledge is built into us by virtue of our creation in God's image, and it's manifested in our hearts and minds externally through creation (Romans 1:19) and internally by a God-given moral conscience (Romans 2:14–15). Unfortunately, because God won't coerce anyone into belief and obedience, people can and do suppress this "general" revelation[1] from God (Romans 1:18). Rather than acknowledging and seeking God, many people turn away from the true Creator and either deny His existence or, more commonly, substitute false gods (Romans 1:21–32).

Nevertheless, because of humankind's "sense of divinity," general revelation represents a point of contact between God and humanity that actually petitions what people intuitively know about spiritual realities—even if they suppress it. Consequently, the "intuitive" argument, which taps into a subjective area of truth acknowledged by many people, can be a valuable apologetic for God's existence. Let me illustrate.

From the mid-1970s until the early 1980s, I was active in the newly emerging environmental movement. I joined the Sierra Club and went on club-sponsored hikes and backpacking trips. During the evenings, Sierra clubbers would typically sit around together and talk about "whatever." Occasionally, someone would make a comment like this: "Don't you feel close to God out here?" Or, "This is my church; this is where you can find God."

Although I was not a Christian at the time, such comments revealed an innate awareness of God in nature and would have provided a wonderful point of contact for apologetic evangelism. Had I been a Christian, I would have responded something like this: "Yes, I do feel God's presence in nature. And you're right, we can draw close to God in the out-of-doors. But I wonder who you think the God of nature is? What is He like, this God who reveals Himself in wild places?" This could have started a conversation on the nature of God and provided an opportunity for me to describe the God of creation—and possibly share Jesus Christ.

When we look at the world around us, as well as into our hearts, we discover that much of what we take for granted makes sense if God exists but it is largely a mystery if He doesn't. In particular, reality as we observe it and live it out is best understood if God exists. Here are a few other examples of how the intuitive argument plays itself out in terms of evidences for God's existence through general revelation and natural law (the moral side of general revelation).[2]

Belief in an Afterlife

Every culture during every period of history, from the most primitive to the most sophisticated, has believed in some form of afterlife and the existence of deity. Quaker scholar, Arthur Roberts, wrote, "Intuitions differ around the world, from myths of eternal return to popular stories about the afterlife, but they abound. . . . Persistent transcultural accounts of heaven point toward a reality difficult to comprehend empirically but less difficult to know intuitively."[3] In short, people recognize that this present world is not our real home; we are only on a journey toward our real home—heaven.

This intuitive knowledge that God exists and that eternal life awaits us after physical death is a basic human understanding. The best and most satisfying explanation for this worldwide phenomenon is that such knowledge was implanted into the human soul by virtue of our creation in God's image. (See Romans 1.) As King Solomon wrote in Ecclesiastes 3:11, God has "set eternity in [men's] heart."

Inner Voice of the Cosmos

Something in us is highly skeptical of the Darwinist's notion that nature and the cosmos are products of accidental, random processes. It is contrary to all human experience and observation. Nature is too complex and too beautiful to have come into being without a Creator. Apart from scientific confirmation (see Part Two), the best explanation is the one we carry in our hearts—that nature is an expression of God. David wrote in Psalm 19:1, "The heavens are telling of the glory of God; and their expanse is declaring the work of His hands."

Our intuitive understanding is confirmed scientifically. Clearly, intelligence is the origin of all that exists. As we saw earlier, the statistical odds of the universe accidentally developing all the conditions necessary to sustain life on earth are impossibly huge. The Anthropic Principle is one of the strongest, and most compelling, arguments for God's existence.

Nature: Designed for Discovery

Remarkably, "the very same conditions that allow for intelligent life on Earth also makes it strangely well-suited for viewing and analyzing the universe.... [This] raises the question of whether the universe has been literally designed for discovery."[4] In other words, are the conditions that allow for intelligent life on earth an accidental by-product of random evolutionary forces or purposeful acts of a cosmic Designer? If the universe is a product of mindless, random processes, there is no obvious reason or physical explanation for why nature's wonders and secrets are so readily available for people to probe and understand, and then utilize for their own well-being. Indeed, as Alister McGrath put it, "It is almost as if the human mind has been designed to grasp the patterns and structures of the cosmos."[5]

It seems probable that the same Intelligence that spoke the universe into existence prepared it in such a way that its scientific secrets and potential technologies await discovery by the very creatures it was created to support. Only if God exists and designed the cosmos for discovery can this phenomena make sense.

The Paradox of Good and Evil

Secular humanists and New Age adherents teach a favorable view of humanity. People are innately good, they claim, and as knowledge (or spiritual insight) grows, we will reach ever greater heights of goodness. At best, this is but a half-truth. A paradox exists between human goodness and human depravity. On the one hand, people are capable of great good—witness the selfless outpouring of money and volunteers to aid the victims of Hurricane Katrina—while on the other hand, people are equally capable of great evil—as Islamic terrorists depict. We have an innate idea of how we ought to behave but struggle to act accordingly. (See Romans 7.) The Bible explains this paradox by revealing that people are created in the image of God—we possess goodness, and yet we are fallen—and we possess evilness. We have a "sin nature" that constantly battles whatever latent good we maintained after the Fall. History confirms this.

People today are just as greedy, covetous, selfish, cruel, and warlike as they were thousands of years ago. The heart of modern man is no different than the heart of ancient man. Indeed, the twentieth century was probably the most bloodthirsty century in history. Well-known Christian apologist, Dr. Robert A. Morey, reported that more than a hundred and fifty million people were killed by *atheistic* governments during the twentieth century.[6] If human beings are products of naturalistic evolution, as the centuries pass, why have we not improved significantly in the area of ethical behavior? Why has our ability to get along as "social animals" failed to evolve?

The best explanation for people's natural disposition to sin is the biblical revelation that the human race is fallen and subsequently possesses a sin nature. (See Romans 3:9–18, 23.) Any other view (secular or religious) contradicts what we observe today, as well as what history reveals. The Christian worldview best explains the paradox of good and evil. This gives tremendous credence to the claim that God not only exists but is the God revealed in the Bible.

Worldwide Moral Conscience

Despite humanity's sinfulness, the Bible also teaches that God endowed the human race with a moral conscience, a sense of right and wrong (Romans 2:13–15). Even people who do not have the Law of Moses (e.g. the Ten Commandants) have God's moral law "written in their hearts, their conscience bearing witness, and their thoughts alternately accusing or else defending them" (vs. 15). People universally and instinctively recognize that certain behaviors are immoral and others are good. All peoples agree that dreadful acts such as indiscriminate murder, rape, cheating, and stealing are immoral but that other acts, such as love, selflessness, sharing, and protecting women and children are virtuous. These values represent a shared moral obligation to do right and condemn wrong. Because these moral values are absolute and independent of personal and cultural parameters, they must have originated *outside* the human mind and experience. A godless worldview provides no such moral absolute. (This concept is developed fully in chapter eighteen.)

The best explanation for these universal moral values is that they are intrinsic to the nature of God Himself, and He passed them to us by virtue of our creation in His image.

Endnotes

1. General revelation is revelation given to all people, at every period of history. It is God's continuous revelation that is made known primarily through the testimony of nature and an innate moral sense of right and wrong. In contrast, special revelation is revelation God makes known to specific people at specific times in history and includes specific information about God, such as salvation through Jesus Christ. The Bible is God's primary avenue of special revelation.

2. For an excellent study on natural law, which is grounded in general revelation, see J. Budziszewski's, *Written on the Heart; The Case for Natural Law* (Downers Grove: InterVarsity Press, 1997).

3. Arthur O. Roberts, *Exploring Heaven; What Great Thinkers Tell Us About Our Afterlife with God* (San Francisco: HarperSanFrancisco, 2003), 67–68.

4. Quoted from an interview with Guillermo Gonzalez and Jay Wesley Richards, in Lee Strobel's *The Case for a Creator; A Journalist Investigates Scientific Evidence That Points Toward God* (Grand Rapids: Zondervan, 2004), 164.

5. Alister McGrath, *Glimpsing the Face of God; The Search for Meaning in the Universe* (Grand Rapids: William B. Eerdmans Publishing Co., 2002), 19.

6. Robert A. Morey, *The New Atheism and the Erosion of Freedom* (Minneapolis: Bethany House Publishers, 1986), 148–149.

NATURE DEMANDS A CREATOR

WITH THE EXCEPTION of the so-called problem of evil, which we will examine in chapter twenty, all arguments against God's existence are actually arguments against evidences that God exists. Evolution is not a direct argument against God's existence. Evolutionists could agree that God may exist even if He isn't the Creator (though they would see God more in line with pantheism than Christian theism). Evolutionists argue against evidences that support creation.

On the other hand, if creation is a fact, there is a Creator (God). Thus, evidences for creation can be used to demonstrate that God does exist. Nature demands a Creator. This familiar teleological argument for God's existence begins with the observation that design is obvious in the world of nature and it points to a cosmic Designer who transcends the world He created.

The second argument for God's existence is to appeal to the evidences for creation outlined in Part Two. We want to present data that requires a Creator: the Anthropic Principle, Intelligent Design, information theory, and the laws of physics. Since we've examined these already, we can move to the next argument for God's existence. However, before we do, let me share an experience I had recently that shows how this information can be used in a witnessing opportunity.

As I waited for my pickup at a car wash, I overhead a woman tell a coworker she was an atheist. I sat down next to them and listened to the conversation. (They weren't aware I was paying any attention.) After a while, I leaned over and said, "I couldn't help overhearing you say that you're an atheist. I'm curious, why?" This, in essence, is how the conversation went from there:

> **Lady:** "I'm a biological evolutionist, and the evidence proves God doesn't exist."
> **Me:** "What kind of evidence are you talking about?"
> **Lady:** "People are prejudiced by their understanding of a lineal concept of time and our three-dimensional perception of the world. Everything is just *here*, it has always been here." (In other words, the universe is eternal so God doesn't exist.)
> **Me:** "That sounds like speculation to me. Actually, the evidence suggests that the universe is not eternal."
> **Coworker:** "Are you from a Judeo-Christian tradition?"

Some Christians may argue that this was an opportune time for me to share my faith, but I didn't think it was. It would have made my challenge appear to be motivated by religion, and I could have been easily dismissed.[1] I wanted them to see that *atheism*, not Christianity, is irrational, so I didn't answer this question directly.

> **Me:** "I'm just interested in your point of view and how you came to it. As I understand it, the Second Law of Thermodynamics and the impossibility of time extending backwards infinitely makes an eternal universe impossible. [Pause] Let me ask you a question. Even if the universe is eternal, where do the laws of physics come from that govern it?"
> **Lady:** "If you were better trained, you would understand!" [Translation: "Gee, I really can't answer that!"]

Actually, this response is typical of many professing evolutionists. She assumed that if I didn't agree with her I was uninformed. After this last comment, they stood up, began looking around to see if their car was finished, and hurriedly walked away. The woman was clearly uncomfortable with having to defend her beliefs.

Was this brief discussion worth the time? Certainly, God could use it to plant a seed of doubt in the woman's mind that may compel her to rethink her reasons for being an atheist. Many tough-minded people need their presuppositions removed before they will consider Christianity. Had we not been strangers at a car wash, and had more time, who knows where the conversation may have gone.

My reason for telling this story is not to share an interesting apologetic discussion, but to illustrate how a combination of facts and Socratic questions can baffle even trained evolutionists. I'm not a scientist, but I've done my homework. Neither the woman nor her companion could give any evidence to support the contention that the universe is eternal or that God doesn't exist. Her opinion really was metaphysical speculation without justification. If I encouraged them to see this, I did my job as an apologist. Perhaps the next apologist or evangelist God sends their way will get a better reception. This is how apologetic encounters often play out. We don't always have the opportunity to share the gospel, but we can lay the groundwork. (See 1 Cor. 3:5–9.) That's why apologetics is often referred to as "pre-evangelism."

Endnote

1. As I have explained elsewhere, we should always try to lead the conversation to the Gospel during witnessing encounters. However, "tough-minded" people (e.g. skeptics, critics, and agnostics) usually reject it. We often have to remove intellectual obstacles first before they will seriously consider the Gospel. In like manner, giving our personal testimony to an atheist will usually be a waste of time, unless we are prepared to give an apologetic defense for the existence of God. Why would atheists give any stock to our testimonies when they reject the existence of God? See my book, *Engaging the Closed Minded; Presenting Your Faith to the Confirmed Unbeliever* (Grand Rapids: Kregel Publications, 1999), chapter one.

MORAL LAW DEMANDS A CREATOR

THIS ARGUMENT stands on the premise that it is impossible to establish any kind of universal and absolute moral laws independent of God. For that reason, if absolute moral laws exist, this fact demonstrates the existence of God (the Moral Lawgiver). This can be expressed as a syllogism.

Premise 1: It is impossible to have universal, absolute moral Laws unless God exists.
Premise 2: Universal, absolute moral laws exist.
Conclusion: Therefore, God (the Moral Lawgiver) must exist.

In a valid argument, if the premises are true the conclusion must be true. So, our apologetic task is to demonstrate that these two premises are true and it is fairly easy to confirm them.

Our Moral Conscience Demonstrates the Existence of God

The simplest way to apply this argument is to point out that everyone (except someone with a serious mental disorder) acknowledges that it *feels* wrong to go against one's own conscience. Where did this self-incriminating conscience come from? If it directs my thoughts and actions, it must be greater than me. If it can motivate me to stand against the pressures of societal norms, it must be greater than society. (An example is Dietrich Bonhoeffer, who opposed the Nazi movement before and during World War II.) The best explanation is that the source of my moral conscience is a transcendent Absolute—God—who is superior to me and not controlled by social institution.

However, to verify the premises in the argument of moral law, we must demonstrate that all people have this same moral conscience and recognize universal moral standards. In other words, people worldwide corporately share a generic moral code, like-mindedness in what constitutes good, evil, right, and wrong. All human beings recognize certain acts as immoral and formulate laws and taboos to curtail such behavior.[1]

Here's how we can demonstrate this.

Comparative studies in anthropology, sociology, and religion have revealed the existence of a universal, worldwide moral code governing the behavior of virtually all peoples, regardless of their cultures, religions, or periods of history in which they existed.[2] This generic moral code is manifested worldwide in prohibitions against indiscriminate murder, rape, stealing, lying, cheating, and other evil acts. It likewise acknowledges that love, sharing, selflessness, and protecting the weak and vulnerable are virtuous. Ethicist Scott Rae explains:

> Values such as justice, fairness, respect for an individual's dignity, the obligation not to harm another, truth telling, and the respect for life in prohibitions against killing are some examples of virtually universal values whose origins predate Scripture.... These values are a consensus that comes out of the observations and conclusions of mankind over the centuries. In the same way that God has revealed truth about the sciences in creation, and revealed truth in the observations of mankind in the social sciences, natural law refers to God's revelation of morality from all sources outside of Scriptures. In this sense, natural law is general revelation applied to moral values [see Romans chapters one and two].[3]

Understandably, these fundamental moral values may be modified as they adapt to distinct cultures. Some societies have allowed people to rape or kill their enemies—but never someone within their own tribe. No culture allows their people to rape or kill anyone they want. Some societies have practiced infanticide, but such practice was stringently controlled and relative to the survival of the society as a whole.[4] No culture allows the random killing of its young. As philosopher and Christian apologist Francis Beckwith pointed out, "it does not follow from different practices that people have different values."[5]

What's important to note here is that there are real, universal moral values and that they are objective, absolute, and obligatory. They are binding on everyone whether or not one wants to obey them. We know this because virtually all cultures apprehend and accept them. In today's increasingly degenerate society, even adulterers and pornographers recognize that murder, rape, and stealing are immoral! If a skeptic denies this, ask him to give a scenario in which torturing babies, genocide, racism, ethnic cleansing, or similar evil acts would be justifiable under any circumstances.

So, where did humanity's corporate moral conscience—its sense of right and wrong—originate? It is highly improbable (and there's no evidence) that blind evolutionary processes, operating within an amoral universe, would result in moral values or produce people who have a sense of moral obligation. Indeed, we would expect just the opposite. A simple story will illustrate this. Suppose three friends were lost in the desert with one quart of water to share. During the night, one man quietly gets up and drinks all the water. Most people would be outraged by his behavior because we instinctively recognize that what the scoundrel did was immoral. It violates our innate (God-give) sense of right and wrong that virtually all people acknowledge. In contrast, according to evolution, such behavior is merely survival of the fittest. The man did nothing wrong. He was under no moral obligation to think about the survival of his friends.

The best explanation for humanity's corporate moral conscience, since universal moral values are absolute and stand in judgment of all human beings, is that they originate from a source outside of the human race—a source *independent* of human thoughts, feelings, and experiences. In short, moral values flow from the mind of a moral lawgiver—God

According to the Bible, God's very nature is perfect in love, wisdom, goodness, and righteousness. Only God, so defined, could judge perfectly what is right and wrong and endow His creatures with similar values. God's eternal, unchanging nature guarantees unchanging, universal moral standards not subject to human capriciousness.

If God Does Not Exist, Evil Cannot Be Condemned

There is a second element to the moral argument. If God does not exist, there is no moral standing from which one person can legitimately tell another person that any particular act is wrong. In fact, if God does not exist, there is no moral obligation to avoid participating in evil.

Within an atheistic worldview, people are supreme beings. In such a society, no higher authority (God) sets standards for good and evil. Hence, cultures are free to determine their own moral conduct. But this creates a grave, far-reaching moral dilemma. What if societies (or even individuals) disagree on what constitutes immoral behavior? Since people are supposedly supreme beings, and no higher authority exists to arbitrate between opposing views, it logically follows that each view must agree to the "moral truth" of the other. This gives birth to moral relativism, and it sounds the death knell for any kind of universal obligation to moral fidelity.

Let's look at this another way. Atheists claim that moral values can exist even if God doesn't. They insist that ethics are simply a projection of people's subjective feelings and experiences. Mankind's "corporate human consciousness" is merely a byproduct of evolution.

In recent years, evolutionary psychologists have increasingly claimed that if physical man is the result of evolutionary forces, so too is his conscience, values, and emotions. This includes every facet of human beliefs and behavior (religious or otherwise).[6] According to evolutionary psychology, cultures condemn immoral behavior, such as torturing babies and incest, not because of a God-given moral conscience but because such behavior is detrimental to the survival of a healthy, evolving society. However, there are numerous problems with this naturalistic worldview. There is not a single iota of evidence that moral values are evolutionary in their origin. Such a preposterous theory is meaningless because the same evolutionary forces that condemn murder and stealing must also justify mothers killing their newborns, sexual relationships between humans and animals, and rape as "an evolutionary adaptation for maximizing reproductive success. . . . After all, to a Darwinist it is simple logic that any behavior that survives must have conferred some evolutionary advantage—otherwise it would have been weeded out by natural selection."[7]

Evolutionists can't have it both ways. They can't justify the evolution of moral values on the one hand and the evolution of contradicting immoral values on the other. A self-contradicting theory is false.

A third problem with an evolutionary origin of morality is that people do not behave according to an imaginary, inbred law of survival. Survival of the fittest does not lend itself to mercy and grace, but to dominance and self-interest. People often behave in ways that violate the principle of survival of the fittest. Such as:

- People give sacrificially to charity.
- People put their lives in danger by dashing into a burning building to rescue perfect strangers.
- People quite their jobs and put their families in jeopardy if called upon to compromise their integrity by lying or stealing.
- People care for sick and dying friends and relatives at great emotional and physical cost.

Two men from the church I attend flew to Thailand to assist other Christian aid workers after the tsunami that killed more than 150,000 people in December 2004. They weren't sure of the availability of food, water, or shelter. They weren't even sure they'd be safe or secure in the area, yet they went to minister to people they had never seen and may never see again. Such selfless commitment to fellow human beings does not arise out of selfish evolution—it is not explained by survival of the fittest—but out of a love for God and the people He created.

A greater problem with the evolutionary explanation of ethics is that it fails to provide any reason why rape, murder, and stealing are morally wrong. What if someone wants to do it? What if an entire culture decides that incest, infanticide, and rape are good (or that killing six million Jews is morally justified)? In the absence of a moral Lawgiver who transcends human relativism, there is no criterion by which to judge and condemn such "values," let alone any objective moral basis *not* to engage in them. Without God, at best, ethics are reduced to the fancy and desires of the most powerful persons or the political group in control. At worse, moral anarchy becomes the law of the land.

Recently, a person told me that he heard about a movement to allow older men to have sexual relations with young boys. Applying the Socratic method, I asked, "Why do you think having sex with a young boy is wrong?"

He thought a moment, then replied, "Because something inside me says it is wrong."

"What if the pedophile said that something inside him says it's okay?"

He thought about this for a few moments and then admitted, "I really can't answer that."

I then pointed out that the only way anyone can legitimately claim that any deviant behavior is immoral is if there is a God who sets moral absolutes that exist outside people's feelings and opinions and therefore sets standards of right and wrong behavior. Otherwise, there is no way to condemn the behavior of anyone—including the pedophile.

In an atheistic society, the concept of absolute, binding moral law is meaningless because there is no objective bases on which to ground it. Without accountability to God, there is morally no obligation to avoid doing anything that one wishes to do. Only if God—a moral Lawgiver—exists can there be any criteria for identifying evil and holding people accountable when they engage in evil acts.

Objective moral laws *do* exist. There is a moral line "in the sand" beyond which no sane person or culture will tolerate certain behaviors. This confirms the existence of God. As William Lane Craig observed, "If moral values cannot exist without God and moral values do exist, then it follows logically and inescapably that God exists."[8]

The Presence of Evil Presupposes That God Exists

A third element of the moral argument for God's existence is that the reality of evil assumes the existence of God. How do we know that something is evil, (and virtually everyone acknowledges that evil exists)? By first knowing what is good. How do we know injustice? By first knowing what is just. There can be no measurement for bad unless there is a standard for good. A simple analogy illustrates this clearly.

Suppose I draw a crooked line on a sheet of paper and ask someone what it is. If he answers correctly, I can ask how he *knows* it's a crooked line. The answer, of course, is that he had to know already what a straight line looked like in order to identify the crooked line.

Similarly, before someone can know something is evil, he or she must first know the good that the evil perverts. As one author put it, "The only way to get a bad thing is to take a good thing and ruin it."[9] Therefore, if evil exists, good necessarily exists. If the ultimate source of good is God (the moral Lawgiver), God must exist. Paradoxically, acknowledgment of evil proves that God exists because, without God, we could not objectively identify evil.

Endnotes

1. The existence of a fundamental understanding of right and wrong does not necessarily prevent individuals—and even entire cultures—from repressing their moral conscience. The apostle Paul wrote in Romans 1:18–32 about people who "suppress the truth in unrighteousness" (vs. 18). Humankind is fallen and vulnerable to the satanic world system that elevates evil over good. Nevertheless, there exists within the human heart a God-given moral conscience that is reflected in a worldwide understanding of right and wrong. People know what is right even when they do what is wrong. It should also be noted that when entire cultures accept gross immorality and suppression, they are godless societies often under the control of a handful of fanatics (e.g. Nazi Germany). The fact is, no society has been able to establish satisfactory moral standards independent of religion.

2. C.S. Lewis demonstrated this fact in his book, *The Abolition of Man* (New York: Macmillan, 1947).

3. Scott B. Rae, *Moral Choices; An Introduction to Ethics* (Grand Rapids, Zondervan Publishing House, 1995), 37.

4. Francis J. Beckwith, *Politically Correct Death: Answering Arguments for Abortion Rights* (Grand Rapids: Baker Books, 1993), 22.

5. Ibid., 24.

6. Nancy R. Pearcey, *Total Truth: Liberating Christianity from Its Cultural Captivity* (Wheaton: Crossway Books, 2004), 208.

7. Ibid., 211.

8. William Lane Craig, "Why I Believe God Exists," in *Why I Am a Christian*, 75.

9. J. Budziszewski, "Why I Am Not an Atheist," in *Why I Am a Christian*, 60.

THE COSMOS DEMANDS A CREATOR

THE BEST PHILOSOPHICAL argument for the existence of God is the cosmological argument. Although it has been used for centuries, this argument has taken on new weight recently. Scientific discoveries during past decades have corroborated the cosmological argument by proving that the universe is not eternal, as evolutionists used to insist.

The cosmological argument may take several forms, but its basic argument (called the Kalam cosmological argument) goes like this:

> Whatever begins to exist has a cause.
> The universe began to exist.
> Therefore, the universe has a cause.[1]

If the premises of a valid argument are true, the conclusion must be true. So, to sustain the cosmological argument we must demonstrate that the above two premises are true.

I'll present the cosmological argument two ways. The first will be "defensive" apologetics—providing philosophical and scientific evidences within the framework of the argument. The second approach will be to apply the Socratic method, an effective apologetic tactic, although it requires a simplified version of the cosmological argument.

Premise One:
Whatever Begins to Exist Has a Cause

Although it's theoretically possible for nothing to exist, things exist. When we contemplate the cosmos and observe nature, we see that everything that began to exist is the product of something else—the effect of a cause. Moreover, the cause is always greater than the effect. For example:

- The power of wind and water causes a canyon to erode.
- Tremendous pressures under the earth's crust causes a volcanic eruption.
- Intense heat from the sun causes glaciers to melt.

Every entity in the observable universe is contingent upon something for its existence. If it exists, it had a cause.

Premise Two:
The Universe Began to Exist

Since everything in observable nature is the effect of a cause, does this principle apply to the universe as a whole? Did the universe begin to exist at a specific point in time? Yes it did.

Why must this be? The universe can't consist of an infinite series of causes and effects (called an "infinite regress") because the universe is finite. Although mathematicians may argue for a *potential* infinite universe (you can potentially keep on counting backward forever), an *actual* infinite (eternal) universe is impossible. There are two ways to demonstrate this.

First, it's impossible for time to extend backward infinitely. Time can be measured as a series of actual events. Unless the universe is finite, any moment in time and any event in history would have already taken place an infinite time ago. There could never be a today. Only if the universe had a beginning could today be actualized, fixed absolutely: "If there were an infinite number of moments before today, then today would never have arrived, but it has."[2] The following chart illustrates this:

Infinite universe:

                  today? today? today? today? today?
No beginning . . . . * . . . . * . . . . . . * . . . . . * . . . . . * . . . . . no end

Finite universe:

                            today!
Beginning _____*_____end

In this simple chart, if the universe were infinite, "today" could never be fixed on a timeline because it would have already occurred an infinite time ago. Indeed, there could be no such thing as time because time itself is married to a finite universe. On the other hand, if the universe had a beginning, any fixed date could be established on a timeline.

An infinite series of causes and effects could never create anything. Why? Because all effects are contingent things—things that depend on something else (causes) for their existence. Somewhere there must be an initiating First Cause, or nothing subsequent could exist. If a First Cause *does* exist, the universe had a beginning.

The second way to demonstrate that the universe is finite may be easier to understand because it can be proven scientifically. Modern science, such as Big Bang cosmology, confirms that the universe is not eternal. If the universe is not eternal, it had to have had a beginning. At some point in time, it began to exist. Moreover, according to the Second Law of Thermodynamics (one of the most reliable laws of science), the universe is a "closed system" with no way to reenergize itself. Consequently, it's running out of energy. It's dying of heat loss; something like a pan of boiling water cooling off when the burner is turned off. If the universe were eternal, this irreversible process would have led to the universe's extinction an infinite time ago. But the universe hasn't expired yet; it's just moving toward extinction. This means that the universe can't be eternal. It must have had a beginning. If it's running down, it will have an end.

Conclusion:
Therefore, the Universe Has a Cause

Building logically on the above two premises, we can conclude that the universe had a cause. Since the universe encompasses the entire cosmos, the cause of the universe must exist independently and outside of the universe—apart from natural processes. Moreover, it must be self-existing or uncaused and not be bound by time and space. Since an effect cannot be greater than its cause, this "First Cause" must also be greater than the universe it created. Now, the question remains: "What is this First Cause?"

According to a theistic worldview, the First Cause is God. If God didn't exist, nothing that exists would exist. If God is the First Cause, in order to create everything that is, He must exist independent of the universe, time, and space and be greater than what He created. In other words, God couldn't be the origin (First Cause) of the universe unless He existed for all eternity apart from the universe He created.

Final Step:
The First Cause Is the Biblical God

At this point, we have only demonstrated the existence of a First Cause, (which we can legitimately refer to as God). However, we must show that the First Cause of creation is in fact the same God who is revealed in the Bible. Let's look at the evidence.

In order to have created everything that exists, this non-contingent First Cause must have had at least the following necessary attributes:

- The First Cause must be supernatural (beyond nature) rather than natural. Because the universe is finite and bound to natural processes, it could not come to be on its own.
- A supernatural First Cause who can choose to create would be a free agent with a free will—thus a living Being with personality.

- In order to create all that exists, this Being must be more intelligent and powerful than the creation itself. (An event cannot be greater than its cause.)
- Because He is the First Cause, "He" must be uncaused and self-existing, changeless, timeless (because He created time), and infinite (must be infinite to be a First Cause).
- To be Creator, He must be omniscient (have all knowledge), omnipresent (be present everywhere at once), and omnipotent (all powerful).
- He must be Spirit rather than material. He could not be a physical Being if He is present everywhere.
- As Creator of moral beings (people), He must be perfect in goodness and love. We could not know that we are imperfect if we could not compare ourselves to a perfect Creator.
- He must be righteous and holy because He created a moral universe. An evil creator would not create a moral universe.
- As a holy Being, He would have to condemn and punish sin.
- As a loving Being, He would have to provide an opportunity to receive forgiveness.

These traits describe the fundamental attributes of God as revealed in the Bible. The cosmological argument, carried to its logical philosophical and theological conclusions, confirms the existence of the God of Abraham, Isaac, and Jacob, and the Father of our Lord Jesus Christ.

A Simpler Way

All of this may seem too philosophical to be used practically during ordinary witnessing opportunities with a "typical" atheist. So let me give you a simpler version of the cosmological argument that lends itself to the Socratic method. It provides three related questions that lead to the inevitable fact of creation:[3]

Question one:

As I see it, there are only three possible ways for the universe to come into existence. I would like you to tell me which one makes the most sense. First, is it possible that the universe created itself? In other words, could the universe be self-caused? Why or why not?

Most atheists will answer "no" because the answer is fairly self-evident. If not, before going further, challenge him or her to explain how something can create itself.

It's impossible for the universe to be self-caused. As we explored earlier, the laws of physics and simple logic prohibit something from coming from nothing. To create itself the universe would have had to exist and not exist at the same time. For Dan Story to be self-caused, I would have to exist in order to create myself, and not exist in order to be created, at the same time. This is impossible. It violates the laws of logic, can't be demonstrated scientifically, and moves from real science to fantasy. (God, of course, is also not self-caused; He is "uncaused" because He has always existed as the First Cause.)

Question two:

The second possible way to account for the existence of the universe is that it's eternal. It always existed. Do you subscribe to this view? Why or why not?

There is a good chance the atheist will answer, "yes." Challenge him (or her) to explain why he thinks the universe always existed.

Remember, in apologetics we're not interested in opinions, we want arguments—evidence. The Christian's biblical position, as data in this book point out, is based on modern scientific evidences, the laws of logic, and sound philosophical reasoning. Big Bang cosmology, the Second Law of Thermodynamics, and the Kalam cosmological argument all confirm that the universe is not eternal. Since most atheists elevate science as the ultimate test for truth (see chapter twenty-six), they are obliged to accept the scientific evidence for a finite universe. To point this out, you might ask something like this: "Do you have any reason for rejecting the scientific evidence that the universe had a beginning—especially since you're an evolutionist?"

Then proceed to question three.

Question three:

If it's impossible for the universe to be self-caused, and if the scientific evidence proves that it's not eternal, how did the universe come into existence?

It seems to me that the only choice left is that the universe was created. Can you think of a fourth alternative? Please explain yourself.

The goal of these three Socratic questions is to guide the conversation to a point where the atheist finally concedes, based on evidence, that the universe is not self-caused or eternal. That leaves only one other option for its origin—it was created. You can now demonstrate that the Creator of the universe is the God revealed in the Bible.

Potential Objections

At this point, an atheist may raise two objections. We need to be prepared to respond to both.

The first objection, which is rather simplistic but almost always asked, goes like this: "If everything is created by something else, then who created God—who made God?"

This question contains what's called in logic a categorical fallacy. As Geisler and Brooks observed, "The category 'before' does not apply to the category 'first'. It is logically impossible."[4] It's like comparing apples and oranges. You see, if God is the "First Cause," nothing can exist before Him. Nothing comes before "first." The Bible says, "In the beginning God created." Nothing can exist before beginning. Only things that have a beginning need a cause. God has always existed so He is uncaused. To ask, "Who made God?" is meaningless and nonsensical. It's like asking what the color blue smells like.

To make this point, you might ask a good Socratic question such as, "What comes before first?" Obviously nothing can come before first!

Another way to respond to the question, "Who made God?" is to point out that whether or not another God made God is not the issue. If we have proven that the universe is not self-caused or eternal, it had to have been created. This rules out atheism and establishes that some kind of First Cause or God must ultimately exist. So we have won our argument but must identify this God with whom we humans must deal.

The second objection to the existence of God is more sophisticated. It is called the "problem of evil," and it's the most common argument used by atheists to deny the existence of God. We'll examine it in detail in the following chapter.

Although evidences for God's existence do not reach mathematical certainty, they are compelling arguments based on sound philosophical reasoning, scientific facts, empirical observations, common sense, and logic. In light of this data, it is vastly more probable that God exists. By any standard, atheism takes more faith than theism!

Endnotes

1. William Lane Craig, *Reasonable Faith; Christian Truth and Apologetics* (Wheaton: Crossway Books, 1994), 92. Other excellent studies of the cosmological argument are found in Norman Geisler's and Winfried Corduan's, *Philosophy of Religions*, 2nd ed. (Grand Rapids: Baker Book House, 1993). Gary R. Habermas and Terry L. Miethe, *Why Believe? God Exists! Rethinking the Case for God and Christianity* (Joplin: College Press Publishing Co., 1993).

2. Norman L. Geisler, "Why I Believe the God of the Bible Is the One True God," in *Why I Am a Christian; Leading Thinkers Explain Why They Believe*, ed. Norman L. Geisler and Paul K. Hoffman (Grand Rapids: Baker Books, 2001), 91.

3. I presented this same apologetic approach to the existence of God using a non-Socratic format in my book, *Defending Your Faith; Reliable Answers for a New Generation of Seekers and Skeptics* (Grand Rapids: Kregel Publications, 1997), 23–26.

4. Normal L. Geisler and Ronald M. Brooks, *Come, Let Us Reason Together: An Introduction to Logical Thinking* (Grand Rapids: Baker Books, 1990), 109.

WHY DO BAD THINGS HAPPEN TO GOOD PEOPLE?
(The Problem of Evil)

A FEW YEARS AGO, a pastor and his wife were called to a small church in a community not far from my home and were killed crossing the street. The first child of a youth pastor in the town where I live died minutes after birth. In a church I attend, a three-year-old drowned in the family pool and a Christian highway patrolman was killed in a tragic motorcycle accident, leaving behind a wife and several children—both of these incidents happened within weeks of each other.

All of us who have lived many years can recall similar, tragic moments. They bring to the surface some issues that most Christians would just as soon not confront. Why do bad things happen to good people, including Christians? Why do the wicked seem to prosper? Even Old Testament saints struggled with this one. (See Jeremiah 12:1–2.)

In this chapter we will examine the most formidable argument against the existence of God, at least as He is revealed in the Bible. It is called the problem of evil. Most atheists consider it to be genuine proof that God does not exist. Admittedly, it is Christianity's one vulnerable spot; some even call it our "Achilles heel."

The problem of evil can be expressed in several ways, including this one:

> Christians say that God is all loving and all powerful. If God is all loving, He would not allow evil and suffering. If He is all powerful, He could stop it. Yet suffering and evil exist. Therefore, God either is not all loving and doesn't want to stop evil and suffering, or He is not all-powerful and can't stop it. Either way, He is not the kind of God described in the Bible.

This is not a simple apologetic issue. It is a potent and emotionally laden challenge to the existence of God. In fact, entire books have been written concerning the problem of evil.[1]

The Problem of Evil

The problem of evil is a seriously compelling argument against God's existence—perhaps the most compelling. All other arguments can be categorized as arguments against evidences for God's existence. Evolution, for example, is not a direct attack against the existence of God. He can exist even if evolution is true. Rather, it's an attack against creation that confirms God exists. Thus, if the problem of evil can be explained satisfactorily, there is no other challenge as serious to the existence of God (other than willful unbelief).

The crux of the problem-of-evil argument is that the presence of evil and suffering is incompatible with God's existence. Therefore, our apologetic task is to demonstrate that the reality of evil and suffering is compatible with the God of Scriptures. We can demonstrate this defensively by providing a reasoned apologetic based on sound theological and philosophical arguments. We can also respond offensively (socratically), challenging atheists to give an explanation for, and solution to, human suffering that is better than the Bible's explanation.

Before considering these two apologetic responses, let's consider a few preliminary observations that help to set the stage for the more complete response to follow.

Preliminary Observations

We may wish to begin by pointing out that God is God. His thoughts and ways, as the prophet Isaiah observed, are much higher than ours—as the heavens are higher than the earth (Isaiah 55:8–9). Job understood this after much anguish and pain. With great passion, he beseeched God to explain why He allowed suffering to explode into his life. Although God never directly answered Job's questions (Job 42:4) and expected Job to trust Him, Job nevertheless came to realize, "Surely I spoke of things I did not understand, things too wonderful for me to know" (Job 42:3, NIV).

Boa and Bowman noted, "There is nothing irrational about admitting that if there is a God, he might know better than we what he is doing."[2] Miethe and Habermas expanded this idea: "What we know about God is sufficient to trust Him in those things we don't know. Not only can such truth keep us focused on the most important matters in the Christian faith, but it can free us from the burden of always having to figure out exactly what God has in mind when people suffer."[3]

A second observation, which mature Christians know, is that God allows difficult times to come into our lives—even suffering and tragedy—as a means of building character and guiding us into greater heights of trust and dependence on Him. After all, our chief purpose is not to live happy, comfortable lives—that would keep many people from even considering God—but to know and serve God. James wrote that the testing of our faith produces endurance (James 1:3). Peter pointed out that trials prove the sincerity of our faith (1 Peter 1:6–7). Paul remarked that our personal suffering can be used to minister to others experiencing similar trials (2 Corinthians 1:7). And, many believers have realized that God uses suffering to open their eyes to sinful attitudes and activities. (See 1 Corinthians 5:1–5.)

It seems as if God is more interested in healing hearts than removing hardships and sickness, and sometimes suffering leads to healed hearts. Furthermore, as Christians know, the joys and rewards of heaven will compensate us infinitely more than we can ever imagine for the physical pain and emotional suffering that afflicts us in this life. The apostle Paul suffered horribly (2 Corinthians 11:24–33), yet called it "momentary, light affliction [that] is producing for us an eternal weight of glory far beyond all comparison" (2 Corinthians 4:17).

A third preliminary observation is that the evil and suffering of this world are not God's fault. Most human suffering is the result of people's behavior. We see evidence of this everywhere we look. At this very hour, millions of people are starving, often not due to a shortage of food but to corrupt governments, civil wars, and selfish administrators who don't care about starving people. The same is true for war, murder, rape, stealing, and corruption. These evils are perpetrated by people against people, not by God.

Now one may ask, "What about natural disasters—so-called 'acts of God'? Isn't God responsible for them?"

First, the number of people killed and/or suffering from natural disasters is low compared to death and suffering at the hands of people. During the twentieth century, more than 150 million people were killed under atheistic governments. This is nearly eight hundred times more people than the number of people killed when the devastating tsunami swept across the Indian Ocean on December 26, 2004

Second, as Christian relief workers testify, God uses natural disasters (as well as persecution and suffering) to bring people into His Kingdom. As philosopher and theologian William Lane Craig observed, "It is precisely in countries that have endured severe hardship [China and Ethiopia, for example] that evangelical Christianity is growing at its greatest rates, while growth curves in the indulgent West are nearly flat."[4] The church I attend sent small relief teams to Thailand after the Indian Ocean tsunami and to Mississippi after hurricane Katrina in 2005. People were led to Christ during both disasters.

Third, natural disasters are, ultimately, a result of the Fall of man. According to Genesis 3:17, nature didn't fall; it was cursed as a result of Adam's fall. One day nature will be redeemed (See Romans 8:19–22). As a result, natural disasters are a result, at least indirectly, of people.

Finally, we should understand that evil, especially natural disasters, is not rational. Evil is gratuitous and nondiscriminatory. It doesn't always choose its victims. You may think of evil as a bomb that terrorists throw into a crowd in order to assassinate a political leader. Many innocent victims are hurt.

Nevertheless, God clearly limits the degree and scope of the pain and suffering we experience. Imagine the potential for evil in a world in which God has no sovereign control. If God allowed Satan full reign, we would quite literally experience hell on earth. Fortunately, God keeps Satan in check. (See 2 Thessalonians 2:7.) Because the source of evil rests squarely on the shoulders of Satan and sinful humanity, we should thank God for His patience and tolerance and seek to cleanse all sinful behavior from our lives. (See 2 Peter 3:9; Ezekiel 18:23.)

The Heart of the Challenge

The fact that most suffering is a result of sinful human behavior explains only part of the problem of evil. We still need to explain why God doesn't stop pain and suffering when He can—even if it *is* people's fault. Or, better, explain why God didn't perpetuate the world He created before the Fall—a world that was free of hunger, accidents, natural disasters, and diseases, and where people never hurt one another?

There is an answer to these questions that is compatible with biblical revelation. Theologians and philosophers alike call it the free-will defense,[5] and it demonstrates that the presence of evil does not contradict the nature of God. Pain and suffering can be a fact of life, and God can exist and still be all loving and all powerful. One does not preclude the other.

The free-will defense can be laid out two ways. It can be explained theologically within the context of historic, biblical revelation, and it can be stated philosophically without direct reference to Christianity. On occasion, you may engage non-Christians who say something like this: "Why should I be blamed for something Adam did? Why didn't God just punish Adam instead of all people?" Since non-Christians voice this objection, the philosophical response, at least initially, may be the better choice.

Part of the answer to this challenge is that all of us are sinful and are held accountable for our own behavior (Galatians 6:7). We all deserve the consequences we suffer as a result of our rebellion and disobedience. (See Romans 3:10–18, 23.) But even if we remove Adam and the biblical narrative from the picture, the free-will defense remains consistent with the existence of God.

The Free-Will Defense

- God exists and is the sovereign Creator of the cosmos. He is perfect in holiness, goodness, love, and justice.
- God created people to love and obey Him.
- In the best of all possible worlds, people will freely choose to love and obey God.
- However, it is logically impossible for God to create a world in which people always and freely choose to love and obey Him. Regardless what the choice is (right or wrong), if one is compelled to make a certain choice, the choice is no longer free. The only way God could have created a world in which people always chose to love and obey Him would have been to create a world *without* free will.
- Consequently, to achieve genuine love and obedience, God created people with a free will. They could choose to love and obey Him (moral good) or reject Him (moral evil). True love depends on free will; otherwise, people would be no more than automated robots.
- Creating people with free will required God to create a world that could potentially harbor moral evil as well as moral good. Unless one could choose not to do good, no real choice could be made.
- People willfully chose to rebel and disobey God. (See Romans 1:20–23.)
- Moral choices require consequences. God would not be holy, good, loving, and just if He ignored rebellion and disobedience (sin).
- The natural consequence of choosing moral evil—that is, of rejecting God's grace and love—is to dwell in a world that has pain and suffering.

The free-will defense explains that God is all loving and all powerful, and yet evil exists (for a time). Nothing is illogical or contradictory about this conclusion. It is entirely consistent that God, within the bounds of His sovereignty, would allow a world to exist in which evil is present.[6] God didn't cause evil, but He permits it for the greater good of allowing people to freely choose to love and obey Him—His purpose for creating them.

The Solution to the Problem of Evil

- In His sovereignty, God knew corporate humanity would "fall" into sin. In spite of this—and out of His immeasurable love—God provided a cure for the sin disease. He prepared a way for all people to be healed from the effects of sin and become reconciled to their Creator: He sent His Son, Jesus Christ, to die on the cross in order to destroy the work and power of sin and restore us to eternal fellowship.
- Although none of us can no longer choose not to sin—because of our sin nature—God gave us a free will choice. We can choose to remain in our rebellion and estranged from God, or we can choose Jesus Christ and be healed and forgiven for our sins. (As a side note, it is important to know that Christians do not have to be in bondage to sin. If we choose Jesus, we have the power of God to resist sin and not submit to it. (See Romans 6:6,12,14.)
- Those of us who accept the atoning work of Christ have a permanent solution to the problem of evil. In this life, we have the power of the Holy Spirit to help us through suffering and pain. In the future, we will live in a new heaven and a new earth where there will be no sin or suffering—the best of all possible worlds. (See Revelation 21:1–4.)

Socratic Response to the Problem of Evil

The free-will defense explains why God allows human suffering and evil in spite of the fact that He could stop it if He chose to do so. However, this apologetic is rather sophisticated and obligates the believer to be somewhat theologically or philosophically astute. It certainly isn't the kind of response you or I could give during a party or other informal meeting. Put simply, the problem of evil is easy to express: "If God exists, there wouldn't be all the suffering in the world!" An adequate response, however, is complex.

Although it doesn't explain why pain and suffering exist in God's world, a second, less-complicated response to the problem of evil is to encourage non-Christians to confront this problem within the perimeter of their own worldviews. It challenges them to come up with a better solution to the problem of evil than the Bible's solution (or admit they have no solution). It's important for them to realize that, in the absence of the biblical understanding of God, there is no solution to the problem of evil. To achieve this, we can begin with the following Socratic reasoning: "Let's remove God from the equation. If there is no God, what is the remedy or solution to the problem of evil and human suffering?"

The obvious premise behind this question is that without God there is no solution to evil and suffering. There are only five possible explanations for, or "solutions" to, the problem of evil.

Atheism. This explanation denies the existence of God. Therefore, all people must live with evil and suffering. There is no God to restrain evil. There is no Holy Spirit to ease and comfort people who suffer. There is no future life where evil and suffering will be absent. In the absurd world of atheism, evil and suffering are products of evolution—survival of the fittest. One can only accept this and live without any hope of a solution. Since evil is an evolutionary by-product, atheists have no objective basis for finding fault with pain and suffering. It's part of reality.

Dualism. This explanation claims that there is a supernatural force other than God from which evil arises. This force is equal to and not controlled by God. This view fails because it creates a separate category for evil that is beyond the ability of God to control. Accordingly, God is incapable of solving the problem of evil and human suffering.

Finitism. This explanation denies that God is all powerful. If He is not all powerful, He is unable to destroy evil or even control its effects. There is no solution here, either.

Illusionism. This explanation denies the reality of pain and suffering and is one of the governing philosophies of Eastern religions and like-minded cults.[7] Evil is thus something we think is real but isn't. Illusionism flies in the face of reality as everyone lives it out. Everyone experiences pain and suffering. What good is it to deny pain and suffering if people must live with them and experience them? Ignoring pain and suffering doesn't make them go away. Merely claiming that pain and suffering are illusions solves nothing.

Theism. Only biblical Christian theism offers a compelling and reasonable explanation for the existence of evil, as people experience it. Only biblical Christian theism accepts the reality of pain and suffering and also offers comfort in this life and the absence of pain and suffering in the next.

Hopefully, a non-Christian who fails to find an alternate solution to the problem of evil will listen to the biblical explanations and remedies. This may be the time to walk him or her through the free-will defense. A follow-up Socratic question can move the conversation in this direction: "If God is all loving and all powerful and yet chooses to allow pain and suffering to remain, He must have good reasons. Wouldn't it be wise to at least see what those reasons are?"

Comforting (Emotional) Response to the Problem of Evil

We can approach the problem of evil from two levels. At the intellectual level, we can discuss pain and suffering around the coffee table or in the classroom without any emotional involvement. We can give the free-will defense in order to explain why a good and loving God allows pain and suffering when He is more than capable of stopping it.

This approach is virtually useless, however, for someone who has just lost a loved one. It only reminds him or her that God could have prevented the tragedy, but didn't. John Feinberg recounts his experience with the problem of evil. After his wife was diagnosed with a horribly debilitating and fatal disease, he wrote:

> At that point, the problem of evil moved from an intellectual problem that I could calmly reflect on in the solitude of my study to a real-life trauma that has to be confronted every day of my life.

... During this time of emotional and spiritual turmoil, none of the intellectual answers proved to be even the least comforting.... I came to [realize that] the crisis of faith precipitated by suffering, at rock bottom is not primarily an intellectual question but an emotional problem."[8]

Because the problem of evil becomes personal when one loses a loved one—when newlyweds are killed in a car accident or when a child develops leukemia—this problem transcends the intellect. No rational explanation lessens the pain. Yet here, in the deepest valley of grief, Christianity offers its greatest hope. The best thing we can offer the bereaved is the love of Jesus Christ. No other religion or philosophy offers a personal relationship with the God who is willing and able to walk us through our darkest hours. No other religion can fulfill its promise of a future life in a glorified body reunited with those who have gone before us.

As recorded in John 11, Jesus' friend, Lazarus, became gravely ill. Jesus could have healed him but purposely waited until he died. Jesus knew He was going to raise Lazarus from the grave. Everything would be fine. Yet as Jesus approached the tomb and witnessed the grief and mourning, what did He do? He *wept*. The God of the universe shed tears of grief.

This is the kind of God we have. He knows pain and suffering because He experienced it. He takes our hands and walks us through times of tragedy and despair. The greatest comfort to be found when tragedy strikes is the love of Jesus Christ.

Soon after I became a Christian, a sixteen-year-old who attended our church was killed in a one-car accident. My wife and I visited the family shortly afterward, and I will never forget a remark the grieving father made. As a new believer, it was a profound lesson on faith: "I don't see how people who aren't Christians survive these things." Here was faith played out during life's darkest hour. He knew that Jesus Christ is the ultimate solution to the problem of evil.

I believe it was the twentieth-century philosopher, Bertrand Russell, who challenged Christians by asking, "What do you Christians say to the parent of a child dying of cancer?"

The real question here is not what can Christians say. Rather, as philosopher William Lane Craig pointed out, what can the atheist say? "Tough luck!"..."Too bad!"..."Gee, what a shame!"

There is no solution to the problem of pain and suffering apart from Jesus Christ.

Endnotes

1. Two books of the Bible, Job and Habakkuk, deal with the problem of evil. Two excellent non-biblical books that examine this issue are: Norman L. Geisler, *The Roots of Evil*, Second Ed. (Dallas: Word Publishing, 1989) and C. S. Lewis, *The Problem of Pain* (New York; MacMillan Publishing Co., 1962).

2. Kenneth D. Boa and Robert M. Bowman Jr., *An Unchanging Faith in a Changing World; Understanding and Responding to Critical Issues that Christians Face Today* (Nashville: Thomas Nelson Publishers, 1997), 81.

3. Terry L. Miethe and Gary R. Habermas, *Why Believe? God Exists! Rethinking the Case for God and Christianity* (Joplin: College Press Publishing Company, 1993), 226.

4. William Lane Craig, *Hard Questions, Real Answers* (Wheaton: Crossway Books, 2003), 95.

5. Alvin Plantinga, who is one of America's greatest philosophers, is the best-known expositor of the "Free Will Defense." His abridged version, more than sixty pages long, was published by William B. Eerdmans Publishing Company in 1974: *God, Freedom, and Evil*.

6. There is good news here in the field of philosophy. As William Lane Craig noted in *Hard Questions, Real Answers*, pages 86–87, "After centuries of discussion, contemporary philosophy has come to recognize this fact. It is now widely admitted that the logical problem of evil has been solved."

7. Most pantheists believe that sin and evil are products of a lower level of existence that is dealt with through the law of karma. Eventually, they believe, everyone will be delivered from the illusions of this life and attain a higher level of consciousness that unites them with the all-encompassing god-essence. See my book, *Christianity on the Offense: Responding to the Beliefs and Assumptions of Spiritual Seekers* (Grand Rapids; Kregel publications, 1998), chapter eight.

8. John S. Feinberg, "Why I Still Believe in Christ, in Spite of Evil and Suffering," in *Why I Am a Christian; Leading Thinkers Explain Why They Believe*, ed. Norman L. Geisler and Paul K. Hoffman (Grand Rapids: Baker Books, 2001), 250.

PART FOUR

JESUS CHRIST: MAN OF HISTORY OR MAN OF MYTH?

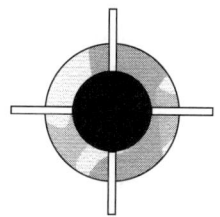

INTRODUCTION TO PART FOUR

PHILOSOPHERS SEEK to know ultimate truth. Scientists seek to discover empirical knowledge. Psychologists seek to understand human behavior. These are important pursuits, yet they pale in significance compared to discovering the answer to the ultimate, far-reaching question confronting the human race in every generation: Who is Jesus Christ (Matthew 16:13)?

Other religions besides Christianity try to answer this question. Islam recognizes Jesus as a great prophet and miracle worker. Hindus consider Him to be an avatar, an incarnation of Vishnu. Buddhists call Jesus an enlightened one. New Agers view him as a man who realized his "divine potential." Jehovah Witnesses claim that Jesus was a lesser god created by Jehovah. Mormons teach that Jesus was the spirit-brother of Lucifer. If these non-Christian religions are correct, if Jesus is a lesser god or a mere human, such as Mohammed, Buddha, or Joseph Smith, Christianity is a sham because only Christians acknowledge Jesus to be God in human flesh, the second member of the Trinity. (See John 1:1,14; Phil. 2:6–8.)

C. S. Lewis, in his lucid and compelling style, has expressed the sum and substance of the debate over the person of Jesus Christ more emphatically and uncompromisingly than anyone I've read:

I'm trying here to prevent anyone from saying the really silly thing that people often say about Him: "I'm ready to accept Jesus as a great moral teacher, but I don't accept His claim to be God." That's the one thing we mustn't say. A man who was merely a man and said the sort of things Jesus said wouldn't be a great moral teacher. He'd either be a lunatic—on a level with the man who says he's a poached egg—or else he'd be the Devil of Hell. You must make your choice. Either this man was, and is, the Son of God: or else a madman or something worse. You can shut Him up for a fool, you can spit at Him and kill Him as a demon; or you can fall at His feet and call Him Lord and God. But don't let us come with any patronising (sic) nonsense about His being a great human teacher. He hasn't left that open to us. He didn't intend to.[1]

The best evidence reveals that Jesus Christ is God. In the following four chapters, we'll explore four challenges related to Jesus.

First, is the Jesus of history the same person as the Jesus portrayed in the Bible? We'll see that liberal critics, typified by the Jesus Seminar, say no. The Jesus of Scripture, they claim, is a fabrication of the early church, presumably in its quest to enhance the community of faith as Christianity began. Our first task, then, is to refute these critics and demonstrate that the Jesus of history is also the Christ of faith. The Gospel authors recorded and passed on an accurate portrait of the historical Jesus.

Second, we must establish the reality of the Trinity. Most people believe in some kind of god; only Christians believe that Jesus is God. A true understanding of Jesus requires that people understand and accept the Trinity.

Third, we must demonstrate that Jesus *claimed* to be God. If He didn't, why explore this further? The deity of Christ would be an invention of the early church, and all related doctrines (virgin birth, Trinity, miracles, fulfilled prophecy, Jesus' resurrection) would have been placed in the Bible by editors contrary to actual history. There would be no Christianity. We will thus look at the evidences Jesus offered as proof that He is God in human form.

Next, we will look at the ultimate proof of the divine nature of Jesus Christ: His resurrection.

Finally, we'll conclude Part Four by examining what for many people—Christian and skeptic alike—is the biggest question surrounding Jesus as Savior: "What happens to people who never had the opportunity to know and accept Jesus as their personal Lord and Savior? Do they automatically go to hell? That doesn't seem fair!"

Endnote

1. C. S. Lewis, *Mere Christianity* (New York: MacMillan Publishing Company, 1944), 55–56.

Jesus
Historical, Fabrication, or Myth?

DURING THE PAST several decades, secular magazines, books, newspapers, and television stations have published or broadcast numerous stories alleging that the Jesus revealed in the Bible is not the Jesus of history. A recent example is the best-selling novel, *The Da Vinci Code*, by Dan Brown. This fictional story, written as if it were grounded in actual history, alleges that Jesus was merely a man who was upgraded to deity almost four centuries after His death. In fact, Brown wrote that Mary Magdalene and Jesus eventually got married, had a daughter, and lived in southern France and that the Catholic Church purposely covered up these important facts.

Although such ludicrous fabrications have no historical support, they nevertheless illustrate the importance of establishing an historical basis for the life and work of Jesus Christ. There are two ways to do this. First, we can establish that the Bible—the primary source material for the life of Jesus Christ—is truthful and reliable. Or, we can demonstrate that the revisionist views have virtually no grounding in objective textual studies or historical facts.[1] Let's explore how we can do both.

Reliable Historical Data

According to New Testament historian Gary Habermas, there are forty-five non-biblical sources for the life of Jesus Christ.[2] However, most of the biographical and historical data we have concerning Christ comes from the New Testament Gospels. So the key to identifying the real Jesus is contingent on the truthfulness of the New Testament. Is the Bible reliable and the Jesus portrayed therein real, or are the critics correct in thinking that the biblical Jesus is a fake?

We have seen in Part One that overwhelming evidence supports the truth and reliability of the Bible. By the standards of acceptable and appropriate historical investigation, we can legitimately conclude that the Jesus portrayed in the Gospels, including the things He said and did, are accurate. So let's flip the coin. Does the revisionist's claim—that the Jesus of history is *not* the Jesus of Scripture—have any *objective* foundation?

The Jesus Seminar

Unfortunately, the evidence that confirms the Bible's truth and reliability is seldom communicated to today's popular culture. More often than not, the Jesus depicted by non-Christians is a watered-down version of the real Jesus. Media spokespersons in popular culture are usually members of the liberal Jesus Seminar, or like-minded people, who preach a Jesus myth. An editorial in the *Christian Research Journal* spoke to this issue:

> The Jesus Seminar is a small group of extremely liberal scholars. Yet they seem to have a lock on the major media outlets so that their pronouncements are taken as the final word by major magazines, newspapers, and public broadcasting programs. As a result, headlines proclaiming that scholars have "discovered" that Jesus never said He'd return (so He won't), and the like, are common fare. What is worse, this kind of material finds its way into the college classroom as the "assured results of critical scholarship," and young Christians are faced with the specter of this imposing group of Bible scholars condemning their faith in a risen Savior as mere myth.

The leaders of the Jesus Seminar confidently proclaim themselves to be the standard bearers of the scholarly consensus. While they are, in reality, far away from the vast majority of biblical scholars.... Sadly, most of the mainstream media never challenge the easy and grandiose claims of the leaders of the Jesus Seminar.[3]

Formed in 1985, the Jesus Seminar set out to identify the historical accuracy of the sayings attributed to Jesus in the Gospels. One governing presupposition of the Seminar is that the Gospels don't provide accurate information about Jesus. Therefore scholars must get "behind" the Gospels, through critical evaluation of the texts (and other alleged sources), to try to determine what is actually true and what is legend. The assumption is that modern critics have a better grasp on who Jesus was and what He said than the biblical authors.

In 1993 the Seminar published a book titled *The Five Gospels: What Did Jesus Really Say?* It included not only the four biblical Gospels but also the non-canonical *Gospel of Thomas*, discovered in 1945 at Nag Hammadi near Cairo, Egypt. Dated between AD 140–170, the *Gospel of Thomas* contains 114 sayings that Jesus supposedly spoke. *The Five Gospels* color code the sayings of Jesus according the Seminar's *opinion* on the probability that Jesus actually spoke these words. Red indicates Jesus spoke a given statement or at least said something similar. Pink emphasizes something close to what Jesus may have said. Gray emphasizes something Jesus didn't say but the ideas expressed were close to His own. Black emphasizes something Jesus never said that was probably derived from later tradition.[4] Only 18 percent of *The Five Gospels* are colored red or pink!

Virtually no historical and textual evidence exists for these liberal scholars' presuppositions, and all their conclusions are unsubstantiated. Gary Habermas wrote, "Seldom do the Jesus Seminar Fellows provide reasons for their opinions or otherwise vindicate their own worldview. Only rarely do they attempt to justify their rules of evidence beyond reporting that certain things are caused."[5]

Virtually all conservative biblical scholars agree that the Seminar's views of Scriptures are not based on normative historical research. Rather, it is a byproduct of a largely naturalistic (antisupernatural) worldview. Moreover, as we'll soon explore, the alleged sources on which the Seminar often depend, such as the so-called "Q" document, are entirely hypothetical. No one has ever seen such documents, nor has any church father ever alluded to or quoted them! Theologian Gregory Boyd wrote:

> The Jesus Seminar represents an extremely small number of radical-fringe scholars who are on the far, far left wing of New Testament thinking. It does not represent mainstream scholarship. . . . To come up with their conclusion that Jesus never spoke most of the words in the gospels, members of the Jesus Seminar used their own assumptions and criteria. . . . There are multiple problems with their assumptions and criteria."[6]

What are some of these problems? Let me highlight a few of them.

Voice of Liberalism

Jesus Seminar[7] scholars have become darlings of the media, as illustrated several years ago when *ABC* broadcast the two-hour special I mentioned previously called "The Search for Jesus," hosted by the late Peter Jennings. The majority of the scholars interviewed were affiliated with the Jesus Seminar. Among other things, they claimed that Jesus did not rise from the dead and that He was not the Son of God. The entire show was little more than a pulpit for liberal scholars—those academics who reject the essential beliefs of traditional Christianity such as the deity of Jesus, inerrancy of Scriptures, and miracles. Participants preached their anti-supernatural dogma to millions of viewers, and in one broadcast, the fundamental beliefs of two thousand years of Christianity were dumped.

The imaginary Jesus of the Jesus Seminar is not the divine, incarnate Son of God but merely an itinerant preacher more interested in an earthly kingdom than "helping people find God, salvation, or heaven."[8] During an interview with Lee Strobel, Dr. Gregory Boyd explained, "There is one picture that they [Jesus Seminar] all agree with: Jesus first of all must be a naturalistic Jesus. . . . Whatever else is said about him,

Jesus was a man like you or me. Maybe he was an extraordinary man.... but he was not supernatural."[9]

Sadly, most non-Christians assume that the liberal Bible critics represent cutting-edge scholarship. Unless they meet loving and thoughtful Christian apologists, rank-and-file unbelievers tend to accept the grossly watered-down caricature of Christ promoted in the secular media.

Philosophical Naturalism

Members of the Jesus Seminar, as well as other liberal theologians, are united by one fundamental presupposition—philosophical naturalism.[10] Professor of philosophy, R. Douglas Geivett wrote, "Radical scholarly opinion about Jesus, abundantly manifested by the Jesus seminar, assumes without justification a naturalistic view of the world."[11]

What does this mean? Liberal Bible critics study the Bible through a worldview filter that denies the supernatural. This inevitably leads them to conclude that anything that relates to the supernatural must be erroneous. Consequently, they reject miracles, prophecy, and anything Jesus said or did concerning the supernatural as unauthentic.

Late-Dating the Gospels

Liberal Bible critics claim that the four Gospels were written a decade or more later than evidence justifies. (See chapter five.) Jesus Seminar spokesman John Dominic Crossan claims that all the Gospels were written from the AD 70s to 90s.[12] Is there valid evidence for this? There is none: his opinion cannot be substantiated.

Understanding this is crucial to understanding why liberal theologians reject Bible prophecy. Let me explain with an example. In Matthew 24:1–2, Jesus prophesized the destruction of the temple in Jerusalem, and in Luke 19:41–44 He prophesized the destruction of the city. Both events occurred around AD 70. If the Gospels of Matthew and Luke were written in the AD 60s, as most conservative scholars believe and evidence indicates, these were genuine, supernatural prophecies that support the divine nature of Christ.

Sadly, liberal critics reject these prophecies as unauthentic. Why? It would mean that the New Testament was written before the destruction of the temple and Jerusalem. That in turn would imply that Jesus predicted future events such as the destruction of the temple and Jerusalem through supernatural foresight. Hence, these critics are forced to conclude that the New Testament was written *after* the fall of Jerusalem and the destruction of the temple.

Unknown Authorship

A third assumption of the Jesus Seminar members and other critics is that the New Testament writers were not the designated authors whom the Bible names. However, this is contrary to the testimony of the early church fathers. As early as AD 130, Papias, Bishop of Hierapolis, confirmed the authorship of the four Gospels, as did Irenaeus, Bishop of Lyons (c. AD 178). Papias was a friend of the apostle John; Irenaeus was a student of Polycarp, who was a disciple of John. They reported that John not only wrote his Gospel but told them that: the Gospel of Mark was written by Mark, the companion and interpreter of Peter; that Matthew's Gospel was published "among the Hebrews [the Jews] in their own tongue;"[13] and that Luke wrote his Gospel as it was "preached by his teacher,"[14] Paul.

The assumption that the Gospel authors were not those named also flies in the face of common sense. New Testament scholar Craig Blomberg observed:

> Given that two of these men were not apostles (Mark and Luke), and that Matthew would have been one of the most "suspect" of the apostles, in light of his background as a tax collector, it seems unlikely that the first Christians would have invented these authorship claims if they were merely trying to enhance the credibility of the documents attributed to them.[15]

Uneducated Apostles

Liberal critics also claim that uneducated men couldn't have written the Gospels. Once again, they offer an assumption that has little support.

Matthew, a tax collector, could well have been educated and Luke—a physician—would certainly have ranked among the better educated segment of society. Moreover, there is no reason why the authors of the Gospels could not have become better educated as they matured and entered ministry. (I didn't return to college to complete my undergraduate and graduate degree until my late thirties.) Ultimately, God authored the Bible and used the words and styles of men. In Acts 4:8, we read that Peter was "filled with the Holy Spirit" as he spoke to the rulers, elders, and scribes in Jerusalem (v. 5). These men were amazed because Peter and John were "uneducated and untrained men" (v. 13). God did, and still does, illuminate the minds of "uneducated" people so they can speak with truth and power.

Alleged Discrepancies

Liberal scholars and other Bible skeptics claim that apparent discrepancies among the four Gospels imply that each original author put his spin on his individual account and that the original manuscripts were later edited (redaction criticism) and embellished from oral tradition (form criticism). Once again, this is pure conjecture. As we have already explored, this theory is wholly subjective and contradicts historical and textual evidence. Unquestionably, there are areas of Scripture that need clarification. Scholars have been doing this, so today there are numerous books that explain virtually every alleged discrepancy in the Old and New Testaments.[16]

We should also point out to Bible critics that no alleged discrepancy—even if it were valid—weakens or discredits the Bible's overall historical reliability and trustworthiness or affects any essential teaching (such as the deity and resurrection of Jesus Christ). Textual critics have demonstrated that the present New Testament is 99.5 percent accurate to the original, inspired manuscripts. Only about four hundred words are in doubt, and none of these affect an essential doctrinal or historical issue.

Hypothetical Source Documents

Jesus Seminar scholars and other liberal theologians insist that ancient documents once existed that predated all four Gospels but did not mention Jesus' miracles or His deity. For example, the so-called Q document (from the German word, *Quelle*) supposedly contained sayings of Jesus written prior to the four Gospels. This document is presumed to account for material found in the Gospels of Matthew and Luke, but not Mark.[17]

The problem with the Q document is that it doesn't exist! Norman Geisler pointed out in the *Baker Encyclopedia of Christian Apologetics*:

> There is not one shred of documentary evidence that Q ever existed. No manuscript or any version of it has ever been found. No church Father ever cited any work corresponding to what current scholars mean by Q.... Apologists can assume with confidence that Q is a modern creation and that no manuscript will turn up next week to prove them wrong.
>
> Obviously, though most Q advocates would be reluctant to admit it, there is an antisupernatural bias behind their view. Following the naturalistic approach to the Gospels that began with David Strauss in 1835–1836, they assume the miraculous events are categorized as later results of myth making.[18]

We should also recognize that contemporary challenges to the New Testament's reliability and trustworthiness are not new. As D. A. Carson observed, many "are not much more than restatements of old-fashioned form and redaction criticism."[19] Conservative scholars dealt with most, if not all, of them by the early part of the last century. Craig Blomberg wrote, "Has there been some revolutionary new find that seriously discredits Christianity? No, not at all. The truth is that the JS [Jesus Seminar] is an anachronism—a throwback to nineteenth-century quests for the historical Jesus, and not even representative of mainstream contemporary New Testament scholarship."[20]

Because the common denominator of all liberal critics is their naturalistic mindset, their premises and conclusions flow from an antisupernatural worldview. Liberal theologians, such as the Jesus Seminar members, rely on a subjective and highly speculative methodology that openly employs circular reasoning. They "know" that miracles and prophecies are impossible because they assume that the Bible is fallible and the Gospels are not reliable. They "know" that the Bible is fallible and the Gospels are not reliable because they assume there is no supernatural revelation. Gary Habermas wrote:

> The Jesus Seminar has made no secret about its contention that the orthodox conception of Jesus is outdated and ought to be rejected. ... Yet seldom are any *reasons* given for such a stance. Mere theological assertion seems to be the order of the day.... Informal logical fallacies abound in statements by the Jesus Seminar.... The lack of careful argumentation begs the question on behalf of the assertions that are made.[21]

In contrast, conservative scholars seek to employ interpretive techniques that allow the text to speak for itself—based on the Bible's proven historical and textual reliability. In the final analysis, the watered-down Jesus of liberal theologians cannot account for the facts of history. The Jesus of the Bible is indeed the Jesus of history.

Endnotes

1. A good study at a popular level of the evidences for the historical Jesus is Josh McDowell and Bill Wilson, *He Walked Among Us: Evidence for the Historical Jesus* (San Bernardino, CA: Here's Life Publishers, 1988).

2. Gary Habermas, *The Historical Jesus; Ancient Evidence for the Life of Christ* (Joplin: College Press Publishing Co., 1999). Summarizing his book, Habermas wrote: "We have examined a total of 45 ancient sources for the life of Jesus, which include 19 early creedal, four archaeological, 17 non-Christian, and five non-New Testament Christian sources. From this data we have enumerated 129 reported facts concerning the life, person, teaching, death, and resurrection of Jesus, plus the disciples' earliest message.... There can be little doubt that this is a substantial amount of pre- and non-New Testament material for Jesus' existence and for numerous facts about his life. In light of these reports we can better understand how groundless the speculations are that deny his existence or that postulate only a minimal amount of facts concerning him," 250–251.

3. Douglas Groothuis, "The Jesus Seminar and the Gospel of Thomas: Courting the Media at the Cost of Truth," *Christian Research Journal*, January-March, 1998, 51.

4. Robert W. Funk and Roy W. Hoover, eds., *The Five Gospels: What Did Jesus Really Say?* (New York: Macmillan, 1993), 36. Quoted in Craig L. Blomberg's, "The Historical Reliability of the New Testament" in William Lane Craig's, *Reasonable Faith: Christian Truths and Apologetics* (Wheaton: Crossway Books, 1994), 201.

5. Gary R. Habermas, "Did Jesus Perform Miracles?" in Michael J. Wilkins and J.P. Moreland, gen. eds., *Jesus Under Fire* (Grand Rapids: Zondervan Publishing House, 1995), 128.

6. Lee Strobel, *The Case for Christ: A Journalist's Personal Investigation of the Evidences for Jesus* (Grand Rapids: Zondervan Publishing House, 1998), 114, 117.

7. For more information about the Jesus Seminar and rebuttals to modern biblical criticism, see: Blomberg, "The Historical Reliability of the New Testament," in *Reasonable Faith*, ch. 6; Habermas, *The Historical Jesus*, ch. 6; Strobel, *The Case for Christ*, ch. 6; Wilkins and Moreland, gen. eds., *Jesus Under Fire*.

8. Dennis Ingolfsland, "Jesus and the 'Earliest' Sources: an Answer to John Dominic Crossan," *Christian Research Journal*, Vol. 25, No. 03, 26.

9. Strobel, *The Case for Christ*, 115.

10. Wilkins and Moreland, gen. eds., *Jesus Under Fire*, 4.

11. Geivett, "Is Jesus the Only Way?" in Wilkins and Moreland, gen. eds., *Jesus Under Fire*, 198.

12. Ingolfsland, "Jesus and the 'Earliest' Sources," 27.

13. John Warwick Montgomery, *History and Christianity* (San Bernardino: Here's Life Publishers, 1983), 32–34. Also see F.F. Bruce, *The New Testament Documents: Are They Reliable?* (Downers Grove: InterVarsity Press, 1984).

14. Ibid.

15. Blomberg, "The Historical Reliability of the New Testament," in R*easonable Faith*, 204.

16. Three popular books that respond to practically every alleged discrepancy in the Bible are: Gleason L. Archer, *Encyclopedia of Bible Difficulties* (Grand Rapids: Zondervan Publishing House, 1982), Norman Geisler and Thomas Howe, *When Critics Ask; A Popular Handbook on Bible Difficulties* (Wheaton: Victor Books, 1992), and John W. Haley, *Alleged Discrepancies of the Bible* (Grand Rapids: Baker Book House, 1983).

17. A good study of the so-called Q document is found in Norman L. Geisler's *Baker Encyclopedia of Christian Apologetics* (Grand Rapids: Baker Books, 1999), 618–621.

18. Ibid., 619–120.

19. D.A. Carson, "Five Gospels, No Christ," *Christianity Today*, April 25, 1994, 32.

20. Craig L. Blomberg, "The Seventy-four 'Scholars': Who Does the Jesus Seminar Really Speak For?" *Christian Research Journal*, Fall, 1994, 34.

21. Habermas, *The Historical Jesus*, 138.

THE TRINITY
Fingerprint of Jesus Christ

THE NEXT STEP in developing compelling apologetics in defense of the deity of Jesus Christ moves from the man of history to the Son of God. Beginning with an understanding of the doctrine of the Trinity, we must now demonstrate that the incarnate Jesus is God. An understanding of this doctrine is crucial to identifying the real Jesus Christ from the Jesus fakes and frauds. (See Matthew 24:4–5; 2 Corinthians 11:4, 13–15.)

Let's begin with a definition of the Trinity. God is one Being in essence who eternally exists as three distinct co-equal, co-eternal Persons—The Father, the Son, and the Holy Spirit. All three Persons share the exact same divine nature.

Several fundamental and essential attributes of Jesus Christ describe exactly who He is. They include His deity, His incarnation and resurrection, His virgin birth, and His position in the Trinity. You might think of these attributes as Jesus' "fingerprint." Just like every person has a unique fingerprint, these particular attributes comprise Jesus' fingerprint. If we removed any of them, including His position in the Trinity, we would not have the same Jesus revealed in the Bible. We would be worshiping a false Jesus.

Taken together, these essential attributes separate the real Jesus from the Jesus of Islam, Mormonism, Jehovah's Witnesses, the Jesus Seminar, and all other non-Christian religions. All of them reject the Trinity. Hence, by definition they are not—and cannot be—Christian.

The doctrine of the Trinity is unique to Christianity. Although some skeptics claim this doctrine was established during the fourth century, the historical fact is that the Trinity has been an essential Christian belief from the beginning of the church. As one author put it, the Trinity was revealed even "*before* the writing of the New Testament so that it is written *by Trinitarians for Trinitarians*."[1]

The earliest Christians accepted and taught the doctrine of the Trinity well before the fourth century, as seen in the writing of the church fathers: Clement, third bishop of Rome (AD 96); Ignatius, bishop of Antioch (AD 90?); Justin Martyr (AD 155); Theophilus, sixth bishop of Antioch (AD 168); Athenagoras, the theologian (AD 177); Irenaeus, bishop of Lyons (AD 180); and Tertullian, early church leader (AD 197).[2]

Is the Trinity Comprehensible?

The doctrine of the Trinity, although recognized as a clear biblical teaching, is not easy to comprehend. In fact, the Trinity is beyond full, human comprehension; there are no human parallels. People have tried to come up with various comparisons to help Christians make intellectual sense of the Trinity, but none accurately illustrates it.

For example, readers may have heard the water analogy. It's observed that water can be in the form of a liquid, a solid (ice), and a gas (vapor) without changing its chemical composition of two parts hydrogen and one part oxygen—H_2O. The problem with this, and similar comparisons, is that the individual forms do not coexist in separate states simultaneously. A single drop of water cannot be a liquid, solid, and gas at the same time. In the Trinity, on the other hand, all three Persons are one God at the same time. The Trinity reveals that the relationship among the Father, Son, and Holy Spirit is a perpetual and eternal relationship.

Perhaps the key to intellectually grasping the Trinity is to discern the difference between *being* and *person*. As theologian James White put it, "Being is what makes something *what* it is. *Person* is what makes someone *who* he or she is."[3] In other words, *being* reflects "what" God is while *person* reflects "who" He is. God is one in essence (one "what") but *three* in persons (three "who's"). It is not illogical or contradictory to say that one Being (God) is shared by three divine, coequal, coeternal Persons, even if we don't fully comprehend it.

Can We Prove the Doctrine of the Trinity?

How did this seemingly incomprehensible doctrine arise? Clearly it must be a product of revelation rather than human reasoning or imagination. If someone wanted to manufacture a religion, who would invent such a perplexing belief? Let's think this through a moment.

Divine revelation is divine disclosure. Its information we receive from God that we can't get anywhere else. We can logically infer a few commonsense assumptions from this. For one, if God is providing such information, we can expect Him to impart it in a way that we can discover. Divine revelation, then, will not be hidden or esoteric. We won't need a priest, a guru, or anyone else to reveal it to us. Moreover, if God were going to reveal something to us as important (yet puzzling) as the Trinity, He would state it clearly so that it would not be open to debate. He would make sure it was permanently documented and accurately recorded so that people could check it out and study it. In fact, the document itself would make such a claim.

Of course, I've just described the Bible. It meets all of these requirements and is the only source of information on the Trinity. What does the Bible say about itself? Second Timothy 3:16 states, "All Scripture is inspired by God and profitable for teaching, for reproof, for correction, for training in righteous." It doesn't say "our feelings," "our ability to understand," or "what someone tells us is inspired by God." The doctrine of the Trinity is something we can know because God has told us. It's not a creation of the early church. Like other crucial biblical doctrines, we know it because God revealed it. We accept it on faith, even

The Trinity

though it remains somewhat a mystery, because it's clearly taught in the Bible. However, this doesn't mean we can't theologically justify the doctrine of the Trinity. How do we do this? First, we can use *inductive* reasoning. We can systematically construct the doctrine from related passages found throughout the Old and New Testaments. Together they reveal the presence and activities of all three members of the Godhead. Consider the following passages:

- Matthew 3:16–17, the baptism of Christ in the Jordan: "After being baptized, Jesus came up immediately from the water; and behold, the heavens were opened, and he saw the [Holy] Spirit of God descending as a dove and lighting on Him, and behold, a voice [the Father's] out of heaven said, "this is My beloved Son, in whom I am well-pleased." Here the Father, Son, and Holy Spirit are all present during Jesus' baptism.
- Matthew 28:19, when Jesus spoke to His disciples just before His ascension:
"Go, therefore and make disciples of all the nations, baptizing them in the name of the Father and the Son and the Holy Spirit." Notice that Jesus said *name*, not *names*. There is only one God (name), but we are to baptize in the *names* of all three persons who comprise the one God.
- Luke 1:35, the angel's prophetic announcement of Jesus' birth to Mary:
"The angel answered and said to her, 'The Holy Spirit will come upon you, and the power of the Most High [the Father] will overshadow you; and for that reason the holy Child [Jesus] shall be called the Son of God.'" Again, all three Persons in the Trinity are active in Jesus' miraculous birth.
- 2 Corinthians 13:14, as Paul ended his letter: "The grace of the Lord Jesus Christ, and the love of God, and the fellowship of the Holy Spirit, be with you all." Again, this verse refers to all three members of the Trinity.
- 1 Peter 1:2, where Peter wrote: "according to the foreknowledge of God the Father, by the sanctifying work of the Spirit, to obey

Jesus Christ and be sprinkled with His blood." All three members of the Godhead are in action: the foreknowledge of the Father, the sanctifying work of the Spirit, and the blood of Christ.

Although not as fully developed, the doctrine of the Trinity can also be glimpsed in the Old Testament. Isaiah referred to all three members of the Trinity: "And now the Lord God [the Father] has sent Me [the pre-incarnate Christ], and His [Holy] Spirit (Isaiah 48:16)."

God also alluded to the Trinity when He referred to Himself in plural terms as *Elohim*: "Then God [*Elohim*] said, 'Let Us make man in Our image.'" "Then the Lord God [*Elohim*] said, 'Behold, the man has become like one of Us, knowing good and evil.'" (Genesis 1:26; 3:22; also see Genesis 11:7 and Isaiah 6:8.)

Together, these passages testify that the biblical revelation of God is one Being in essence eternally revealed as three Persons: Father, Son, and Holy Spirit.

We can also use deductive reasoning to demonstrate, theologically, the doctrine of the Trinity, which can be stated formally in the following syllogism:

1. Only God is omnipresent, omniscient, and omnipotent.
2. The Father, the Son, and the Holy Spirit are all three omnipresent, omniscient, and omnipotent.
3. Therefore, God is triune as Father, Son, and Holy Spirit.

The Father, Son, and Holy Spirit share other attributes, but the three "omni's" are foundational. As the above syllogism illustrates, when we examine the Bible to discover the nature of God, we find that there is only one God. However, when we look at the attributes of God the Father, God the Son, and God the Holy Spirit, we discover that all three share identical attributes. We can only conclude that one God eternally exists as three coequal Persons.

Endnotes

1. James R. White, Loving the Trinity," *Christian Research Journal*, Vol. 21, No. 4, 25.

2. This particular list was compiled in a helpful pamphlet, *The Trinity*, published by Rose Publishing, Torrance, CA, 1999, 4. Rose Publishing offers a variety of pamphlets that cover Christian related topics at an introductory level. For more information on the writings of early church fathers see, L. Russ Bush, ed., *Classical Readings in Christian Apologetics A.D. 100 - 1800* (Grand Rapids: Academie Books, 1983).

3. White, "Loving the Trinity, 23.

DID JESUS CLAIM TO BE GOD?

NOT LONG AFTER my conversion to Christianity, my older brother (who I always looked up to because he was extremely bright and well read) stated that no where in the Bible does Jesus actually claim to be God!

I was certain this wasn't true. I thought Jesus claimed to be God, but I didn't know the Bible well enough to demonstrate it. This was probably one of those unsettling episodes that spurred me into an apologetics ministry!

My brother's challenge reflects another argument skeptics use to deny the deity of Jesus Christ, although I'm not sure that was his intent at the time. Did Jesus really consider Himself to be God? Skeptics say, "No, he didn't." But Jesus did claim to be God—explicitly and dramatically—as we'll see shortly.

One reason why critics fail to recognize Jesus' claim to deity is that they are unaware of, or fail to understand, the historical and theological context in which Jesus made these claims. Critics suppose that Jesus should have more openly said, "I am God," rather than being, to them, so surreptitious about revealing this truth. However, people who expect this declaration don't understand the nature of the Godhead.

As the second Person in the Trinity, Jesus has two, distinct natures. He is not only God the Son, He is also a human being. Jesus is fully God *and* fully man. Christians don't draw this conclusion through human reasoning but from divine revelation. (See John 1:1,14; Philippians 2:6–7; Colossians. 2:8–9.)

The dual nature of Christ is almost as hard to grasp intellectually as the Trinity. Nevertheless, like the Trinity, is does not violate laws of logic. It is not illogical for one person to share two distinct natures. R. C. Sproul wrote, "No formal law precludes the possibility. There is nothing contradictory about Christ's being unitary in A (person) and dual in B (nature)."[1] Moreover, "since the being of God is not limited to a single person, . . . Jesus can likewise be called 'the only true God'" for he fully participates in the same divine being (see John 1:1; 17:5).[2]

This brings us back to the question at hand: If Jesus is God, why didn't He just come right out and say, "I am God"? Actually, He did!

After His arrest, the Sanhedrin asked Jesus, "Are You the Son of God, then?" Jesus answered, "Yes, I am" (Luke 22:70; cf. John 10:36). Likewise, in Mark 14:61–62, when asked by the high priest, "Are you the Christ, the Son of the Blessed One?" Jesus replied: "I am; and you shall see THE SON OF MAN SITTING AT THE RIGHT HAND OF POWER, AND COMING WITH CLOUDS OF HEAVEN."

Some Bible students point out that, to a strictly monotheistic Jew, asking if Jesus was the "Son of God," or "the Christ, the Son of the Blessed One" actually referred to His claim to be the Messiah. However, this doesn't distract from the divine nature of that Messiah. Numerous Old Testament passages implied that the future Messiah would be more than a mortal man. (See Psalm 110:1; Isaiah 9:6; Micah 5:2.) More important, Jesus' response clearly showed His divine self-awareness.

Perhaps the clearest example of Jesus claiming to be God is found in John 8:58, after the Jews asked Jesus how He could have possibly seen Abraham, who lived centuries earlier. Jesus replied: "Truly, truly, I say to you, before Abraham was born, I am." Although this passage may seem rather cryptic to modern readers, the Jews knew precisely what Jesus meant. He was making a direct reference to Exodus 3:13–14. In this passage, Moses asked God what name he should give the Israelites for God.

God replied, "I AM WHO I AM.... Thus you shall say to the sons of Israel, 'I AM has sent me to you.'"

"I AM" relates to the most sacred name of God in the Old Testament. It refers to God's eternal, self-existing nature. So, in John 8:58, Jesus clearly identified Himself as God.

It's true that in the passages where Jesus revealed His deity, He didn't wave a flag and state, "I am God," as critics seem to think He should have. Why didn't He? I think it has to do with His position in the Godhead. Because Jews are monotheists (like Christians), they believe only one God exists. However, Christians, through divine revelation, recognize the triune nature of God. Jesus is one in *essence* with the Father and the Holy Spirit. He isn't a separate God. Otherwise, the Trinity would comprise three separate Gods, not one God. In other words, Jesus knew He was part of the triune Godhead. He knew that He is one in essence with the Father, but He also knew that He isn't the Father. He is the Son in whom "all the fullness of Deity dwells in bodily form" (Colossians 2:9). So, in claiming deity, Jesus apparently preferred to identify Himself with the Father.

Jesus said, "I and the Father are one" (John 10:30).

Jesus said, "He who sees Me sees the One who sent Me" (John 12:45).

Jesus told His disciples, "If you had known Me, you would have known My Father also; from now on you know Him, and have seen Him.... He who has seen Me has see the Father" (John 14:7, 9).

Notice how the Jews reacted to these claims. In response to Christ's statement, "I and the Father are one" (John 10:30), the Jews picked up stones to stone Him. The reason is given in John 10:33: "For a good work we do not stone You, but for blasphemy; and because You, being a man, make Yourself out to be God." Likewise in John 8:59, after Jesus referred to Himself as "I am" in verse 58, the Jews "picked up stones to throw at Him." After Jesus acknowledged He was "the Christ, the Son of the Blessed One" (Mark 14:61–62), the high priest tore his clothes and said, "'What further need do we have of witnesses? You have heard the blasphemy....' And they all condemned Him to be deserving of death" (Mark 14:63–64). John 5:18 records that the Jews were seeking to kill

Jesus "because He not only was breaking the Sabbath, but also was calling God His own Father, making Himself equal with God."

Why did the Jews want to stone Jesus? They knew He was referring to Himself as God, and stoning was the punishment for blasphemy. (See Leviticus 24:16.) Clearly, even Jesus' enemies who denied His deity had no doubt that Jesus considered Himself to be divine.

To help unbelievers see more clearly that Jesus did in fact claim to be God, it may be helpful to point out that His disciples and earliest followers, just like His enemies, had no doubt that Jesus claimed to be God. In various New Testament texts, they referred to Jesus as *theos*, the Greek word for God.

In his prologue, the apostle John wrote, "In the beginning was the Word [Jesus, v. 14], and the Word was with God, and the Word was God [*theos*]" (John 1:1). Thomas called Jesus, "My Lord and my God [*theos*]"(John 20:28). Referring to Christ, Paul wrote, ". . . who is over all, God [*theos*] blessed forever" (Romans 9:5). Later Paul wrote, ". . . our Great God [*theos*] and Savior, Jesus Christ" (Titus 2:13). The author of Hebrews, quoting Psalm 45:6, referred to Jesus when he stated, "But of the Son He says, 'Your throne O God [*theos*] is forever and ever'"(Hebrews 1:8). Peter called Jesus "our God [*theos*] and Savior" (2 Pet. 1:1). (See also Colossians 2:9 and Hebrews 1:3.)

Some cults and fiction books, such as *The De Vinci Code*, claim that Jesus was not considered God until the Council of Nicea in AD 325. The facts prove otherwise. The "explicit application of *theos* to Jesus Christ can be traced from the New Testament period into the second century without interruption. Ignatius, Justin Martyr, Melito, and Athenagoras frequently used the term *theos* of Jesus, as did the early biblical theologian, Irenaeus of Lyons."[3]

The name Jesus used most frequently for Himself also reflects His divine self-awareness. Although Jesus was referred to as the "Son of God" (Matthew 14:33; Mark 3:11; Luke 1:35; John 1:34; 11:27) and even called Himself "Son of God" (John 10:36), He usually referred to Himself as the "Son of Man." Some Bible students see the title "Son of Man" as reflecting Jesus' human nature and "Son of God" His divine nature.[4] Generally speaking, to Christians at least, we may say that this is true because many references to Son of Man in the Gospels refer to Christ's human characteristics. (See Matthew 8:20; 11:19.) However, the title "Son of Man" usually refers to the Messiah and reflects a person who possesses more than mere human characteristics. Moreover, in more than two dozen instances, this title alludes to Daniel 7:13–14, where "Son of Man" plainly refers to a divine, human figure coming from God. It clearly describes a person who is more than a mere man:

> In my vision at night I looked, and there before me was one like a son of man, coming with the clouds of heaven. He approached the Ancient of Days and was led into his presence. He was given authority, glory and sovereign power; all peoples, nations and men of every language worshiped him. His dominion is an everlasting dominion that will not pass away, and his kingdom is one that will never be destroyed (NIV) [cf. Revelation 1:12–18].

Similarly, Isaiah spoke of a future Messiah: "His name will be called Wonderful Counselor, Mighty God, Eternal Father, Prince of Peace" (Isaiah 9:6).

Let's tie this all together. The Bible clearly reveals that Jesus knew He was divine and proclaimed it, but He chose to reveal His deity in a way that would be in harmony with the triune nature of God. Jesus was equal to the Father but wasn't the Father. There is no doubt that Jesus claimed to be God, and those who knew Him personally—His enemies as well as His followers—understood this.

Did Jesus Demonstrate That He Is God?

It's one thing for Jesus to claim to be God; it's quite another to prove it. So our next apologetic task is to demonstrate that Jesus provided evidence that He is God by performing feats only God can perform. Because the Bible is authentic and reliable, the following eyewitness accounts provide valid documentation of the supernatural works of Christ. They unquestionably reveal a man who not only claimed to be God but also proved it.

- *Jesus performed numerous miracles* (Luke 7:18–22). He healed the sick and made the blind see and the deaf hear. He changed water into wine, cast out demons, walked on water, and quieted the sea. He foretold the future (Matthew 24; Luke 24:6–7; John 6:64) and raised Lazarus and others from the dead. Jesus pointed out that His miracles proved His deity (cf. Mark 2:1–12; John 10:36–38).
- *Jesus, who performed acts reserved only for God, claimed to have the authority of God* (Matthew 11:27, 28:18; cf. Romans 14:9; 1 Peter 3:22). He forgave people's sins (Mark 2:5f; Luke 24:46–47), accepted worship (Matthew 14:33; John 20:28), instructed us to pray in His name (John 14:13–14), promised eternal life (John 3:16; 5:39–40), and said that He will act as divine judge (Matthew 25:31–46).
- *Jesus rose from the grave.* This is the greatest evidence that Jesus Christ is who He claims to be (Acts 17:30–31; Romans 1:3–4). It is the ultimate proof that Jesus the man is also, as the apostle Thomas put it, "My Lord and my God" (John 20:28). We will examine His resurrection in the following chapter.

Lord, Liar, Lunatic, Legend, or Guru?

With all this evidence for His deity, you'd think an open-minded skeptic would be convinced that Jesus is God. Unfortunately, most skeptics are not open-minded. Most *assume* that Jesus was just a "good" man who died two thousand years ago. They claim that He was merely a religious teacher, a great prophet, a holy man, or some kind of guru.

How do we deal with people like this? Is there another way to strengthen our argument that Jesus is not just another religious leader like Mohammed or Buddha?

Yes, and it's a tried-and-true, practical, and logical demonstration that Jesus must be God. Moreover, this well-known "trilemma argument" is a demonstration that can be especially effective if applied socratically, as I've done elsewhere.[5]

The trilemma argument starts with a premise that even a skeptic usually accepts. Nearly everyone agrees that Jesus actually lived and that He was an exceptionally wise, good, and honorable man. In other words, at the least, most skeptics admit that Jesus was a virtuous, historical person.

Using this as a point of contact, the traditional trilemma argument points out that there are only three ways to answer the question, "Who is Jesus Christ?" Either He was a liar when He claimed to be God, a lunatic who thought He was God, or He *is* God. Since a liar or lunatic would not make Jesus wise, holy, or honorable, and would contradict everything we know about Him from the Bible, both can be ruled out. Jesus was selfless, loving, and compassionate. Likewise, He doesn't fit the profile of a madman. Jesus was wise, rational, calm, stable, and predictable. What's left? Jesus is who He claimed to be—God incarnate. (The quote by C. S. Lewis in the introduction to Part Four eloquently articulates this argument.)

There are two ways that modern skeptics attempt to get around the logic of this argument.[6] One, they take the position of the Jesus Seminar and assert that the Jesus of the Gospels is different from the Jesus of history. Later editors of the Bible, they declare, inserted supernatural references about Jesus that were not included in the original manuscripts or penned by the original authors.

Second, they claim that Jesus was some kind of a Hindu-like guru. When Jesus claimed divinity, they say, He was actually thinking of Himself in New Age terms. He didn't mean that He was *literally* God. As a man, Jesus possessed the same divine potential that all people do, although He succeeded in perfecting and manifesting this divinity more than most. But the same "Christ spirit," they continue, was perfected in Krishna, Buddha, and other religious teachers and is available to anyone who reaches this elevated level of consciousness.

We have already dealt with the first scenario. The only way skeptics can legitimately claim that the Jesus of history is not the Jesus of the Gospels is if the Bible is in error. But we have already seen that the Bible is the most historically accurate book from antiquity. In particular, we demonstrate that eyewitnesses of Jesus (or their associates) wrote all four Gospels. The Gospels provide accurate, historical information about Jesus. There is no legitimate evidence that later editors tampered with the Gospels or that the Gospels were corrupted by oral tradition. Moreover, not enough time elapsed between when events such as the resurrection took place and when they were recorded to allow for legends to develop.

Likewise, we have seen that the claims of liberal theologians and other skeptics are mostly speculations that flow out of their anti-supernatural bias and are based on hypothetical documents no one has ever seen. No objective basis supports critics' allegation that later Bible editors created Jesus' sayings and deeds. The assertion that the Jesus of history is not the Jesus of the Gospels falls apart for lack of textual and historical evidence. Kreeft and Tacelli provide an additional thought:

> If the events recorded in the gospels did not really happen, then these authors invented modern realistic fantasy nineteen centuries ago. The gospels are full of little details, both of external observations and internal feelings, that are found only in eyewitness descriptions or modern realistic fiction. They also include dozens of little details of life in first-century Israel that could not have been known by someone not living in that time and place (see Jn 12:3, for instance). And there are *no* second-century anachronisms, either in language or content.[7]

The second attempt to escape the Lord, liar, lunatic, legend, or guru dilemma is to assert that when Jesus claimed to be God, He didn't mean "God" in a Jewish or Christian sense. What He really had in mind, skeptics say, was a divine being in the sense of New Age pantheism. In other words, Jesus was making the same claim that New Agers often make today—that He was part of the all-encompassing "god force" that comprises all of reality. He was divine in the same sense that every other person is divine; He just realized it! So, in the New-Age view, Jesus was just a man who reached His "Christ consciousness" and can help us to achieve ours. He is a "guru."

There are several problems with this argument. First, it only makes sense in today's culture. There wasn't a New Age movement during the first century. "No guru was ever a Jew and no Jew was ever a guru."[8] Moreover, there are insurmountable contradictions between eastern pantheism and Judaism.[9] In particular, the Jews were fanatically monotheistic. A Jewish rabbi would never have claimed that the nature of God is pantheistic. Finally, not a shred of evidence reveals that Jesus ever mingled with or was influenced by Eastern, pantheistic religions. Indeed, there is no evidence that Jesus ever left Israel or that Hindus ever lived in Israel.[10]

It can also be added that if Jesus was a New Age-like guru, He was the worst teacher who ever tried to start a new religion. As Peter Kreeft wrote, "No one, not his friends nor his enemies, ever understood what he taught [i.e. He was a guru]—until a few clever persons finally figured it out in the twentieth century."[11] Jesus' followers considered Him to be the Son of God. His enemies considered Him to be a blasphemer who claimed to be God. The second-generation church Fathers (and all orthodox Christians since) considered Jesus to be God. No one considered Him to be a guru until the modern times.

Whether the argument is *trilemma* (Lord, Liar, Lunatic), *quadrilemma* (Lord, Liar, Lunatic, Legend), or *quintilemma* (Lord, Liar, Lunatic, Legend, Guru),[12] if one is willing to go with the evidence (and common sense), there is no way of escaping the conclusion that Jesus Christ is who He claims to be: God incarnate, Lord and Savior. There are no other options.

Endnotes

1. R. C. Sproul, John Gerstner, and Arthur Lindsley, *Classical Apologetics: A Rational Defense of the Christian Faith and a Critique of Presuppositional Apologetics* (Grand Rapids: Zondervan Publishing House, 1984), 77.

2. James R. White, "On the Trinity," *Christian Research Journal*, Vol. 25, No. 01, 29.

3. Paul Hartog, "Jesus as God in the 2nd Century," *Christian Research Journal*, Vol. 29, No. 01, 26.

4. The title, "Son of God," does not mean that Jesus was a created being. Rather it's a reflection of His divine nature and position in the Trinity. Jesus was always the Son of God. In John 17:5, Jesus prayed to the Father, "Now, Father, glorify me together with Yourself, with the glory which I had with You *before the world was*" [emphasis added].

5. I provide a hypothetical dialogue of how the trilemma argument might transpire during a witnessing opportunity in my book, *Engaging the Closed Minded; Presenting Your Faith to the Confirmed Unbeliever* (Kregel Publications, 1999), 96–97.

6. Peter Kreeft, "Why I Believe Jesus Is the Son of God," in Norman L. Geisler and Paul K. Hoffman, eds., *Why I Am a Christian; Leading Thinkers Explain Why They Believer* (Grand Rapids: Baker Books, 2001), 229–230.

7. Peter Kreeft and Ronald Tacelli develop the trilemma argument into the "quintilemma" argument in their *Handbook of Christian Apologetics; Hundreds of Answers to Crucial Questions* (InterVarsity Press: Downers Grove, 1994), 163.

8. Ibid., 165

9. Ibid., 166–170

10. Kreeft, "Why I Believe Jesus Is the Son of God," 230.

11. Ibid.

12. Kreeft and Tacelli in *Handbook of Christian Apologetics*, 158–170, provide an in depth study of the "quintilemma" argument.

RESURRECTION
Fraud, Fantasy, or Fact

NOW WE COME to the climactic event of Christianity and—next to the truth and reliability of the Bible—the most important apologetic issue with which we have to deal.[1] The resurrection of Jesus Christ is the watershed issue in terms of demonstrating that He is God, not merely another religious teacher. According to Romans 1:4, the resurrection is the preeminent evidence that Jesus is the Son of God. Referring to His resurrection, Jesus said, "I have the authority to lay [My life] down, and I have authority to take it up again" (John 10:18). No other religious leader in the world has made such a claim, nor does any miracle have such historical confirmation as Jesus' resurrection. Only God has the power and authority to raise someone from the dead.

The Old Testament prophesied the resurrection of a Jewish Messiah centuries before Jesus' first coming. In Isaiah 53:8–9, the Messiah was prophesied to die. In Acts 2:25–31 Peter quoted King David as saying, "YOU WILL NOT ABANDON MY SOUL TO HADES, NOR ALLOW YOUR HOLY ONE TO UNDERGO DECAY." (See Psalm 16:10.) Since, as Peter pointed out, David was dead and buried, he was referring to "ONE OF HIS DESCENDENTS"—that is, "the resurrection of the Christ" (i.e. the "Messiah").[2]

Resurrection

Jesus predicted His bodily resurrection (Matthew 26:32) and said, "Destroy this temple, and in three days I will raise it up" (John 2:19, cf. vs. 21). He also said, "just as JONAH WAS THREE DAYS AND THREE NIGHTS IN THE BELLY OF THE SEA MONSTER, so will the Son of Man be three days and three nights in the heart of the earth" (Matthew 12:40; cf. 27:63; Mark 8:31; 14:58).

The reality of Christ's resurrection guarantees the believer's resurrection to eternal life. The apostle Paul wrote in 1 Corinthians 15:17–19 that if Jesus did not rise from the grave, our "faith is worthless," we "are still in . . . sins," and "of all men most to be pitied." In verse 42 he stated that with the resurrection of the dead, our perishable bodies will be "raised an imperishable body."

Jesus' resurrection was a *bodily* resurrection. On several occasions after His resurrection, Jesus was touched or offered Himself to be touched. Twice He showed His crucifixion scars; four times He ate food with His disciples. "He literally exhausted the ways it is possible to prove that he rose bodily from the grave."[3] This guarantees that our own resurrection will be physical, not merely spiritual. Paul wrote in 1 Corinthians 15:49 that "just as we have borne the image of the earthly, we will also bear the image of the heavenly."

Finally, Jesus' resurrection qualifies Him to be both judge and Savior. Paul stated that God "has fixed a day in which He will judge the world in righteousness through a Man whom He has appointed, having furnished proof to all men by raising Him from the dead" (Acts 17:31). After proclaiming Jesus' resurrection, Peter boldly stated after that "there is no other name under heaven that has been given among men by which we must be saved" (Acts 4:12).

In light of this decisive doctrine, it's understandable that critics, skeptics, atheists, and false religions have targeted the authenticity of the bodily resurrection of Jesus Christ, sometimes for centuries. In particular, there have been six major challenges to the resurrection of Jesus Christ. Some are centuries old; one is mentioned in the Bible; others are more recent in origin.

In the following pages, we'll explore a defensive and Socratic response to these challenges. Defensively, we'll refute the six attacks. Socratically, we will offer our own challenges to critics of Jesus' resurrection—the most significant, far-reaching, and important miracle of all.

Defensive Response

Virtually all arguments against Jesus' resurrection arise out of an anti-supernatural, naturalistic worldview. Skeptics believe the resurrection didn't occur because they believe miracles are impossible. For the skeptic there are no supernatural realities. Their view of miracles is a philosophical *assumption* that can't be substantiated.

If God exists, however, miracles are not only possible but also likely![4] We must recognize that the truth of any miracle, including the resurrection, is not a matter of philosophy or science. Reasoned assumptions (philosophy), observation, and experimentation (the tools of science) cannot disprove anything that happened in the past. Jesus' resurrection is obviously an historical event, which can only be ruled out by a lack of historical evidence. The same criteria that is used to establish and authenticate other historical events, historical investigation, confirms the resurrection, so we can be certain it happened.

The primary source of information on the resurrection is eyewitness accounts recorded in the Bible. We have seen that the New Testament Gospels are considered by the science of textual criticism to be the most reliable, trustworthy, historical documents from antiquity. According to the rules governing acceptable historical investigation, we can conclude that the resurrection is a fact. When unbelievers challenge its authenticity, we can ask them why. Usually they respond with one of the following six explanations, which we need to understand and be able to refute.

1. Stolen Body Theory

This may be the oldest challenge to Jesus' resurrection. According to Matthew 27:57–66, after His crucifixion Jesus was placed in a tomb, a large stone was rolled over its entrance, and guards were placed in front of it. After the resurrection, the guards reported to the Jewish leaders that the tomb was empty. They were immediately bribed to say that Jesus' disciples stole His body during the night. (See Matthew 28:11–13.)

But why would the disciples steal Jesus' body? What motive would they have had (assuming they somehow got past the Roman guards)? Would they have done it in order to amass followers and invent a fake religion? This is highly unlikely, but let's think it through. Suppose the disciples decided to steal Jesus' body and claim He rose from the dead. Then Stephen is martyred and soon afterward Christians are being persecuted, beaten, imprisoned, and threatened with death. If you were in on the scheme, what would you have done? (I would have produced the body and hightailed it out of town!) The point is, if the disciples stole His body they accepted persecution and even death in exchange for a lie. People will die for a religious belief they think is true (like Muslim terrorists), but no one will die for a religious belief they know is false.

There are other problems with the theory that the disciples stole Jesus' body. For one, in spite of Jesus' predictions, the disciples didn't fully understand that He would rise from the grave until after post-resurrection appearances (John 20:8–10). How could they devise a scheme to preach a resurrected Christ if they did not understand that Jesus would be resurrected in the first place? (Cf. Mark 9:31–32; Luke 18:31–34.)

Here's another consideration. If Jesus' disciples stole His body in order to fabricate a new religion, they would never have used women initially to proclaim Jesus' resurrection. In Jewish culture at the time, most women had little status in society. They were not considered acceptable witnesses and could not testify in Jewish courts. Logically, the Gospel writers reported that women first discovered the empty tomb because it really was empty, and Jesus had risen from the grave.

Other versions of the "stolen body" theory claim that either the Romans or the Jewish authorities stole Christ's body, but these theories don't make sense. What motive would the Romans have had for stealing the body? Pilate ordered that Jesus' tomb be guarded to prevent that very thing. (See Matthew 27:64–65.) More importantly, after Jesus' resurrection the disciples began to preach the Gospel in Jerusalem and refused orders to stop. This incited the anger of the Jews. If the Romans, who were in charge of keeping the peace in Palestine, had known where the body was, surely they would have produced it the moment civil disorder arose.

Likewise, what motive would the Jewish authorities have had for stealing Jesus' body? There is no evidence they did, or any reason they would have done that. Shortly after Pentecost, thousands of Jews began to abandon the synagogues and become Christians. The moment the Jewish leaders' religious authority and social standing was rejected, they would have produced Jesus' body. But they couldn't because He had risen.

The theory that Jesus' body was stolen lacks historical, moral, and psychological merit. William Lane Craig, philosopher and theologian, wrote: "I can't emphasize enough that no modern scholar would defend such a theory today. The only place you read about such things is in the popular, sensationalist press or in former propaganda from behind the Iron Curtain."[5]

2. *The Hallucination Theory*

A second theory which was popular a hundred years ago, and has gained new acceptance in recent years,[6] is the hallucination theory. Its hypothesis is that people who saw the risen Jesus were hallucinating. This preposterous assumption lacks a shred of support. Jesus' post-resurrection appearances occurred during a period of forty days, throughout a wide geographical area, and amidst a variety of environments (indoors, outdoors, at the seashore, and so on). In one instance, as many as 500 people saw Him at the same time. (See 1 Corinthians 15:6.) The hallucination theory demands that all of these people were delusional. This would be nearly as big a miracle as Jesus' resurrection!

Psychologists explain that people hallucinate for one of two reasons. First, drugs, sickness, or physical deprivation such as lack of nutrition, water, or sleep can cause hallucinations. These things can obviously affect the mind. Second, hallucinations are private experiences and not contagious. They usually occur when individuals either want or expect to see something. In other words, in order to induce hallucinations, the mind has to be preprogrammed.

In the first case, there is no historical evidence that the hundreds of people who observed the risen Christ were in any way drugged, sick, or starving. In the latter case, as we've already explored, Jesus' disciples didn't expect to see Him rise from the dead because they didn't fully understand it would even happen. In fact, Jesus' half-brother, James, and Saul (Paul) were antagonistic toward Jesus. Certainly they didn't anticipate, want, or expect Jesus to rise from the grave. Yet after they saw Him, they testified about it. As one author put it, "James the skeptic and Paul the persecutor are exceptionally tough obstacles for the hallucination thesis."[7]

Another convincing evidence repudiating the hallucination theory is that some observers didn't recognize Jesus when He first appeared to them. (See Luke 24:13–31; John 20:15; 21:4.) If they wanted to see Jesus alive so badly that they hallucinated, why did they fail to recognize Him when He showed up?

Finally, if the post-resurrection appearances of Jesus were hallucinations, why didn't the Jews or the Roman authorities produce His body? This would have plainly demonstrated that those who claimed to have seen the risen Christ were delusional (or tricked).

3. The Swoon Theory

This imaginative theory that originated during the mid-nineteenth century claims that Jesus didn't die on the cross. He just fainted, or was drugged, and His followers thought He was dead. Later Jesus revived and appeared to His disciples, convincing them He had risen from the grave.

This hypothesis totally disregards the terrible physical abuse that Jesus encountered prior, during, and (if the swoon theory is true) after His crucifixion. These included:

- Severe beatings and flogging prior to the crucifixion.
- The torture of the crucifixion itself, including spikes driven through His hands and feet.
- The lance thrust into His chest cavity. Blood and water flowed from the wound, indicating that the heart itself was pierced. (See John 19:34.)

- His body wrapped in a hundred pounds of burial material. (See John 19:39–40.)
- The three days He spent in a tomb without food, water, and medical attention.

Could Jesus have survived such abuse? The Roman executioners didn't think so. To expedite death by crucifixion, executioners would sometimes break a victim's legs to hasten suffocation (the main cause of death in a crucifixion). They were about to do this to Jesus so that His body could be removed from the cross before the Sabbath. They didn't, however, because He was already dead. (See John 19:33.) The spear thrust was probably done to make sure of this.

Moreover, the centurion certified before Pilate that Jesus was dead. (See Mark 15:44–45.) Why is this significant? If the executioners or guards had allowed Jesus to survive or escape, they would have been executed. This happened, you may recall, to the soldiers who guarded Peter. After an angel delivered Peter from jail, Herod "examined the guards and ordered that they be led away to execution" (Acts 12:19).

Besides surviving the crucifixion and three days in the tomb, Jesus would also have had to somehow remove the two-ton stone covering the tomb's entrance, overpower the Roman guards, travel forty days over a large track of Palestine, and appear to hundreds of people, all the while looking well enough to convince them that He had risen glorified from the grave. Finally, when His travels were over, Jesus would have had to disappear, never to be seen or heard from again.

Besides the physical impossibility of Jesus achieving these feats, there is not a shred of historical documentation supporting the swoon theory. Nowhere in Roman or Jewish history does anyone claim or even imply that Jesus did not die on the cross. In fact, the swoon theory itself did not arise until eighteen centuries after the resurrection.[8]

4. The Wrong Tomb Theory

This theory arose during the early twentieth century and claims that the women and disciples of Jesus went to the wrong tomb. This explanation is probably the easiest to debunk. If the disciples did go to the wrong tomb, why didn't the Romans or Jews produce the body as soon as people claimed that Jesus rose from the grave? After all, the Romans were supposed to be guarding the tomb. Surely, they must have known exactly where Christ was buried.

Also, Jewish burial grounds were not like modern ones containing thousands of grave sites. It is highly unlikely that Jesus' tomb would have been confused with another.

And if Jesus' followers couldn't find the tomb, why didn't Joseph of Arimathea point it out to them? By the same token, since Joseph provided the grave site, he could quickly have verified whether or not Christ's followers went to the wrong tomb.

Finally, and most damaging to this theory, is the fact that it contradicts the historical account. According to Luke 23:50–56, Mark 15:46–47, and Matthew 27:57–61, the women followed Joseph and saw where the tomb was located. And Peter and John raced to the tomb; so obviously, they knew exactly where it was. (See John 20:3–4.)

5. *The Myth or Legend Theory*

Some critics of the resurrection argue that the resurrection account was incorporated into the Gospels from ancient pagan myths or legends, the so-called "mystery religions." They claim that stories about dying and rising gods parallel the resurrection of Jesus and presuppose that the New Testament authors reproduced the myths. This was a popular attack against Christianity at the beginning of the last century (and still is in some circles), but it has been discredited.[9] It undoubtedly reflects the thinking of liberal theologians and other skeptics who reject the historical Jesus as revealed in the Bible. Because these people are committed to a naturalistic worldview that denies anything supernatural, they, of course, consider a miraculous resurrection mythical.

Denying the miraculous, however, doesn't make the miraculous untrue. The truth of any miracle depends on historical verification based on credible eyewitnesses, and there are overwhelming historical (and other) evidences confirming the New Testament's truth and reliability.

Even setting this fact aside, there are numerous other problems with the hypothesis that Jesus' resurrection evolved from pagan myths.

Most obvious is the fact that the Gospels are free of the tall tales and embellishments so common in myths. The Gospels are specific in their details; unusual events, such as Jesus' miracles, are entrenched in historical narratives rather than fanciful, incredulous episodes. Eyewitnesses recorded in explicit detail the data surrounding the resurrection of Jesus Christ. Philosophy professors Peter Kreeft and Ronald Tacelli wrote, "The style of the Gospels is not the style of myth, but that of real, though unscientific, eyewitness description. Anyone sensitive to literary styles can compare the Gospels to any of the mythic religious literature of the time, and the differences will appear remarkable and unmistakable."[10]

The fact is, as Alister McGrath reports, "Parallels between the pagan myths of dying and rising gods and the New Testament accounts of the resurrection of Jesus are now regarded as remote, to say the least."[11] Moreover, he continued:

> It is at this point that the wisdom of C. S. Lewis—who actually knew something about myths—must be acknowledged. Lewis realized that the New Testament accounts of the resurrection of Jesus bore no relation to real mythology, despite the claims of some theologians who had dabbled in the field. Perhaps most important, however, was his realization that the gnostic redeemer myths—which the New Testament writers allegedly took over and applied to Jesus—[are] dated...later than the New Testament itself.[12]

Gary Habermas and J.P. Moreland agree: "Not one clear case of any alleged resurrection teaching appears in any pagan text before the late second century A.D., almost one hundred years *after* the New Testament was written."[13] Because no resurrection story predates the resurrection of Jesus Christ, one might logically conclude that the mythical stories were borrowed from the biblical accounts. Theologian H. Wayne House added this:

> Various mystery religions did exist from early times in Greece; however, it is only after the first century A.D. that we begin to have

much data on them. It is more likely, therefore, that the mystery religions, observing the success of orthodox Christianity, began to mimic its beliefs and practices, rather than the other way around.[14]

Even if ancient myths are similar to the events surrounding Christ's first advent and resurrection, they pose no threat to Christianity. Kreeft and Tacelli made a good point relative to this:

> For some strange reason, many people think that this fact—that there are many mythic parallels and foreshadowings of the Christian story—points to the *falsehood* of the Christian story. Actually, the more witnesses tell a similar story, the more likely it is to be *true*. The more foreshadowings we find for an event, the more likely it is that the event will happen.[15]

The key defense against the theory that the resurrection is a legend or myth, however, depends on whether or not the New Testament is historically reliable. We have explored this issue extensively, but this is a good time to review key points:

- Either eyewitnesses of the events or their associates wrote the New Testament. Myths and legends cannot be traced to eyewitnesses.
- The events recorded in the New Testament, including the resurrection, were written down within a generation of Jesus' death and postresurrection appearances.
- The apostle Paul related that as many as five hundred people saw the resurrected Christ at one time, and most of them were still alive when he wrote. (See 1 Corinthians 15:6.) There is no record that they, or the enemies of Christ for that matter, ever denied the fact of the empty tomb.
- Oral Christian creeds bridge the gap between the time of Jesus' resurrection and the time when it was recorded in the Gospels. Some of these creeds date within three to eight years of the resurrection.

In short, not enough time elapsed between Jesus' resurrection and when the event was recorded to allow myths or legends to develop. It requires several generations for this to happen, not a mere twenty-five or thirty years. William Lane Craig explained, "Perhaps the greatest difficulty for those who say that the resurrection accounts are legendary is that the time period between the events and the writings of the gospels was too short to allow legend to substantially accrue."[16]

6. The Twin Brother Theory

Perhaps the most far-fetched, preposterous attempt to explain away Jesus' resurrection on naturalistic grounds is the so-called Twin Brother theory. Even critics should be embarrassed by this pitiful explanation. Its hypothesis claims that Jesus had a twin brother (or a look-alike). After Jesus died on the cross and His body was disposed, the imposter walked onto the scene and convinced everyone that he was Jesus recently risen from the grave.

This view creates more problems than it solves. For one, it violates the historical record. Jesus was not a twin. (See Luke 2.) Later, Mary gave birth to His brothers and sisters. Other, more pragmatic problems with this scheme also surface. To succeed, the impostor would have had to get past the Roman guards, roll away the two-ton stone sealing the tomb's entrance, and steal and dispose of Jesus' body undetected. He would then have had to inflict on himself (or let someone do it) the wounds of scourging, the crown of thorns, the nail holes, and the spear thrust. Next, the pretender would have to appear forty times throughout a wide geographical area (being unrecognizable at times) and suddenly disappear forever. And, of course, if the imposter was indeed Jesus' twin brother and not a look-alike, his mother and brothers would have had to willingly go along with the scheme.

What Can We Conclude?

Without exception these six anti-resurrection theories are pathetic attempts to palm off a naturalistic explanation for the resurrection. All of them fail to "explain the data and are refuted by the facts."[17]

What does account for the facts? What is the best explanation for the events surrounding Jesus' resurrection? The obvious answer is that His resurrection was an unprecedented, historical event. This truth will become even clearer as we change tactics and tackle the issue by applying the Socratic apologetic method.

Socratic Response

Sometimes the best defense is a good offense. Let's explore how to "defend" Jesus' resurrection by applying "offensive" apologetics—the Socratic method. (See chapter two.)

At least a dozen established historical facts surrounding the resurrection of Jesus Christ must be explained away if the resurrection never occurred. Most of them are widely accepted by the majority of scholars, including those who deny the resurrection.[18] We'll focus on just six of them. Our challenge to non-Christians, using the Socratic method, is to provide a better explanation for these six historical facts than the resurrection, that is, the empty tomb,[19] the postresurrection appearances, the changed lives of the disciples, the birth of the Christian church around 30 AD, Sunday becoming a day of worship, and Paul's conversion on the Damascus road. Virtually every critical scholar accepts at least these six events as historical facts.[20] Let's examine them briefly.

The Empty Tomb

The contemporaries of Christ, followers and enemies alike, never denied the empty tomb. The fact that the Jewish authorities bribed the guards to claim the disciples stole the body confirms this. (See Matthew 28:11–13.) And, if the tomb was not empty, the Jews or Romans would have produced the body the moment Christ's disciples began to preach His resurrection.

The Postresurrection Appearances

After Jesus' resurrection, people saw, touched, walked alongside of, ate with, and listened to someone they knew to be Jesus Christ. Critics deny it actually was Jesus, but they don't deny that the apostles and others *believed* it was Him. Which view has the best support? We determined that claiming such sightings were hallucinations, or that the person was Jesus' twin brother, are preposterous and without logical or historical justification. The best explanation is that the person seen was Jesus.

The Changed Lives of the Disciples

Most historians agree that the disciples thought Jesus rose from the dead. There is no doubt something happened that first Easter Sunday that transformed eleven cowardly men, hiding in fear of their lives, into bold, outspoken evangelists. These men became willing to risk imprisonment, excommunication, social ostracism, torture, and even death in order to proclaim the resurrection of Jesus Christ in the very city in which He was crucified. Once again, the best explanation is the resurrection.

The Birth of the Christian Church

Where did Christianity come from? What caused it to explode in popularity? What powered the fervent passion of its followers to spread the Gospel throughout the Roman Empire? Scholars have traced the birth of the Christian church to around AD 30. Its rapid spread from Jerusalem all the way to Rome took barely twenty years. Within a few centuries, Christianity became the dominant religion in the vast Roman Empire, purging centuries of pagan practices. What caused this remarkable transformation? Only something as compelling and persuasive as Jesus' resurrection could account for it. Without His resurrection, there would have been no early church. Indeed, the origin of the Christian faith springs from belief in Christ's resurrection.

Sunday Becoming the Day of Worship

The first Christian converts were predominately Jews. After centuries of worshiping on Saturday (the Sabbath), these early followers began to worship on Sunday. (See Acts 20:7; 1 Corinthians 16:2.) Why? The only reasonable explanation is that it celebrated the momentous day when Jesus resurrected from the grave. No other explanation makes sense.

Paul's Conversion on the Road to Damascus

Virtually every scholar acknowledges that something happened to a young, zealous Pharisee named Saul that radically changed the rest of his life. Saul (who became Paul after his conversion) hated Christians. Indeed, his "ministry" was arresting and punishing believers, even to the point of executions (See Acts 7:58–8:3; 9:1–2.) Suddenly, on the road to Damascus, Saul was transformed from being a fanatical persecutor of Christians to the greatest defender, missionary, and evangelist the church has ever known—and the chosen author of thirteen of the twenty-seven books in the New Testament. What caused such a dramatic and abrupt change? Paul related that he encountered the resurrected Christ (cf. Acts 9; 22:2–11; 26:12–18) and was appointed an apostle to the Gentiles (cf. Acts 9:15; Galatians 1:16).

Applying the Socratic Method

Because virtually all Bible scholars (liberal as well as conservative) accept these six historical facts as being authentic, skeptics can't easily shrug them off. Here's where the Socratic method comes into play. The burden of proof is shifted onto the skeptic to give a better explanation for these facts than Jesus' resurrection. Do any naturalistic theories better account for the historical data? Hardly!

Ask the non-Christians if they can suggest a better explanation for these six historical facts than the resurrection. If Jesus didn't rise from the dead, how do they explain the empty tomb, the postresurrection appearances, the changed lives of the disciples, the birth of the Christian church, Sunday becoming the day of worship, and Paul's radical conversion?

If alternate (naturalistic) theories—such as the stolen body theory, swoon theory, hallucination theory, or one of the others we examined—are compared with Jesus' resurrection, it becomes patently clear that His resurrection best accounts for the data and the facts of history. All other theories are merely speculations with no objective corroboration. That's what we want skeptics to see.

Endnotes

1. Although His resurrection is the major evidence for the deity of Jesus Christ, it can only be sustained if the Bible is true and reliable. Hence the Bible's authenticity is the watershed issue in all apologetics. Virtually all Christian beliefs—indeed the entire Christian worldview—rests firmly on the historical foundation of Scripture.

2. Other Old Testament references that imply a resurrection include Job 19:25–27; Isaiah 26:19; Daniel 12:2.

3. Norman L. Geisler and Abdul Saleeb, *Answering Islam; The Crescent in Light of the Cross* (Grand Rapids: Baker Books, 2001), 252.

4. I provide an apologetic response to the denial of miracles in my book, *Defending Your Faith; Reliable Answers for a New Generation of Seekers and Skeptics* (Kregel Publications, 1997), chapter 12.

5. William Lane Craig, *Reasonable Faith; Christian Truth and Apologetics* (Wheaton: Crossway Books, 1994), 278.

6. Gary R. Habermas, "Explaining Away Jesus' Resurrection: Hallucinations; The Recent Revival of Theories," *Christian Research Journal*, Vol. 23, No. 4, 2001.

7. Ibid., 47

8. Norman L. Geisler, *Baker Encyclopedia of Christian Apologetics* (Grand Rapids: Baker Books, 1999), 713.

9. Alister E. McGrath, *Intellectuals Don't Need God & Other Modern Myths* (Grand Rapids: Zondervan Publishing House, 1993), 121.

10. Peter Kreeft and Ronald Tacelli, *Handbook of Christian Apologetics; Hundreds of Answers to Crucial Questions* (InterVarsity Press: Downers Grove, 1994), 163.

11. McGrath, *Intellectuals Don't Need God*, 121.

12. Ibid.

13. Gary R. Habermas & J. P. Moreland, *Morality; the Other Side of Death* (Nashville: Thomas Nelson Publishers, 1992), 62.

14. H. Wayne House, "A Summary Critique: The Mythological Jesus Mysteries," *Christian Research Journal*, Vol. 26, No. 01, 57.

15. Peter Kreeft and Ronald Tacelli, *Handbook of Christian Apologetics; Hundreds of Answers to Crucial Questions* (InterVarsity Press: Downers Grove, 1994), 153–154.

16. Craig, *Reasonable Faith*, 284.

17. Gary R. Habermas, *The Historical Jesus; Ancient Evidence for the Life of Christ*, (Joplin: College Press Publishing Co., 199), 253.

18. Ibid., 158. Habermas reported that because of the testimony of the "early Christian creeds, as well as other data [such as early non-Christian historians and ancient Christian writings] even contemporary critical scholars recognize a certain amount of historical facts surrounding the death, burial, and resurrection of Jesus." In chapter seven, "Primary Sources: Creeds and Facts," he provided examples of the numerous creeds circulating "before the writing of the New Testament. ... and later written in the books of the New Testament," 143.

19. Habermas explained, "Although not as widely accepted, many scholars hold that the tomb in which Jesus was buried was discovered to be empty just a few days later," 158. In his summary he added, "The historical evidence for the empty tomb is also very strong (even from secular sources alone)" 254.

20. Ibid., 160.

DO PEOPLE GO TO HELL WHO NEVER HEARD OF JESUS?

AS MANY OF us have experienced, family members can be our strongest critics. When I was a new believer, my sister (who has become a Christian) said something like this: "I don't understand why God sends people to hell just because they're not Christians. That doesn't seem fair!" It was a good question and one I wanted to answer. In fact, I've since discovered that even seasoned Christians would like an answer to this question.

The core issue here concerns the eternal destiny of people who die without hearing about Jesus Christ—including those who lived before His first coming. Do they go directly to hell, or has God provided another way by which they might be saved? If He hasn't, then the "fate of the heathen," like the problem of evil, seems to contradict God's perfect love. How *can* an all-loving God reject "good" or "religious" people just because they never heard about Jesus Christ or practiced another religion?

Preliminary Considerations

Before going further, I need to preface what follows. The Bible does not give us all the information we'd like to have regarding the eternal destiny of people who had no opportunity to accept Jesus as Savior. Hence, any position on this issue is necessarily speculative. We simply do not know for certain how God will ultimately deal with these people. As C. S. Lewis observed, "The truth is God hasn't told us what His arrangements about the other people are. We do know that no man can be saved except through Christ; we don't know that only those who know Him can be saved through Him."[1]

Second, the points of this chapter should not be misconstrued to imply that anyone can be saved independent of Jesus Christ. If a person, Christian or non-Christian, is ultimately saved, salvation is only through Christ's work on the cross. Jesus and His apostles clearly taught this. (See John 14:6; Acts 4:12.) Universalism—the belief that ultimately all people will be saved, regardless of religious beliefs—is untrue.

Third, we should not conclude that salvation is easily accessible to the unevangelized or even that they are likely to be saved. In Romans 10:14–15, Paul emphasized the importance of direct, verbal evangelism. In fact, independent of hearing the Gospel, salvation appears to be extremely unlikely. William Lane Craig noted that "the testimony of Scripture is that people do not in general live up to even the meager demands [of general revelation] and therefore are lost.... Perhaps some do access salvation by means of general revelation, but if we take Scripture seriously we must admit that these are relatively few."[2] (See Romans 1:18–32.)

Finally, I'm not going to give a specific, theological response to the fate of non-Christians. I'll give an apologetic response. I'm primarily interested in providing adequate apologetics designed for people who view this issue as a defect in Christianity. There is more leeway in apologetics than in theology. As explained in chapter one, the goal of apologetics is to identify and remove intellectual obstacles to Christianity. When a debatable issue arises, we are not obligated to give definitive theological answers or even our own personal positions on the topic. We must give answers that are theologically legitimate and will bear up under biblical scrutiny. If these conditions are met, apologetic responses that avoid dogmatic theological positions are acceptable means of lovingly removing obstacles that prevent unbelievers from seriously considering Christianity.

The fate of people who never received Jesus as Lord and Savior before they died encompasses three related issues:

- What happens to people who followed other religions?
- What happens to people who lived beyond the reach of Christian missionaries and evangelists and never heard about Jesus?
- What happens to people who heard the Gospel but outright rejected it?

This third question is easy to answer—they are eternally condemned. The Bible clearly states that anyone who has the opportunity to receive Jesus Christ as Savior and rejects Him has no hope. (See Mark 16:16; John 3:18, 36; 1 John 2:23.) Christians don't make the rules; God does. Let's look at the other two issues now.

What Happens to People Who Follow Other Religions?

The Bible is clear regarding this issue, too. People who heard the Gospel and rejected it in favor of another religion have the same fate as anyone who rejects Jesus Christ. They go to hell. But what about people who practiced other religions and never had the opportunity to meet Jesus Christ and receive Him as personal Savior? And what about those who lived before Jesus' first coming? Are these people condemned to hell?

At this point, it's important for us to understand that just being "religious" does not automatically save anyone, just as being "good" does not earn a person salvation. As R. C. Sproul observed, "The fact that people are religious does not in itself mean that God is pleased with them. Idolatry represents the ultimate insult to God."[3]

According to Romans 1:18–25, people who suppress truth about God embrace some form of idolatry (vs. 23). It appears, then, that practitioners of non-Christian religions and cults are lost because they rejected God and turned to substitutes. Explained Sproul: "If Paul is correct, the practice of religion does not excuse the pagan but in fact compounds his guilt."[4]

However, this Roman passage refers to people who suppress the truth of God. So, are there people who never met Jesus and did not suppress that truth? In other words, are there people who sought the one true God within the perimeters of the light they had?[5] If so, after they die, do they have an opportunity to be saved through the blood of the Savior they never personally met?

What Happens to People Who Never Heard about Jesus?

Unbelievers often express this challenge by saying something like this: "I can't accept a God who sends people to hell just because they never heard of Jesus Christ."

Like all other apologetic challenges, we can respond to this question defensively or offensively (the Socratic method). In terms of a Socratic response, we can reply with questions such as: "Is it worth losing your own salvation because you don't like how God saves people?" Or, "Why shouldn't salvation be on God's terms?"

Honestly, I doubt if either of these responses will get you far in removing this obstacle in a loving, sensitive way. It doesn't explain a thing. It merely stumps the non-Christian by forcing him or her to respond in a way that removes the question without a legitimate answer. If the unbeliever is truly seeking spiritual truth, obviously he doesn't want to risk losing his salvation. But such a response is unlikely to change his belief that God's unfair.

A *defensive* response may address this particular issue better, and I'll outline such a response below. Nevertheless, it is still good to start with a Socratic question, such as this one: "Why do you think Christians believe that everyone who never met Jesus goes to hell?" The goal of this question is to encourage the non-Christian to see his or her basic assumption. It provides an opportunity to explain an alternate Christian position on this issue, one they probably never have heard. Not all Christians believe that people who never heard of Jesus automatically go to hell. As I've pointed out already, most unbelievers get their opinions about Christianity from popular culture, which wrongly may assume that Christians believe all categories of non-Christians end up in hell. In my experience, few Christians take this position.

There are three apologetic responses concerning the eternal destiny of people who never had the opportunity to meet Jesus. I call these responses "hard-boiled," "over-easy," and "soft-boiled."

The Hard-Boiled Response

The hard-boiled response claims that people who never had the opportunity to choose or reject Jesus Christ are lost. In other words, only those who hear the Gospel and personally receive Jesus Christ as their Lord and Savior are saved. All others enter a godless eternity. These poor souls are simply not the "elect." If they were predestined to salvation, God would have sent Christians to bring them the Gospel.

Unfortunately, this response will not sway many non-Christians to receive Jesus. They don't understand anything about people's inherent sin nature, their rebellion against God, and their guilt before a holy and righteous God. To them, God is unfair.

The Over-Easy Response

A second response concerning the eternal destiny of people who never heard of Jesus Christ is sometimes called "middle-knowledge." This view holds that God "arranged this world ... [so that] those who never hear the Gospel would not have responded to it even if they had heard it."[6]

According to the thesis of this response, God knows that many individuals will never have the opportunity to meet Jesus Christ. Nevertheless, in God's sovereignty, He knows what response these people would have made if they had heard the Gospel. Thus, "those who would respond to the Gospel in any *possible* world are given the opportunity to do so in this *actual* world. God engineers the world in such a way that those who would freely receive Jesus Christ would be placed in the position of hearing about him."[7] Hence, "no one is eternally lost because he was born in the wrong place at the wrong time."[8]

Apologetically, this response is better than the hard-boiled response for a couple reasons. "So long as this scenario is even *possible*, it proves that it is entirely consistent to affirm that God is all-powerful and all-loving and yet that some people never hear the gospel and are lost."[9] It also answers the question about, "What happens to people who never heard the Gospel but would have responded favorably to it if only they had had the chance." People who would have responded favorably to the Gospel heard it. Those who would not have accepted it didn't hear it.

However, this response is a theological construction and will be almost as unconvincing to non-Christians as the hard-boiled response. It still seems to preclude any hope of salvation for vast numbers of people, and it says nothing about the fate of people who lived before the incarnate Christ.

The Soft-Boiled Response

The third response regarding the fate of people who never met Jesus Christ is much more conducive to effective apologetics. It's softer and more likely to remove this issue if it is an obstacle to Christianity. I believe it's the best apologetic response—even for Christians who theologically accept the hard-boiled position. Remember, we're doing apologetics, not theology. Once a non-Christian becomes a Christian, he or she can wrestle with the theological implications of their position and adjust their views accordingly.

I will first present this response as I would say it during an apologetics conversation. Afterwards I'll provide Scripture to support it.

* * * * * *

"It's true that the Bible teaches that no one is saved apart from Jesus Christ. If anyone is saved at all—people who heard of Jesus or people who didn't—it's only because of the work of Christ on the cross. Jesus said, 'I am the way, and the truth, and the life; no one comes to the Father, but through Me.' In fact, even unsaved people will one day recognize and confess that Jesus Christ is Lord and Savior (Philippians 2:9–11).

However, the Bible doesn't clearly explain how God deals with people who couldn't make a commitment to Jesus because they never heard of Him. I believe that to say they automatically go to hell is reading more into the Bible than the Bible actually says.

There seem to be passages in the Bible that indicate God may have provided an opportunity for people to be saved who never heard of Jesus Christ. We can be sure, from what we know about God in the Bible, that He will deal with these people fairly. I'll gladly show you some verses that speak to this issue."

* * * * * *

The soft-boiled response points out that the Bible appears to teach that people will be judged according to the degree of revelation they have received from God and what they have done with it. In other words, people are judged according to what they knew, not according to what they didn't know. Rather than short-circuiting the chance to establish fruitful dialogue, this response is more likely to lead the conversation beyond the fate of unsaved people to the Gospel itself. This is the goal of all apologetics, which facilitates discussions rather than stifling them.

Scriptures Supporting the Soft Response

Since I believe this response is the best of the three, I want to provide Scripture that supports this view.

Ezekiel 18:32, 33:11; 1 Timothy 2:3–4; 2 Peter 3:9

The Old and New Testaments clearly teach that God wants everyone to have eternal life. Of course, this doesn't mean that everyone will be saved. People who have had the opportunity to receive Jesus and rejected Him will perish (which, by the way, may include the person you are talking to).

Genesis 18:25; Exodus 34:6; Deuteronomy 32:4; Psalm 103:8

The Old and New Testaments testify that God is just, righteous, compassionate, and loving. Although we don't know exactly how God will deal with people who never met Jesus Christ, we know that He will be fair. (Notice that the above passages are all from the Old Testament. Many non-Christians think that God in the New Testament is loving and compassionate but that God in the Old Testament is wrathful and vengeful. Hence they have contradictory views of God. These passages demonstrate that the God of the Old Testament is the same loving, compassionate, and long-suffering God of the New Testament.)

Luke 12:47–48; John 9:39–41; 15:22–24; 1 Timothy 1:12–16

Although not explicit (the Luke passage addresses degrees of punishment), these passages nevertheless reflect a key biblical principle—

people are accountable for the knowledge they have. I believe it can be argued theologically that this implies that people who knew God's will, to accept Jesus Christ as Lord and Savior, and refused to do so will receive greater punishment than those who did not know God's will (never heard of Jesus Christ). Does this mean the latter will have an opportunity to be saved? Certainly these passages don't explicitly say so. However, the principle of accountability relative to knowledge fits the hypothesis.

In Matthew 10:5–15, Jesus sent His twelve apostles to heal and to preach the Kingdom of Heaven. He told them that any house or city that did not receive their words positively will be worse off on the day of judgment than Sodom and Gomorrah (v.15), the most depraved cities in Old Testament. Why does Jesus declare this? "They have had the benefit of a clearer call to repentance, God's last word, and so the guilt of their failure to respond is greater."[10]

Psalm 19:1–2; Acts 14:16–17, 17:22–31; Romans 1:19–20; 2:13–16
These key passages support the soft-boiled position. The Bible teaches that all people have the opportunity to know God through general revelation, that is, through nature and a divinely placed moral conscience.[11] Consequently, people who reject general revelation actually "suppress" truth about God and choose not "to acknowledge God any longer" (Romans 1:18, 28). In order for people to suppress truth about God, they must first have that truth. Hence, general revelation must provide true knowledge about God. Rejecting God's general revelation is not a matter of ignorance. Moreover, according to Romans 1:20, there is enough information about God available through general revelation to hold people accountable. They are "without excuse" if they reject it.

Finally, it can be argued that if the Father, Son, and Holy Spirit are the one God, rejecting the Father is tantamount to rejecting the Son. In other words, although unsaved people may never have had the opportunity to hear the Gospel message and therefore know Jesus Christ personally, they did have the opportunity (through general revelation) to know God. If this view is correct, non-Christians will be judged by how they respond to God the Father through general revelation, not according to how they responded to Jesus. R.C. Sproul wrote, "If a person in a remote area has never heard of Christ, he will not be punished for that. What he will be punished for is the rejection of the Father of whom he has heard and for disobedience to the law that is written in his heart.[12]

A Few More Words About General Revelation

General revelation reveals information *about* God and is not, in and of itself, a means by which people can develop a personal relationship with Jesus Christ. Nevertheless, the premise of general revelation is that God has provided enough information about Himself through nature and our moral conscience so that the unevangelized have genuine opportunities to find God if they seek Him. (This is sometimes referred to as "prevenient grace.") Oxford theologian Alister McGrath explained:

> God's revelation is not limited to the explicit human preaching of the good news, but extends beyond it.... Where the word is not or cannot be preached by human agents, God is not inhibited from bringing people to faith in him, even if that act of hope and trust may lack the full orbed character of an informed Christian faith.[13]

As David said nearly thirty centuries ago, "The Lord searches all hearts, and understands every intent of the thoughts. If you seek Him, He will let you find Him; but if you forsake Him, He will reject you forever" (1 Chronicles 28:9). Likewise, the prophet Jeremiah offered these encouraging words from God: "You will seek Me and find Me when you search for Me with all your heart" (Jeremiah 29:13).

In light of general revelation, it appears possible that God will judge people who never had the opportunity to meet Jesus Christ according to the revelation they received and how they responded to it. God does not send anyone to hell. A person chooses hell by rejecting the revelation that God has provided for him or her, either through general revelation or the gospel.

R. C. Sproul wrote: "We can rest assured that no one is ever punished for rejecting Christ if they've never heard of Him.... People are not rejected for what they haven't heard but for what they have heard."[14]

Not all Christians agree with this position or agree that the above passages imply the *potential* salvation of people who never heard of Jesus Christ. That's not the point here. I'm not declaring the only legitimate theological position on the fate of the unsaved. That issue can be argued out charitably within the family of Christ. Rather I'm supporting an effective, Bible-based, apologetic strategy to use with non-Christians. I'm suggesting a tactic that will remove this issue so it is not an obstacle to placing faith in Jesus Christ. When we use good apologetics, we avoid debatable theological issues that stifle our evangelism and seek to communicate the Gospel as quickly and efficiently as possible to non-Christians.

Endnotes

1. C. S. Lewis, *Mere Christianity* (New York: MacMillan Publishing Co.), 55.

2. William Lane Craig, "Politically Incorrect Salvation," in *Christian Apologetics in the Postmodern World*, Timothy R. Phillips and Dennis L. Okholm, eds. (Downers Grove: InterVarsity Press, 1995), 89.

3. R.C. Sproul, *Reasons to Believe* (Grand Rapids: Zondervan, 1982), 55.

4. Ibid., 54.

5. Missionaries report that it is not unusual to encounter people groups who have never met Jesus Christ and yet entertain a latent monotheistic concept of God. Sometimes these people appear to have been prepared to hear the Gospel. See, for example, Don Richardson, *Eternity In Their Hearts* (Ventura: Regal Books, 1981).

6. Paul Copan, *"True For You, But Not For Me"* (Minneapolis: Bethany House Publishers, 1998), 128. Chapter 20 examines the middle-knowledge response in detail.

7. Ibid., 127.

8. Ibid., 130.

9. Craig, "Politically Correct Salvation," in *Christian Apologetics in the Postmodern World*, 94.

10. R.T. France, *Tyndale New Testament Commentaries; The Gospel According to Matthew, An Introduction and Commentary*, gen. ed. Leon Morris (Grand Rapids: William B. Eerdmans Publishing Co., 1986), 181.

11. General revelation, according to Romans 1:19–20 and Romans 2:12–16, reveals that God created and governs the universe, is infinite and almighty, and judges evil. He has also placed within the hearts and minds of all people an innate sense of right and wrong by which they will be held accountable. (See the moral argument for God's existence in chapter eighteen.)

12. Sproul, *Reasons to Believe,* 56.

13. Alister E. McGrath, "A Particularist View: A Post-Enlightenment Approach," in Okholm and Phillips, gen. eds., *Four Views on Salvation in a Pluralistic World* (Grand Rapids: Zondervan Publishing House, 1996), 178–179.

14. Sproul, *Reasons to Believe,* 50, 56.

PART FIVE

Modern Issues: The World Beyond The Church

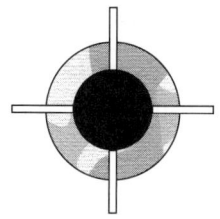

INTRODUCTION TO PART FIVE

DURING RECENT years, attacks against Christianity have increased in dimension. In addition to challenging specific doctrinal beliefs, such as the reliability of the Bible and Jesus' resurrection, cutting-edge apologetic issues today include Christian ethics and other values. The Christian stand against abortion, homosexual marriage, cohabitation, Internet pornography, euthanasia, embryonic stem-cell research, cloning, and similar moral issues have come under increasingly strong criticism, due primarily to dramatic sociological changes that have taken place in Western culture since the 1960s. Prior to the mid-twentieth century, Christianity was not only the dominant religious belief in America but set standards for moral and social behavior. Until the 1960s, even non-Christians generally accepted and obeyed Christian values.

Recently, I watched an episode from the late 1950s television show "Leave it to Beaver." This weekly comedy centered on the day-to-day life and adventures of a mid-twentieth-century American family. The main character was a boy nicknamed "Beaver" (Jerry Mathers). During this episode, Beaver tore his pants and lied to his parents about how it happened. Of course, he was found out. As the show concluded, his mother reminded Beaver that God sees his actions and knows when he lies, even if no one else does. The show ended with Beaver and his brother, Wally (Tony Dow), at home from Sunday school, reflecting on the lessons learned.

Today, as in the 1950s, television is a major barometer of American values. What one sees there usually reflects current values—or at least those the media wants us to accept. Practically every episode of pre–1970s sitcoms, including "Leave It to Beaver" and "The Andy Griffith Show," presented implicit lessons on honesty, courage, sacrifice, kindness, and other values intrinsic not only to Christians but to American culture in general. The shows often included scenes in church, showed pastors in respectful roles, and frequently ended with moral lessons.

When was the last time you saw a modern sitcom encouraging godly behavior? Rarely, if ever. Most openly promote adultery, fornication, homosexuality, cohabitation, swearing, lying, cheating, pride, self-centeredness, disrespect for parents, and much more. Go to the movies, scan magazines at a grocery store checkout line, or attend a play. Clearly, American culture no longer promotes biblical morals and values. The syndicated advice column, *Dear Abby*, illustrates this. In a single column during November, 2004, Abby tackled homosexual relationships, children being checked for weapons at a public school, and a woman who was pregnant by a married man,

Today, Christianity no longer sets the standard for moral behavior in America. It has been shoved off center stage and replaced by a godless worldview called secular humanism. As a distinct ideology, secular humanism promotes a brand of "morality" that is largely antithetical to Christianity.[1] Because the values and the political agenda of secular humanism dominate and direct popular culture—especially academia, the media, and the entertainment industries—Christians are struggling just to maintain a vibrant voice and influence in modern culture, especially in the area of morality.[2] Thus, as we consider apologetics, we must be prepared to address a host of moral issues rarely encountered forty or fifty years ago.

Modern Worldviews

Two formidable worldview adversaries of Christianity fuel secular humanism and create its philosophical infrastructure. Both would like nothing better than to remove Christianity entirely from the public square. I'm speaking here of naturalism and postmodernism. These may be new concepts for some of you, but whether you recognize them or not, you probably encounter these worldviews from the moment you leave for work or school in the morning until you turn off your television at night. Their influences on modern culture can't be exaggerated, and their attacks against Christianity are unrelenting.

It's crucial that Christians understand these worldviews, identify how they permeate our thinking and behavior, and prepare successful apologetic responses. This is especially important for high school and college students. As I observed earlier, up to 80 percent of kids raised in a Christian home fall away from the faith when attending secular universities.[3] As Chuck Colson warned, "We'd better ground our students in worldview thinking before they leave for college, where professors challenge everything they believe."[4]

In the next four chapters, I'll explore the basic tenets of naturalism and postmodernism and then prepare adequate apologetics responses.

Endnotes

1. I included a chapter on secular humanism in my book, *Christianity on the Offense; Responding to the Beliefs and Assumptions of Spiritual Seekers* (Grand Rapids: Kregel Publications, 1998), chapter 11.

2. As I pointed out in the introduction to this book, other factors have contributed to the loss of Christianity's moral and intellectual leadership in American culture. In particular is the anti-intellectualism that denominates much of evangelicalism today. See note seven on page xiv.

3. I mentioned in the endnotes of chapter one that I attended a seminar hosted by the Institute of Creation Research. Dr. John Morris, president of ICR, pointed out that seventy-five percent of children reared in Christian homes fall away from the faith after entering secular colleges. This was later confirmed in Rick Cornish's *5 Minute Apologist: Maximum Truth in Minimum Time* (Colorado Springs: NavPress, 2005), p. 17.

4. Charles Colson, "Worldview Boot Camp; Evangelical Young People Need Training in Truth about Truth," *Christianity Today*, December 2004, p. 80.

NATURALISM
The Collapse of Christian Dominance

I WAS BORN IN June, 1945, one of the last of the "war babies." As I look back on my life, it seems as if I'm living on an entirely different planet than the America of my youth. No time in the history of humanity has a culture experienced such profound ethical changes during such a short span of time as America has experienced since World War II, especially after the 1960s. Readers who are my age know exactly what I'm talking about. Who would have imagined in the 1960s that Americans could freely kill their unborn children. Who would have dreamed that a person could marry someone of the same sex—but could not discuss their religious beliefs in public schools and governmental agencies. No one in the 1960s would have forecast that in forty-five years people would be allowed to engage openly in public pornography in the name of freedom of speech.

By every cultural indicator, America prior to the 1960s was a safer place to live. It was more emotionally stable and less violent. It embraced greater personal and political integrity and healthier moral behavior. It had less crime, less divorce, less child abuse, and fewer teenage suicides. There was less drug and alcohol addiction. Out of wedlock pregnancies were rare. Graphic sex and violence on television and in the movies was virtually nonexistent. William Bennett described the situation well:

> The nation we live in today is more violent and vulgar, coarse and cynical, rude and remorseless, deviant and depressed, than the one we once inhabited. A popular culture that is often brutal, gruesome, and enamored with death robs many children of their innocence. People kill other people, and themselves, more easily. Men and women abandon each other, and their children, more readily. Marriage and the American family are weaker, more unstable, less normative.[1]

It's no coincidence that during the same four decades that we witnessed the collapse of Christianity as the guiding moral light in American society, we also witnessed the decay of the moral health in America. As a recent editorial in *Christianity Today* described it:

> The spiritual decline has only accelerated in the 23 years since [1978]. We live in a political/economic nexus that not only permits but actually protects those who practice evil. In the slavish and mindless pursuit of liberty, we've ended up with a system that guards the rights of pornographers to commodify sex, of advertisers to entice people to hedonism, of executives to pursue a life of greed, of abortionists to kill innocent human life."[2]

Remove God and biblical values from society, and elevate godless secular humanism in their place, and civilization crumbles. This brings us to naturalism. The philosophy of naturalism is expressed as a distinct worldview through secular humanism. It is the philosophical justification for a godless worldview that elevates people to the status of supreme beings. Let's see how it works and what we can do to combat it.

Naturalism

Naturalism, an anti-supernatural worldview, alleges that everything that exists is a product of nature and is governed by natural laws.

Naturalists deny the deity of Jesus Christ, the existence of a soul, life after death, angels, demons, miracles, and answered prayer. All reality, naturalists preach, is material—even our thoughts. The human mind is no more than physiological and neurological processes. "You and I are merely particles that have somehow evolved consciousness and a sense of personal identity."[3]

Although one can be a "mythological" naturalist and not an atheist, yet to a naturalist, "if God exists at all, he acts only through inviolable laws of nature and adds nothing to them."[4] Phillip Johnson, who wrote extensively on philosophical naturalism, explained:

> Naturalism assumes the entire realm of nature to be a closed system of material causes and effects, which cannot be influenced by anything from "outside." Naturalism does not explicitly deny the mere existence of God, but it does deny that a supernatural being could in any way influence natural events, such as evolution, or communicate with natural creatures like ourselves.[5]

Naturalism—Philosophy, Not Science

Most people associate naturalism with modern science, biological evolution in particular, because many of the battles between naturalism and Christianity involve the creation/evolution debate. The truth is science is only one area in which naturalism exerts influence.

The first thing we must understand about naturalism, in order to formulate an effective apologetics, is that naturalism is not science—*it's philosophy*. It's a way of looking at all of reality, not just the origin of life. When the late Carl Sagan voiced his now famous dictum on the *Cosmos* television program, "The cosmos is all that is or ever was or ever will be," he wasn't making a scientific statement. There is no scientific proof that the cosmos is all there is. Sagan was speaking philosophically. He was expressing a metaphysical, naturalistic, materialistic view of the universe that omits the supernatural.

Naturalism in Modern Society

Philosophical naturalism has moved far beyond the limits of science and invaded modern society in numerous areas. It's the secular infrastructure—the foundational presupposition—of ethics, psychology, sociology, education, and law. Its influence, however, is particularly powerful and significant in three areas. It's the philosophical basis of evolutionary science, the justification for moral relativism, and provides an epistemological basis for rejecting the existence of God and other religious truths. This last effect has been accomplished by elevating science as the only reliable truth-test in all areas of knowledge. Since we explored the philosophical role of naturalism in evolutionary science earlier in this book (see chapter ten), let's focus on the latter two issues.

Naturalism: Justification for Moral Relativism

Because naturalism is a philosophy rather than science, it freely roams about and permeates all facets of modern society. Nowhere is this more obvious and dangerous than in the area of ethics. The godless world of naturalism is foundational to moral relativism and the rejection of absolute standards of right and wrong. Follow these thoughts:

- If naturalism is true, there is no God.
- If there is no God, people are elevated to supreme beings, and there is no basis for moral absolutes. (See chapter eighteen.)
- Without absolute standards of right and wrong, and if people are supreme beings, ethics arise from human feelings and experiences.
- Since individual cultures and people differ in their acceptance or rejection of particular moral behaviors (e.g. abortion and homosexuality), and since no absolute higher authority exists to say whose view is correct (e.g. God), it logically follows that all moral perspectives must be equally true and acceptable.

This is moral relativism, and here's the danger. Without God, there is no ultimate "good" to identify what is ultimately "bad." Moral behavior becomes *descriptive* rather than *prescriptive*. It's how we act, not how we ought to act. "Sin" in an absolute sense is nonexistent. Moral behavior is determined by the whims of the most powerful—the physically (or militarily) strongest, the most influential, the richest, or the dominant political party. In naturalistic terms, what people think is immoral or evil is actually the fruit of natural selection—"survival of the fittest." It's merely nature.

The roots of moral relativism dig deeply into a naturalistic worldview void of God. We'll examine moral relativism more fully in the next chapter. For now, let's recognize that the cultural pacesetters in America today, especially in academia, are increasingly endorsing this moral philosophy. Here are a few examples.

The late Francis Crick, who with James Watson won a Nobel Prize in the 1962 for the discovery of the double helix structure in DNA advocated, "that all newborns be screened to determine who should live. All who fail to reach a certain level on the Apgar test, used to determine the health of newborns, should be euthanized."[6]

Princeton University professor Peter Singer openly advocates infanticide:

> In 1993 . . . Singer shocked many Americans by suggesting that no newborn should be considered a person until 30 days after birth and that the attending physician should kill some disabled babies on the spot. . . . In 1979 he wrote, "Human babies are not born self-aware, or capable of grasping that they exist over time. They are not persons," therefore, "the life of a newborn is of less value than the life of a pig, a dog, or a chimpanzee."[7]

> If babies are nonpersons, as Singer believes, they are "'replaceable,' like chicken or other livestock. . . . [In fact, Singer advocates] killing incompetent persons of any age if their families decide their lives are 'not worth living.'"[8]

Following are two other illustrations of the logical consequences (moral degradation) prompted by relativism gone amuck. They are quoted in Nancy Pearcey's superb book on contemporary culture, *Total Truth*. They refer to Terri Schiavo, who died after her feeding tube was removed by court order in 2004.

> In a television debate, bioethicist Bill Allen was asked point blink, "Do you think Terri is a person?" He replied, "No, I do not. I think having awareness is an essential criterion of personhood" (Court

TV Online, Mar. 25, 2004). [This pathetic disregard for life is a principle that is increasingly being used to support abortion, now that many abortionists are admitting, medically speaking, that the unborn child is fully human.] Those who favored letting Terri die included some, like Dr. Ronald Cranford, who have openly defended denying food and water even to disabled people who are conscious and partly mobile, like the case of a Washington man who could operate an electric wheelchair (see Robert Johansen, national Review Online, Mar. 16, 2005).[9]

The growing endorsement of euthanasia (and according to some reports, infanticide) has reached fruition in the Netherlands, which in 2002 became the first country to legalize euthanasia. Read a portion of a recent Internet article:

> The Dutch practice of euthanasia is not restricted to voluntary euthanasia for the terminally ill, but has been shown to include nonvoluntary euthanasia for the "never-competent" adults and minors, non-terminally ill, disabled, depressed and the elderly.... Doctors have opted to abandon care, and instead, euthanized their patients even though the patients had not requested to be killed. In response, the government plans to codify the practice of involuntary euthanasia.[10]

As Crick, Singer, and others illustrate, the godless philosophy of naturalism, carried to its logical and lethal conclusion, results in a total disregard for the sanctity of human life. If there is no God, and if matter and the forces of nature are all there is, why not eliminate the weak and dependent? In their book on relativism, Francis Beckwith and Greg Koukl expressed this well:

> What Darwinists [naturalists] cannot do is give us a reason why we ought not simply copy nature and destroy those who are weak, unpleasant, costly, or just plain boring. If all moral options are legitimate, then it's acceptable for the strong to rule the weak. No moral restraints would protect the feeble, because moral restraint simply wouldn't exist.[11]

"Why not carry this idea a step further?" a naturalist might ask. "Why even honor people by giving them a higher status in nature than animals?" Many naturalists don't. Phillip Johnson wrote: "Many scientists and philosophers now say that to award a special status to human beings ... is an anthropocentric sin called *speciesism*, akin to racism and sexism."[12] In other words, if Homo sapiens, like all other animals, are a product of random evolutionary forces, "to declare humans to have some unique status above that of other species may be as arbitrary as to declare one race of humans beings superior to the others."[13] If all creatures are products of biological evolution, and all share the earth equally, there is no basis for human rights above animal rights. Think of the ramifications of this. Medical experimentation using animals would be outlawed. Eating flesh would be immoral. Breeding dogs, cats, and cattle would be considered rape.

It could be even worse. Peter Singer has been an animal rights activist since the 1970s. In his unashamed zeal to refute biblical morality and elevate the status of animals to that of people (after all, an evolutionist believes that people *are* merely another species of animal), Peter Singer has even supported bestiality (sexual relations between humans and animals).[14]

This brand of ethics and morality is what American students are being taught in our most distinguished universities. It's frightening to imagine what this nation, and others, will be like when these students become the moral pacesetters in society. (We'll see how to respond to moral relativism in chapter twenty-nine.)

Naturalism: Rejecting the Existence of God

Having established that philosophical naturalism is the governing principle behind evolutionary science and modern ethics, we can now examine its role as an adversary of religious truth.

God (at least a personal, creator God) and naturalism are mutually exclusive; if a creator God exists, naturalism as a worldview can't be true. Naturalism leads to evolution, not creation. So, it is in the interest (the very survival) of naturalism to deny the existence of God and other religious truth-claims.

The primary means naturalists use in denying the existence of God (or at least denying the plausibility of religious knowledge) is promoting science as the only reliable source of truth. In other words, if nature and matter is all there is, there is no transcendent, supernatural "Personality" to reveal truth. Science must explain reality as it is. This is called *Scientism*, and refuting Scientism is a key apologetic response to naturalism.

Scientism

According to Scientism, anything that can be considered true or factual must pass through the grid of scientific testing. If something can't be explained by modern science—that is, can't be proven scientifically—it can't be considered true or even rational. Naturalists usually say it something like this: "You can't know for sure if something is true unless you can prove it scientifically."

The most serious fallout from this dogma is that it elevates scientific truth above religious truth. Science, on the one hand, is supposedly objective knowledge. It's "impartial fact-finding, the objective and unprejudiced weighing of evidence.... [It] relies on careful observations, calculations, and above all, repeatable experiments."[15] Religion, on the other hand, falls into the category of things that cannot be known for sure because it can't be demonstrated scientifically, observed in nature, or tested in a lab. Religious truth is said to be subjective, merely feelings and experiences. It's considered to be faith, values and beliefs, not objective fact and knowledge. According to Scientism, theological study in search of spiritual knowledge is "not a rational enterprise."[16] To put it bluntly, Scientism views science as fact and religion as fiction, or at best a relativistic and subjective value system. Religion can give no true knowledge about the cosmos; it has no basis in reality as science defines it.[17]

Besides the fact that this perspective is clearly untrue (Christianity says much about science in the realm of origins and human behavior), what we need to realize here is that the statement, "You can't know for sure if something is true unless you can prove it scientifically," is not a scientific statement. It's a philosophical statement *about* science. It's a worldview philosophy that denies anything can be proven outside of scientific testing. Obviously, if Scientism writes the rules, it can declare anything to be irrational.

Thus, in popular culture, scientists radiating wisdom and confidence are contrasted with flashy-dressed televangelists. The unruffled, dispassionate scientist presents an entirely different image than the sweaty, shouting evangelist with his threatening talk of apocalypse and sin.

Now think about this. Why should we think of reality as only what can be seen? Why should truth and knowledge only be in the realm of empirical science? There is no logical, philosophical, or scientific reason *not* to recognize that truth and knowledge can reside in the unseen world as well as in the natural world. Let's look at evidence that demonstrates this.

Apologetics to Scientism

How do we counter Scientism's claim that religious truth falls outside the realm of the factual and that science is the only valid avenue for discovering and verifying truth? Let's explore three responses to Scientism that demonstrate it has nothing to say about religion—or any nonscientific topic for that matter. As a test for truth, science is limited to the scientific arena alone.

1. Scientism Is Self-refuting

The first response is purely logical—Scientism is self-refuting; it falsifies itself. Listen carefully to this statement: "Only something that can be proven scientifically is true." Can this statement be proven scientifically? Of course not! It's not a scientific statement. It's an assumption that imposes its own definition as to what can be considered true. By its own tenets, Scientism can be rejected because it can't be proven scientifically. The creed of Scientism (science is the only valid avenue for discovering and verifying truth) can't be tested or verified. So it dies the death of inconsistency. It commits suicide. As J. P. Moreland put it, "Self-refuting propositions are necessarily false; that is, it is not possible for them to be true."[18]

2. Scientific Knowledge Is Limited in Scope

In today's popular culture, science is held in such high esteem that it is often granted an undeserved authority. As a result, science renders judgment in areas where it isn't qualified to comment. This leads to a second way of disproving Scientism's claim that science is the ultimate truth-test in all areas of knowledge. We can easily demonstrate that science is incapable of proving anything outside of scientific matters.

Scientism claims that before anything can be considered factual, it must pass through the grid of scientific testing. If something cannot be explained in terms of modern science, if it can't be investigated scientifically, it can't be considered factual.

At this point Scientism as a truth-test flounders. To prove something scientifically, according to science, one must be able to test it, observe the results, repeat the experiments, and come up with the same conclusions each time. But this kind of test cannot be applied to non-scientific matters, including things that people instinctively know are true. Indeed, science routinely makes assumptions that are not derived from direct empirical observations. Has anyone actually observed electrons, quarks, quantum events, black holes, and so on? They are simply inferred from other empirical studies.

Numerous areas of truth and knowledge are not open to scientific verification. Can observation and experimentation be applied when investigating historical matters? No—yet historical facts exist. Can observation and experimentation determine guilt or innocence in a crime? No—legal reasoning and eyewitness testimony are called for. Can aesthetics (the reality of beauty), ethics (moral behavior), and philosophy (the search for guiding principles) be tested scientifically? Of course not. Yet most people agree that truths can be identified in these areas.

Laboratory studies can reveal much about the physiology of the human body, but they can say nothing about humor, cultural taboos, or why one chooses a particular spouse or is drawn toward particular music. More importantly for our purposes, science has no means of proving or disproving the worldwide phenomenon of belief in spiritual realities.

J. P. Moreland in his book, *Love Your God with All Your Mind*, pointed out that "some propositions believed outside science ... are better justified than some believed within science."[19] Moreland correctly understood that there are some things about reality in which we have a stronger sense of their truthfulness than what science can teach us. I know innately, without a shadow of doubt, that it was wrong for Islamic terrorists to destroy the World Trade Center and kill thousands of innocent people (moral truth). This fact is far more real to me than my understanding of the process of photosynthesis (a scientific truth). And it is infinitely more real to me than many scientific claims that are merely speculation, such as abiogenesis.

3. Nonscientific Truth Can Be Ascertained

A third response to Scientism is to demonstrate that areas of knowledge in which science has no authority, such as religion, can be confirmed to be factual.

In my book, *Christianity on the Offense*,[20] I explain how the inductive approach for determining truth is the methodology applied in most areas of knowledge. Historical truth, legal truth, religious truth, and most of the decisions we make in everyday life all depend on inductive reasoning. In fact, the application of inductive reasoning is the same method used by science to determine scientific truth. This procedure is called the "scientific method."

The scientific method (inductive reasoning) is the process of accumulating a preponderance of reliable evidences in order to reach a probable conclusion—to reach the highest level of certainty attainable in the area under investigation. In science, this involves observation, experimentation, and verification. But the scientific method is not limited to just empirical science. This same truth-test is used to verify everything from the odds of winning the lottery to the guilt or innocence of a murder suspect. It's the method used to ascertain the historicity of George Washington as well as to establish the likelihood of dying in a plane crash. It is the same truth-test doctors use to diagnose an illness, stockbrokers use to direct their investments, and consumers use to select a reliable used car. In all these instances, decisions are based on their probable outcome—not absolute, mathematical certainty.

Religion is no different. We can't prove or disprove religious truth through scientific observation or experimentation because that approach doesn't apply. Yet the vast amount of accumulated evidence demonstrates "to a moral certainty beyond reasonable doubt" (to use the legal phrase), that Christian truth-claims are valid. To the highest level of certainty attainable in the area of religious truth, we can demonstrate that God exists, the Bible is His only authentic written revelation, and that Jesus Christ died for our sins and rose from the grave to redeem us.[21]

Because we can't verify something "scientifically" doesn't mean it can't be proven or that it's not true. If naturalists reject knowledge that does not pass through the filter of Scientism, to be consistent, they will also have to deny all legal, historical, aesthetic, philosophical, and other nonscientific truths.

Endnotes

1. William J. Bennett, *The Index of Leading Cultural Indicators; American Society at the End of the 20th Century* (New York: Broadway Books, 1999), 5.

2. "One Nation Under God—Sort of," *Christianity Today*, January 2004, 34.

3. Nancy R. Pearcey, *Total Truth: Liberating Christianity from Its Cultural Captivity* (Wheaton: Crossway Books, 2004), 111.

4. Phillip E. Johnson, *The Wedge of Truth; Splitting the Foundations of Naturalism* (Downers Grove: InterVarsity Press, 2000), 13.

5. Phillip E. Johnson, *Darwin on Trial* (Downers Grove: InterVarsity Press, 1991), 114–115.

6. Quoted in Charles Colson and Nancy Percey, *How Now Shall We Live?* (Wheaton: Tyndale House Publishers, 1999), 122.

7. Quoted in Scott Klusendorf, "Death with a Happy Face: Peter Singer's Bold Defense of Infanticide," *Christian Research Journal*, Vol. 23, Num. 3, 2001, 25.

8. Quoted in Colson and Percey, *How Now Shall We Live?*, 123.

9. Nancy R. Pearcey, *Total Truth: Liberating Christianity from Its Cultural Captivity*, Study Guide Edition (Wheaton: Crossway Books, 2005), 493.

10. Cheryl Eckstein, ed. "Infanticide: Part One. Infanticide and Nonvoluntary Euthanasia As Practiced in the Netherlands," CHN [Compassionate Healthcare Network] Info Series. (downloaded 12–13-05, http://www.chninternational.com/chninfo3.htm), 1.

11. Francis J. Beckwith and Gregory Koukl, *Relativism; Feet Firmly Planted in Mid-Air* (Grand Rapids: Baker books, 1998), 160.

12. Phillip E. Johnson, *The Right Questions; Truth, Meaning, & Public Debate* (Downers Grove: InterVarsity Press, 2002), 36.

13. Ibid., 37.

14. Pearcey, *Total Truth*, 214.

15. Johnson, *The Wedge of Truth*, 14.

16. J.P. Moreland, *Love Your With All Your Mind; The Role of Reason in the Life of the Soul* (Colorado Springs: NavPress, 1997), 145.

17. Pearcey, *Total Truth*, 110, 176–177.

18. Moreland, *Love Your God with all Your Mind*, 146.

19. Ibid., 147.

20. Dan Story, *Christianity on the Offensive: Responding to the Beliefs and Assumptions of Spiritual Seekers,* (Grand Rapids: Kregel Publications, 1988), chapter 6.

21. The same criteria that demonstrates Christianity is true falsifies all non-Christian religions, philosophies, and worldviews. I also develop this theme in my book, *Christianity on the Offense: Responding to the Beliefs and Assumptions of Spiritual Seekers,* (Grand Rapids: Kregel Publications, 1988), chapter 6.

Postmodernism
Moral Relativism, Religious Pluralism, and the New Tolerance

I BEGAN TO STUDY Christian apologetics in the early 1980s. Back then, tough-minded non-Christians typically responded to the Gospel by saying, "How do you know Jesus rose from the dead? Can you prove it?" Or they'd say, "The Bible is full of contradictions. Its been copied and changed for so many centuries, you can't possibly know it's true."

At this point, Christian evangelists trained in apologetics would switch from the Gospel to apologetics.[1] We would demonstrate why Christians know for sure that Jesus rose from the dead. We would harmonize alleged contradictions with the biblical text. We would provide evidence that the Bible is historically reliable. With the aid of the Holy Spirit, we tried to convince people that Christianity is *true*. This approach worked well until the 1990s. Most people—Christians and non-Christians—accepted the reality of objective, absolute truth. They differed over what constituted truth, but they agreed that truth existed and appealed to evidence and reasoned arguments to support their perspectives.

This is not always the case today. Successful apologetic tactics used during the twentieth century are sometimes ineffective now. Why? Because during the last decades of the twentieth century, a profound and socially jarring worldview shift occurred relating to how people view truth. Modern critics of Christianity repeatedly deny the effectiveness of human reasoning and reject the notion of absolute truth. As a result, it's common for a person to say something like this, "You're so intolerant! What gives you the right to claim Jesus is the only way to God? Even the Bible says, 'Do not judge so that you will not be judged.' Muslims, Mormons, Buddhists—all are equal. What difference does it make if they see God differently?"

Called postmodernism, this new, politically charged, and highly influential worldview is a radical departure from "modernism," and it has ushered in a revolutionary new set of presuppositions and values that we must confront. Before we learn how to do this, however, we need to explore why postmodernism is rapidly dominating a society that for centuries acknowledged absolute truth in most areas of knowledge and trusted in people's ability to reason and understand.

Modernism

In order to fully understand postmodernism, we must first understand modernism. Postmodernism arose from the ashes of modernism.

The Christian worldview generally was unchallenged in Western culture from the fourth century until the eighteenth century. By the eighteenth century Enlightenment, Christianity began to lose its standing as the dominant worldview in Western culture. Many people's interests moved away from religious issues toward philosophy and science. Human reasoning began to take precedence over divine revelation. Ultimately, most people came to view science as the supreme source of truth and knowledge. Modernism, then, is the term used to delineate the period of history that began during the eighteenth-century Enlightenment and continued until the last decade of the twentieth century. Modernism, as a worldview, attempted "to subsume all reality and all knowledge under the rubric of rationalistic scientific objectivity."[2]

In some ways, modernism and Christianity have similar views of reality. Both reject the irrational subjectivism and relativism of postmodernism, and both acknowledge that universal, absolute truth exists and can be discovered. However, modernism rejects God and anything that smacks of the supernatural. Secular humanism, with its naturalistic underpinnings, is a progeny of the modernist era.

The Industrial Revolution greatly influenced the modernist era. At the same time secular and scientific revolutions were taking place, the Industrial Revolution exploded on the scene. By the end of the nineteenth century, people widely believed that science and technology would solve the world's problems. Together, they would eliminate disease, feed the world's hungry, abolish poverty, and end war. It was a time of great optimism and immense faith in the capabilities of humanity. This helped to push religious beliefs to the fringes of society and elevate human reasoning and science as being sufficient unto themselves for discovering and understanding all truth. Who needs God?

Unfortunately (for secularists), but not surprising to many Christians, the modernist's "pie in the sky" became mud on the face. By the end of the twentieth century, it had become increasingly clear that modernists' goals had failed. Rather than science and technology leading to utopia, the twentieth century had become worse off in many ways than during the nineteenth century. Humankind experienced economic collapse during the Great Depression, two World Wars, the butchery of Nazism and Communism, the proliferation of nuclear weapons with the potential for doomsday, terrible worldwide environmental degradation (in spite of technology that could halt it), the spread of new and deadly diseases, and widespread greed, political corruption, moral decline, and famine. These things convinced many in the West that modernism, in spite of its scientific and technological gains, could not solve the world's problems. Consequently, during the last decades of the twentieth century, secular humanists turned to a new paradigm of reality called postmodernism.

Postmodernism is a present-day reaction to the failure of modernism. Sadly, rather than returning to the West's Judeo/Christian roots, increasing numbers of secular humanists (especially in academia) are embracing postmodernism as a replacement for bankrupt modernism.

Postmodernism

Largely a Western intellectual phenomenon, postmodernism has dramatically impacted contemporary culture. It's responsible for an ongoing worldview shift of such magnitude that it is radically changing the way people think and behave in practically every area of knowledge including science, history, law, education, sociology, psychology, entertainment, ethics, and religion. The greatest danger with postmodernism and where it most aggressively attacks Christian values is academia. Many Christian apologists believe that *postmodernism is the most dangerous adversary* of the church today. As one author writing for the *Christian Research Journal* states, "Today the church faces a challenge far greater than the Renaissance, potentially more divisive than the Reformation, and more insidious in its inroads into the life of the church itself than the secularist rationalism of the Enlightenment. I am referring to postmodernism."[3] Two key presuppositions form the philosophical infrastructure of postmodernism. Both directly oppose the governing principles of modernism and lay a foundation for the principle doctrines of postmodernism.

1. There Are No Absolute Truths

Modernism subscribes to the belief that absolute, universal truths exist that can be apprehended intellectually and established scientifically.[4] The laws of logic are valid and foundational to thinking and communicating. Truth is objective and true whether one believes it or not. It's not situational, nor relative to one's culture milieu. Truth exists independent of people's personal beliefs, feelings, and experiences; it's "out there" waiting to be discovered by science and applied through technology. People can gain real knowledge about nature and the cosmos that are universal in application and content.

Postmodernism, on the other hand, rejects the existence of absolute truth in any area of knowledge—including science, history, law, psychology, education, sociology, ethics, and religion—and assumes that no area of knowledge produces absolute truth. Objective facts are nonexistent. "Truth" is relative, situational, and subject to redefinition and reinterpretation.

Today, American courts play loosely with the U.S. Constitution, because it is no longer viewed as absolute authority. What's important now is how the courts decide to interpret it. Activist judges read into the Constitution "freedoms" such as abortion and same-sex marriage that the original intent of the Constitution never had. As a result, some judges no longer interpret laws; they make laws according to their own moral and social prejudices. Consider, for example, that the U.S. Courts of Appeals declared the Federal Partial Birth Abortion Ban unconstitutional. The majority of Americans believe that aborting a baby that's almost completely out of the womb is appalling, as did the legislature that passed the ban. But a handful of judges disagreed, so the ban was thrown out.

We see a similar philosophy at work in our educational system. Many students are taught that all moral values are equally legitimate and that they should "clarify" their own values. They are encouraged to bypass "religious and moral dogmas" that tell students how they ought to behave and instead "probe their own subjective feelings and values" and select those values which they personally prefer.[5]

In postmodern, secular America, ethics are largely in the eyes of the beholder. A postmodernist may say, "Pornography may be wrong to you and right to someone else," and that's acceptable. Abortion and homosexuality were considered evil in the past, but are no longer today because we are now living under the umbrella of a morally relativist worldview.

2. *"Truth" Is Culturally Conditioned*

The second key postmodern presupposition is likewise the antithesis of modernism. Postmodernism rejects the faculty of human reasoning as a means to discovering absolute truth (even if it did exist). Why? Because postmodernists believe that what people think is objective knowledge is actually a byproduct of their own cultures—the thoughts and feelings they are conditioned to believe by the societies in which they live.

According to postmodern thinking, people can't escape their personal life history and the influence of the traditions, interpretations, and corporate experiences of their cultural heritage. People are so immersed in their cultures that "reality" (what is real) and culture are inseparable. Consequently, people are a product of what their culture makes them; cultures actually determine—"script"—people's thoughts and attitudes. As pastor and apologist Craig Loscalzo put it, "Reality is a mental construct. . . . [and] absolutes are a myth of an earlier, naive generation."[6] The following chart illustrates fundamental differences between modernism and postmodernism.

Modernism vs. Postmodernism

Modernism	**Postmodernism**
Absolute truth exists in many areas of knowledge.	No absolute truth in any area of knowledge.
Truth is objective.	Truth is subjective.
Truth is attained through human reasoning.	Human reasoning does not lead to truth.
Truth is universal.	No universal truths.
People are primarily physical beings.	People are primarily social beings.
Intrinsically bound to naturalism and secular humanism. Denies the need for God.	Grounded in naturalism and secular humanism. Gives rise to moral and religious relativism. Can have spiritual dimensions.

Flowing from the two key presuppositions of postmodernism are three closely related doctrines that permeate virtually all aspects of modern society: moral relativism, religious pluralism, and a redefined philosophy of tolerance.

Moral Relativism

Relativism, the cardinal doctrine of postmodernism, is intrinsic to every dimension of this worldview. In fact, relativism is the foremost apologetic issue of our times. It is not the most important apologetic issue we must confront (defending the Bible's truth and reliability, Jesus' resurrection, and His deity are far more crucial issues), but it is arguably the most common apologetic related obstacle we as Christians will encounter in popular culture.

Conforming to the postmodern presupposition that there are no absolute truths in any area of knowledge, moral relativism teaches that acceptable moral behavior depends on the circumstances that define it. In other words, because peoples' beliefs and experiences vary and are culturally conditioned, moral "truth" is relative to individual and cultural choices. Ethics are situational. Consequently, what was true in the past may not be true today. During my own lifetime, I have seen views on homosexuality evolve from it being a sin to a sickness to an alternative lifestyle to an act that people are encouraged to try.

Not only does moral relativism assert that what was true in the past may not be true any longer, it also declares that what is true for one person may not be true for another. A woman named Karen opposes cohabitation, but people next door who wish to live together prior to marriage consider cohabitation to be perfectly legitimate.

Professor Francis Beckwith, who has written extensively on ethical issues, offered a good working definition of moral relativism: "Moral relativism is the view that when it comes to questions of morality, there are no absolutes and no objective right or wrong; moral rules are merely personal preferences and/or the result of one's cultural, sexual, or ethnic orientation."[7]

To fully grasp how such an alien view of morality evolved into prominence in American culture, we have to understand the formative role played by philosophical naturalism. (See chapter twenty-six.) The roots of moral relativism dig deeply into the twentieth-century's naturalistic worldview. Let's recall the following observation:

- If naturalism is true, there is no God.
- It there is no God, people are elevated to supreme beings, and there is no basis for moral absolutes.
- Without absolute standards of right and wrong, and if people are supreme beings, ethics arise from human feelings and experiences.

Since individual cultures and people differ in their acceptance or rejection of particular moral behaviors (e.g. abortion and homosexuality), and since no absolute higher authority exists to say whose view is correct (e.g. God), it logically follows that all moral perspectives must be equally true and acceptable.

See how this works? If people are supreme, they set the standards even if they are in opposition to each other. And you and I are supposed to accept all as valid because there is no higher authority to say that anyone's views are wrong.

In a word, without God there is no ultimate "good" to identify what is ultimately "bad." Moral behavior is descriptive rather than prescriptive. It's how we act, not how we ought to act. "Sin" in an absolute sense is nonexistent. As Nancy Pearcey wrote, "Many people do not believe in a transcendent moral standard; if you speak about guilt, they think you're talking about a psychological problem that requires therapy, not about true moral guilt that requires forgiveness."[8]

We'll explore an apologetics to moral relativism in chapter twenty-nine.

Religious Pluralism

Although modernism and naturalism, as worldviews, are essentially atheistic, postmodernism is not. In fact, many postmoderns are open to religious beliefs and are spiritual seekers. Unfortunately, however, most postmodern spiritual seekers are gravitating toward New Age ideologies rather than Christianity. New Age thinking is simply more in harmony with their beliefs.[9] Religious postmodernists seek subjective experiences rather than objective revelation. This New Age reasoning leads naturally to religious pluralism.

Pluralism is the word used to describe the belief that reality consists of many instead of one. Religious pluralism, then, teaches that "the major world religions provide independent salvific access to the divine Reality."[10]

This can mean two things: that all of the diverse, distinct religious beliefs are independently true and legitimate, and that there is only one "Ultimate Reality" to which all world religions relate but in different ways.[11] The Hindu god, Krishna, supposedly expressed this view in the *Bhagavad-Gita*: "In any way that men love me, in that same way they find my love: for many are the paths of men, but they all in the end come to me."[12]

In popular parlance, religious pluralistic philosophy is expressed in remarks such as:

- "Jesus, Buddha, Mohammed—all are prophets of God."
- "All religions are paths to the same mountaintop."
- "All religions are true; they're just different."
- "Christianity may be all right for you, but I prefer Hinduism [or whatever]."

And Christians and like-minded people who recognize and highlight the irrationality of such claims are quickly categorized as bigoted:

- "What gives you the right to claim that Christianity is the only true religion."
- "You Christians are so intolerant; you think you have a monopoly on God."

Religious pluralism is relativism played out in the spiritual arena. In postmodern America, it has become fashionable to promote this view. It's "politically correct" to accept all faiths as equally legitimate and to denounce religions—in particular Christianity—that refuse to accept this pluralistic philosophy. Religious pluralism is a serious obstacle to Christianity. It not only destroys the unique, saving work of Jesus Christ on the cross but opens the door to universalism—the fatal belief that everyone will eventually be saved.

In chapter twenty-nine we'll also explore an apologetics to religious pluralism.

The New Tolerance

In his book, *The New Absolutes*, William Watkins observed that the traditional definition of tolerance has changed dramatically in this generation. "I call it new [tolerance] because it is not the kind of tolerance of less than thirty years ago."[13] This "new" tolerance, another doctrine of postmodernism, is a governing policy of both religious pluralism and moral relativism. Let's start by comparing yesterday's definition of tolerance with today's.

Prior to the 1970s, the idea of tolerance had to do with how one person treated another person. We might have disagreed with a person's viewpoint—even opposed and tried to refute it—but "being tolerant" meant that we shouldn't demean him and try to prevent him from having and expressing his viewpoint. In a democratic society, people were expected to treat each other with respect and allow each other to have—and even voice—their own opinions without fear of persecution. However, this did not mean that everyone's moral and religious beliefs were equally true and legitimate. Nor did tolerance extend to harmful behavior. People were free (and expected) to debate opposing viewpoints and stop practices that were illegal, dangerous, and detrimental to society. In short, people were free to think as they liked, but they weren't free to behave as they liked.

This is no longer the case. In today's postmodern society, the definition of tolerance has drastically changed. Watkins described this new tolerance:

> The tolerant person is someone who is broad-minded, open to other beliefs, lifestyles, claims to truth, and moral conviction. The tolerant person makes room for others to do as they wish, even if their behavior contradicts or mocks his own. The tolerant person believes in "live and let live." The new tolerance doesn't just put up with contrary beliefs or behaviors. It accepts them, makes room for them, honors them, and even strives to protect them. The tolerant person may not adopt any of these beliefs or behaviors as his own, but he will go to the mat to uphold the desires of others to live them out. In short, the new tolerance is non-condemning and

all-protecting *as long as the matters involved are PC compatible* [emphasis his].[14]

So, to say that someone's ideas or behaviors are wrong is to be intolerant. According to postmodern philosophy, everyone's moral values, religious beliefs, and political alliances are equally legitimate and valuable. One never criticizes, disparages, or rejects as illegitimate or wrong anyone's beliefs or behavior. If you do, you're being intolerant. You're bigoted, narrow-minded, and ought to be ostracized from mainstream society. Indeed, you ought to be punished. If people violate the codes of the new tolerance, they are "open to ridicule, rebuke, lawsuits, jail time, fines, and a host of other means to intimidate you into coming in line with the PC [politically correct] standard."[15]

A recent article in *Christianity Today* reported that the Rutherford Institute was representing a "handful" of employees who "lost their jobs for refusing to condone employment policies they found biblically immoral."[16] The article went on to report that, "The cultural war over homosexuality in America has moved to a new front—the workplace. Christian observers say millions of employees are being commanded not just to tolerate homosexual behavior but also to respect and even promote it."[17]

In Sweden, radical egalitarianism has moved to frightening new levels. "A Swedish court sentenced a Pentecostal pastor to one month in prison after finding him guilty of offending homosexuals in a sermon. The case was the first trial test of the national law against incitement as applied to speech about homosexuals."[18]

This so-called tolerance is plainly absurd, unlivable, and inconsistent. Postmodern gurus who promote the new tolerance violate the principles they claim to endorse. They insist that everyone is free to think and behave as they please, and that no one should interfere or try to foist his or her views on another person. But in the next breath, they condemn Christians, and other like-minded people, who adopt a view of reality in which objective, absolute, moral, and religious truth exists. In other words, these people actually teach that the belief and practices of some individuals and groups are more equal than the beliefs and practices of other individuals and groups. This isn't tolerance. As apologist Greg Koukl pointed out:

> Most of what passes for tolerance today is not tolerance at all, but rather intellectual cowardice. Those who hide behind the myth of neutrality are often afraid of intelligent engagement. Unwilling to be challenged by alternate points of view, they don't engage contrary opinions or even consider them. It's easier to hurl an insult "you intolerant bigot" than to confront the idea and either refute it or be changed by it.[19]

This redefined philosophy of tolerance tremendously pressures individuals to conform to postmodern values. William Watkins forcefully describes how intolerant proponents of the new tolerance are toward "nonconformers."

> Nonconformers are considered racists, sexists, homophobes, Victorian prudes, religious zealots, terrorist-like fundamentalists, anti everything that PC [political correct] considers good. Non-PCers are never allowed to be pro anything. If we call ourselves pro-life, we are labeled anti-choice. If we say we are pro-family, we are told we are anti-women or anti-gay. If we present ourselves as pro-marriage, we are reported as being intolerant moralists and antagonistic toward single mothers. If we say we are for parental involvement and choice in education, then we are said to be against children's rights and quality education. If we uphold character and performance as the true measure for job placement and advancement, then we are looked upon a racists or suppressors of the poor and needy. If we are not PC, we are ostracized in the name of tolerance and diversity.[20]

This new paradigm of tolerance/intolerance, which attacks the fundamental values and principles of biblical Christianity, is now widely taught in American colleges and universities. Growing numbers of academic leaders apply the iron rod of this new tolerance to force conformity to moral and political agendas of postmodernism. This is nowhere more evident than the ideology referred to as multiculturalism and its bedfellow, political correctness.

Endnotes

1. There are three primary approaches one can choose in evangelism: law, Gospel, or apologetics. During every witnessing opportunity, one (or a combination) will be selected. I develop this principle in my book, *Engaging the Closed Minded* (Grand Rapids: Kregel Publications, 1999), chapter one.

2. Donald T. Williams, "The Great Divide; The Church and the Postmodernist Challenge," *Christian Research Journal*, Vol. 26, No. 02, 35.

3. Ibid.

4. The belief in absolute, universal truths is not the offspring of modernism. Classical philosophers such as Socrates, Plato, and Aristotle believed that knowledge was objective and that eternal ideals such as truth and goodness existed. Likewise the Old and New Testaments unequivocally taught absolute, transcendent truths—spiritual and moral.

5. Nancy R. Pearcey, *Total Truth: Liberating Christianity from Its Cultural Captivity* (Wheaton: Crossway Books, 1004), 239–240.

6. Craig A. Loscalzo, *Apologetic Preaching; Proclaiming Christ to a Postmodern World* (Downers Grove: InterVarsity Press, 2000), 68.

7. Francis J. Beckwith, "Why I Am Not a Moral Relativist," in Normal L. Geisler and Paul K. Hoffman, eds., *Why I Am a Christian; Leading Thinkers Explain Why They Believe* (Grand Rapids: Baker Books, 2001), 15.

8. Pearcey, *Total Truth*, 119.

9. Dennis Hollinger, "The Church as Apologetic; A Sociological of Knowledge Perspective," in Timothy R. Phillips & Dennis L. Okholm, eds., *Christian Apologetics in the Postmodern World* (Downers Grove: InterVarsity Press, 1995), 186.

10. Dennis L. Okholm and Timothy R. Phillips, gen. eds., *Four Views on Salvation in a Pluralistic World* (Grand Rapids: Zondervan Publishing House, 1996), 17.

11. Ibid.

12. Quoted in Paul Copan, *Deflating the Slogans That Leave Christians Speechless* (Minneapolis: Bethany house Publishers, 1998), 74.

13. William D. Watkins, *The New Absolutes* (Minneapolis: Bethany House Publishers, 1996), 209.

14. Ibid.

15. Ibid.

16. North American Report: "Corporate thought police," *Christianity Today*, January, 2004, 26.

17. Ibid.

18. Lars Grip, "No Free Speech in Preaching," *Christianity Today*, September, 2004, 23.

19. Greg Koukl, "The Intolerance of Tolerance," *Southern California Christian Times*, March 2000, 7.

20. Watkins, *The New Absolutes*, 209–210.

POSTMODERN POLICE
Multiculturalism and Political Correctness

IT'S IRONIC THAT a worldview that supposedly promotes tolerance has resulted in a rigid, enforced political stronghold in American culture. Whereas most Christians believe people should be free to pursue their own religious and political agendas (even when we disagree with them), postmodernism exerts tremendous pressure (especially on college students) to comply with freedom-stifling ideologies. This is vividly seen in multiculturalism and its enforcer, political correctness.

Multiculturalism

Multiculturalism literally means "many cultures." However, in popular parlance it implies more than just a society being composed of many distinct cultures or ideologies, as in Europe and America. Nor does it merely imply, as some believe, that people should seek to understand and appreciate other cultures. Rather this word carries definite connotations that are loaded with philosophical, educational, and political goals and meanings. As Colson and Pearcey observed, "Multiculturalism is not about appreciating folk cultures; it's about the dissolution of the individual into the tribal group."[1]

Like other postmodern doctrines, multiculturalism rests on two key presuppositions we examined earlier: objective, absolute, universal truth is nonexistence because (second) everyone's interpretation of reality (what they mistakenly perceive as "truth") is actually scripted by the experiences, opinions, and perspectives of their cultural landscape.

Building on these foundational presuppositions, multiculturalism goes a step further. If truth is relevant only to one's cultural interpretations, and since entire cultures differ in beliefs, opinions, and so on, no single culture (especially dominant ones such as American culture) is superior to any other. Thus, all cultures are equal. Beliefs, traditions, and customs in one culture are just as "true" and legitimate as those in any other culture. No culture, according to multiculturalism, has a right to impose its beliefs and practices on another culture, and no culture has a right to suppress the beliefs and practices of another culture.

This philosophy also encompasses minority groups within larger societies such as gays, lesbians, blacks, feminists, and so on (or a combination of one or more). In particular, multiculturalists emphasize that progressive, dominant cultures such as American and European (or white Anglo-Saxons) cultures have no right to impose their values or religious beliefs on repressed or less-dominant cultures and groups.

This philosophy is particularly prevalent, proclaimed, and propagated in Western universities and colleges. William Watkins commented on this:

> Under the guise of a new approach to education, they [multiculturalists] want to rid the classroom of what they call a eurocentric, ethnocentric, white-male-dominated, racist, heterosexist education. The emphasis on Western civilization—its history, religious foundations, intellectual and political movements, and achievements—must be marginalized in the curriculum and radically reinterpreted. In addition, they want to inaugurate studies that deride the West as bigoted and oppressive, as they uphold non-Western societies and other "oppressed peoples" as monuments to human fulfillment and keys to freedom. The multiculturalists want Euro-

Americans to stop looking at the rest of the world through Western glasses, which they justly identify with the Greco-Roman-Judeo-Christian heritage. Instead, they want us to evaluate all non-Western cultures according to the standards of those cultures alone. In other words, multiculturalists are opposed to the old absolute: *Western civilization and its heritage should be studied and valued above others.* They want everyone to accept the new absolute they embrace: *Non-Western societies and other oppressed peoples and their heritage should be studied and valued above Western civilizations* (emphasis his).[2]

Students who disagree with this philosophy, who fail to recognize its legitimacy or challenge its inconsistency and irrationality, are pigeon-holed as narrow-minded and intolerant (i.e. racists, homophobes, male chauvinists, and so on).

Now we can understand why Marxist ideology still thrives in American universities, observed Nancy Pearcey:

> Marxism retains a powerful influence in many places of the world—especially on the American university campus. A French political philosopher recently said that nowadays when he wants to debate a Marxist, he has to import one from an American university.... These liberation movements [multiculturalism, feminism, and political correctness] ... apply Marxist forms of analysis to groups identified by race or gender, urging them to raise their consciousness and throw off their oppressors. The characters have changed, but it's still the same play.[3]

Not All Cultures Are Equal

Multiculturalists err when they assume that every cultural ideology is equally true or legitimate. As apologists Beckwith and Koukl observed, "Some cultures, like some individuals, have discovered more knowledge and truth than others."[4] Moreover, these authors pointed out, it is wrong to assume that "all cultures have contributed to human progress and knowledge equally.... Western values—

whether scientific, philosophical, economic or moral—have proved to be vastly superior. Those societies that have embraced Western values, whether geographically in the Far East or in the West, reveal this."[5]

Multiculturalism, especially as it plays out in university and college campuses, fosters a radical egalitarianism where even the most bizarre and degenerate behavior is endorsed and legitimized. Ultimately, this variety of multiculturalism can only lead to nihilism, social anarchy, moral relativism, and censorship. Beckwith and Koukl concluded, "Strong multiculturalism ... forces us to tolerate barbarism in order to avoid being accused of ethnocentrism. On the authority of flimsy dogma, it requires that we become closed-minded to the possibility of objective truth, all in the name of inclusiveness, tolerance, and sensitivity."[6]

Political Correctness

Multiculturalists view human history as being dominated by the attempts of various cultures to manipulate and impose their beliefs on other cultures. Multiculturalists believe that the "Christianized" West is exerting its power by oppressing and marginalizing non-Western societies and subgroups (non-Christian religions, ethnic groups, homosexuals, women, etc.) to maintain its own status in world civilization. "This ought not to be," clamor the multiculturalists. "This must be changed, and political correctness is a means of achieving this change."

So, to be "politically correct," one must adhere to the creeds and dogma of multiculturalism. This requires that:

> One must be pro-feminists, pro-gay rights, pro-minority studies, mistrustful of tradition, scornful of Dead White European males and deeply skeptical toward the very idea of a "masterpiece," because it implies that one idea, culture or human being can actually be better than another. . . . [For example,] Shakespeare is deemed to be racist, sexist, and classist—a product of the ultimate evil, Western civilization."[7]

In order to impose their ideologies on society, multiculturalists advance a rigid language code—especially in universities and colleges.

The idea is to dictate what is permissible to say (correct) and what is impermissible to say (incorrect) in the community. This, claim multiculturalists, will remove certain words and phrases that may be interpreted as denigrating people's racial and ethnic backgrounds, religious beliefs and practices, sexual orientations, and so on. For example, the University of Michigan sought (and failed because it violated First Amendment rights) to punish "any behavior, verbal or physical, that stigmatizes or victimizes an individual on the basis of race, ethnicity, religion, sex, sexual orientation, creed, national origin, ancestry, age, marital status, handicap, or Vietnam-era veteran status."[8]

If the genuine (and only) intent of political correctness were to remove racial and ethnic barriers, it would be a noble quest. But there is a sinister side to political correctness that strives not just to create an atmosphere of peace and acceptance among divergent cultures and groups, but to radically transform societies to fit the political and moral ideologies of multiculturalism. This is done by controlling how people speak.

Postmodernists recognize that people communicate and think through language—words. However, languages vary from culture to culture. For this reason, postmodernists believe people interpret reality differently according to the words used in their respective cultures. However, here's where the perverse side of political correctness comes into play. If it's true that language determines how people think and communicate, if you want to change society what would you do? You'd change the language—the way people talk—in order to change the way they think and behave.

This is exactly what multiculturalists try to accomplish under the guise of politically correct speech. Contrary to what many people think, a key goal of political correctness is not just to teach sensitivity to people's feelings and beliefs, but rather its purpose is to transform society. Words, multiculturalists realize, don't just allow us to apprehend truth; words change or create "truth." So, changing the language actually creates a new reality. For instance, if you want to change people's negative view of abortion, you redefine a fetus. Instead of calling it an unborn baby, one calls it "a product of conception," or "reproductive tissue." Gradually, people no longer think of a fetus as a human being or baby, but as a piece of tissue without a soul.

Likewise, if you want to change people's views on homosexuality, you don't call a homosexual by admittedly derogatory terms such as "queer" and "fag," rather you use the terms "gay" or "lesbian." It's not "abnormal behavior"; it's an "alternate lifestyle." Soon people are thinking of homosexuality in positive terms, not in negative terms.

This is political correctness undressed, and it demonstrates why we must oppose it in spite of its positive features. The agenda of political correctness, like multiculturalism, is to destroy moral and religious principles that have successfully guided Western civilization for two millenniums.

Endnotes

1. Charles Colson and Nancy Pearcey, *How Now Shall We Live?* (Wheaton: Tyndale House Publishing, 1999), 23.

2. William D. Watkins, *The New Absolutes* (Minneapolis: Bethany House Publishers, 1996), 194.

3. Nancy R. Pearcey, *Total Truth: Liberating Christianity from Its Cultural Captivity* (Wheaton: Crossway Books, 2004), 135.

4. Francis J. Beckwith and Gregory Koukl, *Relativism; Feet Firmly Planted in Mid-Air* (Grand Rapids: Baker Books, 1998), 81.

5. Ibid., 94.

6. Ibid., 95.

7. Probe Ministries, *Survival Mind Games Course* (Richardson, TX: Probe Ministries, 1998), VI–19.

8. Quoted in Ibid., VI–21.

APOLOGETICS TO POSTMODERNISM
Refuting Secular Beliefs and Morals

FOR CENTURIES, rational arguments supported by objective evidences have been the foundation of Christian apologetics.[1] These arguments have been successful because most people, until fairly recently, accepted the existence of absolute truth, the authority of logic, and the efficacy of human reasoning.

Today, however, some Christian apologists tend to abandon evidential and classical apologetic tactics under the pretense that people today view reality differently. "Past apologetic tactics," they say, "are not effective today because many postmodernists, especially in academia, are unwilling to accept truth statements, especially Christian." Is this an accurate assessment? Are traditional apologetic arguments and evidences no longer effective in postmodern America? Let's explore this.

Is Traditional Apologetics Useful Today?

The concern that traditional apologetic tactics may not be useful today has prompted some Christian apologists to suggest that Christians must avoid making any propositional truth-claims and must make their case from a wholly *subjective* point of view because the worldviews of many people ignore logic, seek to circumvent rational discourse, and deny the possibility of discovering absolute truth. These people often shrug us off with quips such as:

- "Well, that may be true for you, but it's not for me."
- "It's okay if you want to be a Christian; I don't mind, but it's not for me."
- "That's your interpretation; I have my own."
- "Judge not lest you be judged."

Although successfully communicating apologetics in our postmodern world may necessitate adding a few subjective weapons to our apologetic arsenal, I disagree that traditional apologetics are ineffective today. In fact, Christian apologists who sidestep the issue of absolute truth, especially in terms of Christian truth-claims, are making a serious tactical error that will greatly diminish their effectiveness in countering postmodernism.

Christianity, after all, is a history-based religion grounded on specific historical events that actually occurred. (See 1 Corinthians 15:3–8.) One cannot separate the first coming of Jesus Christ, the Day of Pentecost described in Acts 2, Jesus' resurrection, and other historical events from the spiritual truths that flow out of them. This historical "rootedness" separates Christianity from all other religions. If we can't demonstrate, therefore, that the Bible reveals genuine knowledge, wisdom, and absolute truth, Christianity becomes just one more dish in the smorgasbord of available religions. Rather than hiding from the reality of absolute truth and the veracity of sound reasoning, our first apologetic task, when confronting postmodernism, is to establish that Christianity rests on verifiable historical facts and presents absolute, objective truth—not subjective opinions.

Fortunately, in spite of what critics may say, this approach works. As C. S. Lewis pointed out,

> One of the things that distinguishes man from the other animals is that he wants to know things, wants to find out what reality is

like, simply for the sake of knowing.... Christianity claims to give an account of *facts*—to tell you what the real universe is like.... If Christianity is untrue, then no honest man will want to believe it, however helpful it might be: if it is true, every honest man will want to believe it, even if it gives him no help at all.[2]

Most ordinary people we meet still maintain beliefs that depend on absolute truth. Even people who verbally endorse postmodernism and preach relativism do not (as we'll see) live consistently with this philosophy. It's easy to tout moral relativism at a party or in a classroom, but in the real world most people still think and behave in terms of moral absolutes and still accept the trustworthiness of logic and reason in most areas of life.

Six Apologetic Responses to Postmodernism

Although these responses are not purely "evidential apologetics"[3] in their entirety, because they are tailored to a postmodern non-Christian, the reader will notice that each employs sound logic, assumes that absolute truths exist, and credits non-Christians with the ability to use their brains rationally and objectively.

1. Postmodernism Is Destroying the Moral Fabric of America

The first and simplest way to respond to postmodernism, as well as the whole secular/naturalistic worldview, is to demonstrate that it is destroying the moral fabric of America.

A worldview is not just a philosophy of life; it's a blueprint for living. It sets the moral and social standards by which people in a culture think and behave. All worldviews must possess several necessary ingredients if they are to sustain a healthy, civilized society.[4] One of these is that it must promote moral virtues. History has shown that civilizations that degenerate morally ultimately collapse. Is today's postmodern world healthy? Decidedly no. Consider these statistics from William Bennett's, *The Index of Leading Cultural Indicators*:

Since 1960, our population has increased 48 percent. But since 1960, even *taking into account* recent improvements, we have seen a 467 percent increase in violent crime; a 463 percent increase in the numbers of state and federal prisoners; a 461 percent increase in out-of-wedlock births; more than a 200 percent increase in the percentage of children living in single-parent homes; more than a doubling in the teenage suicide rate; a more than 150 percent increase in the number of Americans receiving welfare payments; an almost tenfold increase in the number of cohabiting couples; a doubling of the divorce rate; and a drop of almost 60 points on SAT scores. Since 1973, there have been more than 35 million abortions.[5]

These kinds of statistics give ample evidence that America's moral stability under the flag of postmodernism has rapidly declined during the past few decades.

As we noted earlier, it is no coincidence that during the same four decades in which the influence of Christianity in America declined, the moral health of America deteriorated. The moral decay in American culture parallels the diminishing influence of the Christian worldview and its role as moral standard-bearer in society. Remove God from the picture and put people in His place, as postmodernists and naturalists do, and civilization crumbles. Christian apologists can prove this. A wealth of figures available on the Internet, in journals, and in recent books provide ample fodder to support the argument that America (and the rest of Western civilization for that matter) is on the threshold of moral collapse because society as a whole has rejected biblical values and principles.

2. *Believing in Something Doesn't Make It True*

The second response to postmodernism is to point out that believing something is true doesn't automatically make it true. A person can sincerely believe in something and be sincerely wrong. Just because moral relativism and religious pluralism are widely accepted in postmodern society doesn't make them true. Let's look at examples.

A common complaint among postmodernists is that Christians are intolerant of other religions. The postmodern party line is that any religion that meets people's spiritual needs—that "feels" right to them—is just as legitimate as Christianity. The danger here is that people make what amounts to crucial truth-related decisions based on feelings rather than thinking and facts. What if religions other than Christianity are false?[6] Someone may believe that all religions lead to salvation, but a little thoughtful reflection shows that is nonsense. Although the major world religions sometimes share similar beliefs, especially in the area of moral behavior, these religions nevertheless differ dramatically in terms of the nature of God and how they perceive "salvation." The impersonal, abstract, non-creating god of Hinduism is not compatible with the personal, knowable, creator God of the Bible. They cannot be reduced to a common denominator. Any attempt to do so only succeeds if one distorts both religions.

This same principle applies to ethical issues. The postmodern perspective on moral behavior has more to do with feelings than facts. But "feeling" that a certain behavior is morally acceptable doesn't make it true. Examples of this are legion. Consider these common statements:

- "My husband no longer meets my sexual and emotional needs, so why shouldn't I find fulfillment in another man?"
- "The company has hundreds of pens; why not take a few home?"
- "I'm a good person; God will let me into heaven even if I . . ."
- "So what if I look at pornography, it's not hurting anybody!"
- "I think a woman has a right to have an abortion if she feels like it!"

All of these justifications presuppose moral relativism based on feelings, that is, belief that if something feels okay it must be "true." However, merely believing there is nothing immoral about certain behaviors doesn't necessarily mean it's true.

At first, pointing out that someone can sincerely believe in something and be sincerely wrong may seem like a weak apologetic. But when applied using the Socratic method, it can be an effective tactic to challenge postmodern relativism. Consider the following Socratic questions that challenge beliefs based on feelings rather than on reasoning and evidence.

- "Why do you feel that all religions are true?" (It's logically impossible.)
- "Why would you choose a religion without having any tangible evidence that it's true? What if it's false?" (There is overwhelming evidence demonstrating that only Christianity is true.)
- "Why do you believe an unborn child is not a human being?" (No scientific evidence supports this assumption.)[7]
- "Why do you believe Jesus didn't rise from the grave when He was certified to be dead, was buried, and eyewitnesses talked to him three days later? (Overwhelming historical evidence confirms His resurrection.)

We want postmodern non-Christians to recognize that beliefs based solely on feelings are usually distorted or outright false. Without evidential justification, such beliefs are merely opinions. Asking questions that require thoughtful reflection moves the discussion out of the realm of feelings and unsubstantiated beliefs into the realm of rational thinking. This can lead to more effective apologetic opportunities because thinking people are more likely to consider Christianity—a faith that rests on objective, verifiable facts and absolute truths.

3. Relativism Is a Self-refuting Proposition

A third apologetic response to postmodernism is to demonstrate that relativism—its cardinal doctrine—is a self-refuting proposition. It is stuck in a quagmire of contradictions and inconsistencies.

Relativists claim that absolute truth is a myth and that what people assume to be true are actually subjective interpretations of their cultural experiences and personal feelings. This view is expressed in fashionable statements such as:

"All truth is relative."
"There are no absolutes."
"People have different interpretations; you shouldn't judge them."

Now if I say, "There are no absolute truths," I am making an absolute statement about truth. By claiming there are no absolutes, postmodernists contradict themselves because they make an absolute statement (not a relative statement) about truth! When postmodernists make comments such as, "You can't judge," "you can't be intolerant," "everything is relative," and so on, they are actually making absolute statements about reality. They are endorsing a different set of absolutes.[8]

No one can affirm relativism without refuting it in the process. Indeed, to attempt to persuade someone that relativism is true is to become an absolutist. Norman Geisler expressed this well:

> Those who deny the absolute nature of truth do not believe their view is just another relative view. They claim, at least implicitly, that it is absolutely true. In short, total relativism is self-defeating. Relativism of truth cannot be affirmed as truth unless relativism is false, for it is self-defeating to affirm that it is objectively true for all that truth is not objectively true for all. Absolute truth, therefore, is literally undeniable.[9]

The self-refuting, inconsistent nature of postmodernism permeates many of its dictums. Recognizing and pointing this out is the key to this particular apologetic tactic. The best way to do this is to apply the Socratic method—to challenge a relativist to justify his or her claims. In particular, we want him or her to see the inconsistencies—even hypocrisy—of this position. Here are some scenarios.

    PM: (**postmodernist**): "It's wrong for you to impose your morals on other people!"
    CA: (**Christian apologist**): "Isn't that exactly what you're doing when you tell me that?"

    PM: "No one's beliefs are better than anyone else's."
    CA: "Does this mean my beliefs are as valid as yours?"

    PM "People have a right to believe whatever they want."
    CA: "Then why are you trying to convince me of your view?"

PM: "There is no right or wrong."
CA: "What about that statement? Is it right or wrong?"

PM: "Nothing can be known for sure."
CA: "Does that include your statement?"

PM: "There are no absolutes."
CA: "Are you absolutely certain there are no absolutes?"

PM: "All religions are equally true!"
CA: "If all religions are equally true, then Christianity is false because it claims to be the only true religion. And if Christianity is false, then it's not true that all religions are equally true!"

4. Postmoderns Can't Hide from Logic

Postmodernism also breaks down because relativism violates the most fundamental law of logic, the law of non-contradiction. This basic first principle of logic states that contradicting statements can't both be true.

"A" cannot be both "A" and "non-A" at the same time and in the same relationship.

I'm married to my wife—or I'm not. I can't be married and unmarried at the same time. Likewise, according to the law of non-contradiction, two contradicting religions or moral claims cannot both be correct. It is a violation of this law to claim that "all paths (all religions) lead to God." Either Christianity is true, or another religion is true. They may both be false, but both can't be true. Similarly, a fetus cannot be an unborn child in some cases and mere tissue in another (as our courts insist). This schizophrenic view of the fetus was recently illustrated by the court case, McKnight v. South Carolina, where a homicide conviction was upheld for a drug user's stillbirth.[10] Yet in the case of more than 43,000,000 abortions since the U.S. Supreme Court decision, *Roe v. Wade* (1973), fetuses were obviously considered nonhuman.

Without the law of non-contradiction, and the other laws of logic, it would be impossible to live and think consistently. In a postmodern world, understanding and communication would be unattainable. If contradictions actually existed but were not recognized, there could be no difference between true and false, black and white, or up and down. We can be "logically" justified to insist the street is paved when it's gravel, claim it's sunny when it's overcast, and say our dog is in the yard when he is in the house. Indeed, without the laws of logic and absolute truth as points of reference, it would be impossible to separate lies from the truth.

In spite of this, many postmodernists are simply not influenced by arguments based on logic, such as the self-refuting nature of relativism. The irrationality of their position does not bother them. They assert that rational thought is passé, out-of-date, old fashioned, and no longer relevant in contemporary culture.

A similar response comes from New Agers and others who espouse forms of Eastern religion. They dismiss appeals to the laws of logic by claiming that such laws are merely a Western view of reality. When a person reaches higher levels of consciousness or encounters different realities, they claim, he or she moves beyond Western logic and into a realm of existence where contradictions are meaningless.

Don't let such pseudo-intellectual responses intimidate you. They are merely the same relativistic assertions dressed in different clothing, and our response should be the same—loving people and challenging their assumptions by asking Socratic questions. How do relativists know, for instance, that rationality is passé? Obviously, they just assume it.

Denial of logic is nonsensical and unlivable. People who attempt to do this actually endorse the very laws of logic they deny. Indeed, whatever getting beyond logic entails would require logical thinking to accomplish. As philosopher Mark Hanna put it, "There is no way to escape the horns of the dilemma. The employment of logic in the attempt to refute logic is an implicit acknowledgment of the certainty and absoluteness of logic."[11] Philosopher Thomas Nagel agreed: "Any challenge mounted against reasoning would have to involve reasoning of its own, and this can only be evaluated rationally."[12] Because we are created in the image of God, the laws of logic are built into us. Everyone uses them and lives by them, whether or not people accept or deny their validity.

5. Postmodernism as a Worldview Is Inconsistent

In the broadest sense, a worldview is a set of presuppositions (assumptions) that altogether create a standard by which individuals and their societies interpret all data in order to maintain a consistent and coherent understanding of the whole of reality. However, the presuppositions that form the infrastructure of a worldview are not automatically true. They may be partially true or absolutely false. Obviously, if its foundational presuppositions are false, the worldview that rests on them will also be false. As I pointed out in my book, *Christianity on the Offense*, "What people individually and culturally perceive as reality and believe to be true is largely determined by their particular worldview. Thus, if a worldview distorts reality, truth is likewise distorted."[13]

This brings us to our fifth apologetic response to postmodernism. In order for a worldview to correspond to reality, it must pass at least three tests: (1) it must be internally *and* externally consistent and coherent; (2) answer crucial questions about life and the cosmos that correspond to human nature and experience as universally understood and lived out; and (3) be emotionally and spiritually satisfying.[14]

As we've already seen, postmodernism is consistently *inconsistent* because it's self-refuting and violates the laws of logic. Postmodernism has no legitimate and consistent answers to life's great questions, it promotes beliefs that are out of sync with human nature and experience (e.g. there are no absolutes), and, as we'll see next, is unlivable. The Christian worldview, on the other hand, passes all three "tests." Moreover, unlike postmodernists, Christians can verify their presuppositions apologetically.

The apologetic tactic here is to challenge non-Christians to point out any inconsistencies in the Christian worldview. When they can't, we can lovingly bring them face to face with *their* worldview's inconsistencies. More important, when non-Christians fail to identify inconsistencies in the Christian worldview, the door is open for us to provide biblical perspectives on life's great issues: Why are we here? Where did we come from? What happens to us after death? Why is there so much pain and suffering? Why do we need a Redeemer and Savior?

6. Postmodernism Is Unlivable

Now we come to what I believe is the most effective and clearest demonstration that postmodernism is false—and inconsistent. As we explored earlier, the cardinal doctrine of postmodernism is relativism, which is the underlying assumption of religious pluralism, multiculturalism, political correctness, and moral relativism.

Nevertheless (and here's the key to this apologetic response), regardless of how popular relativism has become in Western culture, it is an unlivable philosophy and lifestyle. In day-to-day life, no one consistently follows the precepts of relativism. It's easy to endorse relativism in the ivory tower where it's safe, no one gets hurt, and where one can argue without committing one's life to it. But bring this philosophy out of the ivory tower and into the real world where it must be lived out—where it affects one's personal life—and suddenly commitment to relativism evaporates.

It's easy to say:

- "A woman has a right to do what she wants with her own body."
- "A homosexual lifestyle is just as legitimate as a heterosexual lifestyle. Why not marry someone of the same sex?"
- "Pornography is guaranteed by freedom of speech. As long as a person doesn't harm anyone else, it's his business what he does in private life."
- "You Christians are living in the Dark Ages. So what if people want to live together before they marry."

But, if the same relativistic principles behind these statements are applied to other areas of life, relativism is suddenly unacceptable. It won't be tolerated.

It's important for us to provide real-life scenarios that demonstrate where postmodern relativism will lead if people were actually to live it out consistently. Postmodern unbelievers need to recognize (and admit) that they won't abide many tenets of unabridged relativism. For example, virtually every civilized person condemns child abuse, rape, cannibalism, slavery, and human sacrifice in the name of religion or moral freedom. Yet if relativism is a valid philosophy of life, all behaviors and religious conduct must be sanctioned. Remember, according to a postmodern worldview there is no absolute, transcendent law from which to condemn these atrocities or any other sick and hideous forms of behavior. All deviant behaviors must be sanctioned in a truly relativistic society. If not, the disciples of relativism are hypocrites and the postmodern worldview is false.

To get around the dilemma that individuals in a relativistic society are free to nurture their own brands of ethics, postmodernists argue that relativism in the moral arena functions on a broad, cultural level. Individuals are not free to behave as they choose. Society, not individuals, sets moral standards, and people must obey the "laws of the land" as dictated by their respective cultures. This evasion doesn't change anything. For one thing, it contradicts relativism. When a culture sets standards that apply to everyone within its control, it's making laws. Laws reflect absolutism, not relativism.

Relativism on a cultural scale still provides no valid means by which immoral actions of an entire society can be condemned (such as keeping slaves, oppressing women, and gassing Jews). Relativism on a cultural scale simply means that the entire society is free to behave as it chooses in spite of doing harm to other cultures. Suicide attacks sponsored by some Middle Eastern nations are a present-day example of cultural sanctioned immorality.

The best way for us to point out the unlivable nature of postmodernism is to ask Socratic questions that move the debate out of the moral comfort zone toward the hard choices a person would have to make in order to live consistently using a relativistic framework. In other words, as Francis Schaeffer suggested, compel them to face the logical conclusions of postmodernism. He wrote, "We ought not first try to move a man away from what he should deduce from his position but towards it.... We try to move him in the natural direction in which his presuppositions would take him. We are then pushing him towards the place where he ought to be, had he not stopped short."[15]

Here are some examples:

- "Do you have any doubt that murder and rape are wrong?"
- "Is sexual relations with children okay?"

- "Is torturing babies for religious purposes acceptable behavior?"
- "Should cannibalism and headhunting in the name of religion be accepted in civilized society?"
- "It was popular in India during the nineteenth century to burn the widow of the deceased on his funeral pyre. Should this be reinstated if East Indians want to practice it again?"
- "Is the degradation of women as promoted in some cultures as good for society as Christianity's teaching on the equality of women?"

Not one person in ten million will endorse such behaviors, regardless of whether rejecting them violates the ideological precepts of postmodern relativism. There are limits to human conduct that apply to everyone. People may talk the talk of relativism, but in most areas of life they live according to absolute standards. In the real world, no sane person will tolerate the ultimate consequences of moral relativism, and no civilized society will allow its people to exercise consistent religious pluralism. There are certain laws that civilization must impose and demand that all people obey. This is absolutism, not relativism!

Remember, an unlivable worldview is a false worldview.

The Cardinal Postmodern Assumption

There's one other thing we must notice before moving on. As you discuss moral issues with non-Christians, a common assumption will underlie practically every argument they muster. They assume that either God does not exist or that He has nothing to say about moral issues. Consider these statements, for example: "If two gay men want to live together, it's no one's business. They're not hurting anyone!" Or, "If a single man sleeps with a prostitute, it's a 'victimless crime'; no one gets hurt."

What's wrong with these statements? They are only valid if a holy, righteous God does not exist. If God does exist and lays out moral guidelines, both choices are immoral. Non-Christians need to see this and understand that these types of statements are only true if God is out of the picture.

A good Socratic question you might use to drive this point home is, "If God exists and says such behavior is wrong, is it okay to disobey

God?" This question can refocus the issue because most Americans believe in a personal God as He is revealed in the Bible.

Subjective Apologetic Tactics

In previous chapters, we've reviewed the fact that postmodernism represents a way of thinking that rejects the concept of absolute truth and the ability of people to reason objectively and independent of cultural parameters. In spite of this, the apologetic tactics we've examined will be effective with most postmodernists. All of us live in a world bound by the laws of logic. All of us necessarily make real-life decisions that depend on reasoning, evidences, and absolutes. In most cases, sharing apologetics with postmodernists is a matter of encouraging them to make religious and moral decisions the same way they make other crucial life decisions.[16]

However, rational arguments and objective evidences do not always convince postmodernists. Some of them want nothing to do with appeals to common sense. These postmodernists generally view "truth" as something that can be known primarily through experience. Therefore, they tend to make decisions, including religious and moral decisions, based primarily on feelings rather than thinking. How do we convince these individuals that Christianity is true? Since they rely almost entirely on feelings and experiences, we must establish a point of contact that reveals Christian truth-claims subjectively. We must provide *evidence* that appeals more to their emotions and feelings than their intellect.

So, the final apologetic response to postmodernism is different from the previous six. Rather than appealing to statistics, logic, and persuasive reasoning, it is subjective in nature, petitioning the emotional side of a person's personality rather than the cognitive side. I'm going to suggest three avenues for doing this.

Lifestyle Evangelism

Nancy Pearcey observed correctly that "it is all but impossible for people to accept new ideas purely in the abstract, without seeing a concrete illustration of what they look like when lived out in practice."[17] We can do this through lifestyle evangelism, providing concrete illustrations of Christianity "lived out in practice." Living out our faith with love and service is a powerful testimony to the truth of Christianity—and it can also provide apologetic opportunities. Non-Christians, drawn to Christianity by our love for them and our lifestyles, are going to be more willing to share their intellectual concerns with an open mind rather than with criticisms.

Lifestyle evangelism is a natural outgrowth of the love God gives us for other people. It has always been the Christian's most successful evangelistic tool. How we live out our beliefs and faith before non-Christians demonstrates that Christianity is true at all levels. It gives meaning and purpose to our lives. It heals us. It changes our behaviors and transforms our minds. The sinful things we once loved to do we avoid doing. We're the same people outwardly, but we are different on the inside because of God's redemptive work.

Non-Christians notice how we respond to life's challenges, how we talk and behave. Our lifestyle can make a tremendous impact on them. If we demonstrate that we possess an inner strength and peace the world can't offer, Christianity can become extremely appealing to people—including those who have never been responsive to direct witnessing or apologetics.

When we become involved in people's lives, reaching out to share in their suffering, coming alongside them during times of tragedy to comfort and encourage, taking time to listen to their worldviews, and offer new directions of thoughts, we create an environment that sets the Holy Spirit free to soften people's hearts and open their minds to Christ.

The apostle Peter wrote in 1 Peter 3:15, "Sanctify Christ as Lord in your hearts, always being ready to make a defense to everyone who asks you to give an account for the hope that is in you." Unfortunately, many apologists stop with this first part of the verse. But Peter added these crucial words, "yet with gentleness and reverence." Paul agrees. He wrote in 2 Timothy 2:24–25, "The Lord's bond-servant must not be quarrelsome, but be kind to all . . . with gentleness correcting those who are in opposition." Gentleness, reverence, kindness—these are the lifestyle attributes of love that must always be expressed in our apologetics.

Personal Testimony

There is something in human nature that causes people to love to hear true-life stories. Thus, the popularity of reality television shows, celebrity magazines, and exposés. Every person—Christian or not—has his or her own story to tell. This can create an apologetic point of contact.

Each one of us as Christians has a story about how we came to faith in Jesus Christ. Our personal testimonies make the objective truths of our faith subjectively real. Sharing how Jesus healed our emotional wounds, delivered us from bondage to addictions, healed our marriages, brought us closer to our children, restored family relationships, improved our standing among coworkers, delivered us from pornography—all such personal encounters with the living Christ demonstrate the reality of Christianity and its power in all areas of our life.

Fiction Stories

The late Bill Bright, author of more than sixty books, co-wrote two novels with Ted Dekker. Referring to them, Bright wrote:

> I have come to the conclusion that a good novel on biblical themes can reach many more people than most theological works. God Himself, upon coming to earth in the form of Jesus of Nazareth, chose stories as His primary mode of communication. He used fiction. We call them parables, but they are stories either way.[18]

Sadly, it's almost impossible to get non-Christians to read Christian books, especially those that openly promote Christian values and beliefs. However, over the last few years, numerous Christian authors have begun to write novels that are subtle in their presentation of the Christian worldview. Many of these novelists, such as Ted Dekker, Randy Singer, and Frank Peretti, are every bit as skillful as popular secular authors in creating exciting, suspenseful plots built around interesting, real-life characters, but without the language and sex that pervades secular novels. Even most secular bookstores carry a selection of popular Christian novels.

In a newsletter essay, Christian apologist Gretchen Passantino commented on "Discovering God Through Stories:"

> Some of the most profound personal and spiritual insights I've ever experienced have grabbed me from the pages of a story. In exquisite story telling I see the creational image of God reflected in authors who created worlds of ideas never pondered before. As a spiritual novice and moral ingenue I encountered and came to understand faithfulness, integrity, courage, humility, and self-discipline through good characters; and betrayal, deceit, cowardice, pride, and self-indulgence through evil ones. I can't count how often God has sneaked up on me in a powerful story, and taught me lessons I wouldn't have willingly learned had he been so obvious as to challenge my stubbornness directly through a Bible study. My actual conversion to Christ came through a fairly ordinary encounter with the straightforward gospel, but the Holy Spirit softened me beforehand through literature, and nurtured me long after through the same manner.
>
> I've used outstanding stories to share some of my most important beliefs with non-Christians who would never listen to an overt preaching of the gospel, but who can be enticed by a good story into thinking for the first time about life after death, justice, morality, and redemption. Mainstream, popular contemporary fiction—if it's good—is a valuable tool of pre-evangelism, seed planting, "soft" apologetics.[19]

Encourage your postmodern friends, or any non-Christian, for that matter, to read a fiction book or attend a play that portrays Christianity in a positive light. Start a book club that meets every week or two to discuss a novel. The idea is to encourage non-Christians to consider aspects of the biblical worldview and compare them with the principles of postmodernism. Which worldview best explains the human condition?

Which one best accounts for people's natural tendency to sin, seek power over other people, put self first, be greedy and lustful, and so on? Which worldview best accounts for the commonality of religious experiences—that is, the worldwide craving for a relationship with God? Most importantly, which worldview—Christian or postmodern—best explains life's great mysteries: Where did I come from? Why am I here? Is there life after death? How do I attain it? These topics often arise in the plots of many novels. All are evangelistic points of contact in which the Christian positions can be corroborated by apologetics.

Not only is Christianity objectively and historically true, it is subjectively true. Instead of only mustering objective evidences and engaging in rational arguments, we can demonstrate through our words and deeds, our personal testimonies and experiences, and even fiction novels that Christianity is true. It meets not only our intellectual needs, but our deepest emotional and spiritual needs. It explains the world in a way that is in complete harmony with reality as most people understand it and live it out.

Our goal in subjective apologetics is to convince non-Christians *from their own points of view*—in their own hearts as well as their minds—that biblical Christianity offers solutions to the issues postmodern relativism can't solve. Biblical Christianity provides the moral guidelines and intellectual gratification that modern society needs.

Spiritual truth is attainable, and we can demonstrate that Christianity is the only path. There is no other option.

Endnotes

1. Many early Christian theologians, such as Thomas Aquinas (thirteenth century) and John Calvin (Reformation era) were apologists. See L. Russ Bush, ed., *Classical Readings in Christian Apologetics, A.D. 100–1800* (Grand Rapids: Academic Books, 1983).

2. C.S. Lewis, *God in the Dock; Essays on Theology and Ethics* (Grand Rapids: William B. Eerdmans Publishing Company, 1994), 108–109.

3. Kenneth D. Boa and Robert M. Bowman, Jr. in their book, *Faith Has Its Reasons: An Integrative Approach to Defending Christianity* (Colorado Springs: NavPress, 2001) provide an outstanding study of various apologetic traditions. With regard to evidential apologetics, they make the following comment on page

159: "In the modern period American evangelical apologetics has been dominated by the **evidentialist** approach. Its emphasis is on the presentation of Christianity as *factual*—as supportable or verifiable by the examination of evidences.... More specifically, evidentialist apologetics argues that these crucial truths can be shown to be highly probable."

4. For a discussion on the necessary ingredients of a valid worldview, see my book, *Christianity on the Offense* (Grand Rapids: Kregel Publications, 1998), chapter four.

5. William J. Bennett, *The Index of Leading Cultural Indicators; American Society at the End of the 20th Century* (Colorado Springs: WaterBrook Press, 1999), 4.

6. Unlike other religions, as I demonstrated throughout this book, Christianity is able to verify its truth-claims with objective, testable evidence.

7. Francis J. Beckwith, "What Does It mean to Be Human," *Christian Research Journal*, Volume 26, Number 03.

8. William D. Watkins, in his book, *The New Absolutes* (Minneapolis: Bethany House Publishers, 1996) developed the thesis that modern society is not so much rejecting absolutes as it is merely trading in old values and beliefs for new values and beliefs: "new absolutes."

9. Norman L. Geisler, "Why I Believe Truth Is Real and Knowable," in *Why I Am a Christian; Leading Thinkers Explain Why They Believe* (Grand Rapids: Baker Books, 2001), 45.

10. Ted Olsen, "Supremely Rejected," *Christianity Today*, Dec. 2003, 19.

11. Mark M. Hanna, *Crucial Questions in Apologetics* (Grand Rapids: Baker Books, 1981), 115.

12. Thomas Nagel, *The Last Word* (New York: Oxford University Press, 1997), 25.

13. Dan Story, *Christianity on the Offensive: Responding to the Beliefs and Assumptions of Spiritual Seekers* (Grand Rapids: Kregel Publications, 1998), 38. Chapter four examines the characteristics of a valid worldview and the importance of understanding the role worldviews play in Christian apologetics.

14. Ibid., 48.

15. Francis A. Schaeffer, *The God Who Is There: Speaking Historic Christianity into the Twentieth Century* (Downers Grove: InterVarsity Press, 1968), 127.

16. I develop this concept fully in my book, *Christianity on the Offensive*, chapter six.

17. Nancy R. Pearcey, *Total Truth: Liberating Christianity from Its Cultural Captivity* (Wheaton: Crossway Books, 2004), 354–355.

18. Ted Dekker and Bill Bright, *Blessed Child* (Nashville: West Bow Press, 2001), 349.

19. "Discovering God through Stories," Gretchen Passantino, *Answers and Action*, 995, 1.

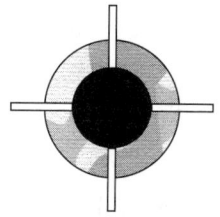

APPENDIX
Practice Socratic Responses

NON-CHRISTIANS frequently raise the following questions or make the following statements during witnessing opportunities. They are listed according to the five divisions of this book. Before you read the suggested responses that follow each question, try to think of your own Socratic counter-questions that challenge the non-Christians to justify and explain their positions. This exercise can be used for individual study, group discussions, and role-playing formats.

Part One

1. **I don't believe the Bible!**
    - Have you read or studied the Bible?
    - If person says no: Then are you saying you don't believe in something you know nothing about?
    - If person say yes: What don't you believe about the Bible, and why don't you believe it?

2. **You don't take the Bible *literally*, do you?**
    - Why wouldn't God say what He intends to mean?

- If the Bible is God's revelation to people about Himself, His plan for salvation, and His guidelines for how He wants *all people* to live, why wouldn't He make it literal?
- Why would God make us guess what the Bible means if He wants to communicate truth to us?
- What reason would God have for *not* making the Bible literal?

3. **Everyone knows that the Bible's unreliable because it's been translated so many times during the centuries!**
   - How do you know the Bible is unreliable?
   - Where has the Bible been translated incorrectly?
   - Thousands of Bible scholars believe the Bible is reliable and translated accurately. Why do you think they're wrong?
   - Have you studied how carefully the Bible has been recopied and translated?
   - Why do you think the scholars who did this made mistakes?
   - The science of textual criticism says that the Bible is 99.5 percent accurate to the original manuscripts. Why do you think they are wrong?

4. **Everyone knows that the Bible is full of contradictions!**
   - What contradictions are you talking about? Here's my Bible. Can you show me some examples?
   - How do you know there are contradictions in the Bible?
   - What difference would it make if a few minor contradictions did exist, as long as they don't affect the historical accuracy and doctrinal truths of the Bible?
   - Since alleged contradictions in the Bible have nothing to do with the Bible's cardinal teachings, such as the deity of Jesus Christ, how do they discredit Christianity?
   - Even if a few minor copyist errors do exist, how does that prove Jesus Christ isn't God and Savior?

5. **The Bible is full of scientific inaccuracies!**
   - Can you show me one?
   - Where, for example?
   - What kind of inaccuracies?

6. **Science proves miracles never happened!**
   - How does science prove miracles never happened?
   - Miracles are a matter of history and are verified by eyewitnesses. Can science prove anything that is historical in nature, like the existence of George Washington?
   - If a transcendent, personal God exists, aren't miracles possible—even probable?

7. **You can't believe the Bible; it was written thousands of years ago!**
   - Where is the Bible historically, scientifically, or in any other way untruthful?
   - What does age have to do with truth?
   - The Bible has been proven to be more historically reliable than any other ancient text. So if you reject the Bible, you must also reject the writings of Plato, Aristotle, and the Greek and Roman historians. If you are willing to reject the Bible and not them, why would you do this?

8. **You can't trust the Bible because it was written by men.**
   - Are you saying that no book written by men or women is trustworthy?
   - Are you saying that if there is a God, He couldn't use people to record His eternal truths?
   - Don't you consider other books written by people trustworthy?
   - If you throw out the Bible because it was written by men, why shouldn't you throw out other books?

Part Two

1. **Evolution best explains the origin of life!**
   - How can something come from nothing?
   - How can order evolve from disorder?
   - How can life emerge from non-life?
   - Where are the transitional fossils?

2. **Evolution is science; creation is religion!**
   - Why should I believe that when the facts and evidences of science can be used to prove creation?
   - The debate is not about my religion or anyone else's; it's about the facts and evidences of science. If evolution is science, how does it explain . . . (e.g. how something came from nothing? how order evolved from disorder? how life emerged from non-life?)
   - Can you provide any testable scientific evidence that shows one kind of animal evolving into another kind of animal? If not, aren't you making an assumption, and what impact might that assumption make on your perspectives?
   - Can you give me even one example from the fossil record of a truly transitional fossil?

3. **Evolution is a fact of science!**
   - If it can't be demonstrated that life originated and developed through purely natural processes, isn't that belief *faith* rather than fact?
   - Why do so many leading evolutionists disagree on how evolution works (e.g. Gould, Dawkins, Crick)?
   - Scientific facts arise from repeatable observations and experimentation. Evolution depends largely on assumptions and speculations. How can you say evolution is a *fact* of science?

4. **All serious scientist are evolutionists!**
   - If that's true, how do you explain the scientific work of Michael Behe, Stephen Myers, Jonathan Wells, Henry Morris, and thousands of other scientists—many of them well known in their respective fields—who are not evolutionists?
   - How does that make evolution true? Two hundred years ago evolution was unknown and creation was the accepted model of origins. Why should being an evolutionist make someone a "serious scientist?"
   - If your view is true, why are there thousands of highly educated scientists who are creationists? Why do you think many of them

were originally evolutionists? (Hint: the evidence convinced them that creation is true!)

5. **The fossil record proves evolution!**
   - All fossils—including fish, amphibians, reptiles, birds, and mammals—are fully developed when they first appear in the fossil record and there are no transitional fossils between these major groups. How does the fossil record prove evolution?
   - Can you give me one example of a transitional fossil between fish and amphibians, or between amphibians and reptiles, or reptiles and mammals? If not, why not since you say the fossil record proves evolution?

6. **The universe began with the Big Bang!**
   - How can something come from nothing?
   - Where did the laws of physics come from that caused the Big Bang?

7. **Life emerged billions of years ago when nonliving chemicals accidentally combined to form tiny, one-celled animals!**
   - Has that theory been verified? [Note: It has never been observed in nature or performed in a laboratory.] What scientific evidence do you have to support that claim?
   - How do you explain the statistical impossibility of life emerging from non-life and then evolving into multi-celled organisms?
   - How can non-living chemicals evolve?

8. **Intelligent Design is all about a divine Creator, and therefore religion, which makes this theory a subject outside the scope of science.**
   - If Intelligent Design is religion, why do nearly all Intelligent Design proponents refuse to bring their religious beliefs into the debate, or even mention God? And why do they keep their evidence strictly scientific?
   - If the scientific evidence leads to creation, why is Intelligent Design unscientific?

- If science defines any evidence that is anti-evolutionary as outside the scope of science, doesn't that make it more of a philosophical position than a scientific one?

Part Three

1. **I don't believe that God exists!**
   - If I gave you evidence that demonstrates beyond reasonable doubt that God exists, would there be any reason for you to reject God's existence? If so, I'd like to know why.
   - Draw a circle and ask the person you are speaking with to think of the circle as representing all knowledge in the universe. Ask him or her to fill in the amount of the circle that represents his total personal knowledge. (Will probably put in a dot.) Then ask, "How do you know that God does not exist in the vast area of knowledge beyond the scope of your personal comprehension or experience?"

2. **There is no proof that God exists!**
   - Modern science says that the universe had a beginning—that it's not eternal. If God didn't create it, how did the universe come into existence? As I see it, there are only three possible ways for the universe to come into existence. It created itself, it always existed, or God created it. Since the laws of physics and logic demonstrate that the universe is not eternal and could not have caused itself to come into existence, what other option is there other than that the universe was created by God?

3. **If everything that exists has a cause, God must have a cause!**
   - Only things that have a beginning have a cause. The God of the Bible is self-existing and eternal. Why would God need a cause?
   - If God is the First Cause, what came before "first?"

4. **Atheists can be just as morally upright as Christians. We don't need a God to tell us how to behave!**
   - It's true that atheists can be just as morally upright as Christians, but why should they? If there is no God to communicate eternal

truths that set standards for moral behavior, and hold people accountable if they violate those standards, why shouldn't atheists do as they please?
- If people disagree over what's moral and immoral, and if God doesn't exist and didn't set moral standards, on what basis do we condemn pedophilia or infanticide?
- In Western civilization, traditional moral standards have their source in the Judeo/Christian religions. Doesn't this mean that the moral standards atheists accept come from God? If not, where do they come from?

5. **How can you claim that God exists when there is so much pain, suffering, and evil in the world?**
   - For the sake of argument, let's say that God doesn't exist. Now what is the solution to the problem of evil and human suffering?
   - If God *is* all loving and all powerful and yet chooses to allow pain and suffering to remain, He must have good reasons. Wouldn't it be wise to at least see what those reasons may be?
   - Why do you blame God for evil acts that people are clearly responsible for—such as war, murder, rape, and child abuse?

Part Four

1. **According to a magazine article I recently read, second-century Bible editors fabricated the stories and sayings of Jesus!**
   - How do you know the article is true? Was it written by a qualified biblical scholar or by a reporter? Who did the reporter interview?
   - Where or how are the words of Jesus fabricated?
   - Who in particular did the fabrication?
   - Why would anyone want to change the Bible?

2. **The doctrine of the Trinity arose during fourth century!**
   - Why are there numerous references to the Trinity before the fourth century?
   - What evidence do you have for saying that? Why would people invent such a perplexing belief if they wanted to manufacture a religion?

- If Jesus claimed to be God and has all the characteristics of God, why would He not be God?

3. Jesus never claimed to be God!
- If Jesus didn't claim to be God, why did His enemies (the Jewish leaders) try to stone Him and eventually had Him crucified for blasphemy?
- Which makes the most sense to believe: the eyewitnesses who wrote much of the New Testament and said that Jesus claimed to be God and proved it, or people writing two thousand years later?

4. Jesus may have been a good man or a prophet, but He isn't God!
- If Jesus claimed to be God, claimed to have the authority of God, had all the characteristics of God, and performed miracles only God can do, why do you say He isn't God?
- Let's think about this. If Jesus claimed to be God, He either is God or He was a liar or mad man. Tell me, what is there about Jesus that makes you think He is a liar or a lunatic?

5. The Gospel stories about Jesus are just religious myth!
- Since Jesus' birth, life, and resurrection are recorded by eyewitnesses (the Gospels), why do you think they're myth?
- How can a legend or myth about Jesus develop within thirty years?
- Why do you believe a documentary on a television program or a magazine article written by non-Christians instead of biblical scholars who have demonstrated that the Gospels are true?
- Since the entire Bible has been proven to be an historically reliable document, why do you think the Gospel accounts are mythical?
- If Jesus claimed to be God and proved He is God by miracles, such as the resurrection and by fulfilling hundreds of Old Testament prophecies, on what basis do you claim the Gospel accounts are mythical?

6. **Jesus' resurrection is a myth. There is no evidence that He rose from the grave!**
   - If Jesus was certified dead and buried by the Roman authorities but was later seen alive by hundreds of eyewitnesses (and no one could produce His body), how can you say that the resurrection is a myth?
   - If the resurrection is a myth, can you give a *better explanation* than the resurrection for the empty tomb, postresurrection appearances, changed lives of Jesus' disciples, birth of the Christian church around A.D. 30, and Sunday becoming a day of worship?

   Note: After asking this question, unbelievers may respond with one of the six alternate explanations we examined. Be prepared to refute each one in order to substantiate that Jesus' resurrection *is* the best explanation for the historical facts.

7. **I can't accept a God who would send people to hell just because they never heard of Jesus. That's unfair!**
   - Before you reject God, shouldn't you at least try to understand why Jesus Christ is the only way God chose to save people?
   - Where did you hear that God sends people to hell who never had the opportunity to hear about Jesus? Where does the Bible say that?
   - You don't fall into the category of people who never heard of Jesus. Shouldn't you be more concerned with your own salvation and leave it up to God to deal fairly with people who never heard of Him?
   - The Bible teaches that God does not send anyone to hell. People choose hell by rejecting the revelation that God has provided them. Would you like to hear how you can have eternal life?
   - If someone chooses to reject God, why should God take away their free will and force them to go to heaven?

8. **If people live good lives and are good persons, God will accept them into heaven!**

- How good would you have to be? What would be the criteria?
- Where did you learn that? Where did God say that in the Bible?
- How do you know that God saves people based on how good they are?
- What is there about your life that makes you so extraordinarily good that God will let you into heaven independent of Jesus Christ—when He doesn't let other people?

Part Five

1. **All religions are just as true and good as Christianity!**
   - If your view is true, it would mean that cannibalism, headhunting, and child sacrifice should be acceptable religious practices. If you reject these practices, how can you say that all religions are as true and good as Christianity?
   - If your view is true, on what basis can we condemn the degradation of women and slavery that are practiced in some religions?
   - Do you think that the traditional Hindu prohibition against reaching out to the so-called "untouchables" in their society was just as virtuous as the biblical teaching to help poor and starving people?

2. **You Christians have no right to judge other people's behavior!**
   - If people can't judge other people's behavior, how can teachers condemn students who cheat on tests?
   - If people can't judge other people's behavior, how can laws be formulated to condemn people who murder and rape?
   - If people have no right to judge other people's behavior, why shouldn't sexual relationships with children be permissible?
   - If people have no right to judge other people's behavior, why can't torturing people for fun be on reality television programs if the public wants to watch it?

Note: In the responses above, I have purposely constructed exaggerated scenarios that few, if any, non-Christians will endorse.

The idea is to help non-Christians understand that moral relativism, carried to its logical conclusion, is an unlivable worldview. No one will live consistently with moral relativism. By rejecting these practices as immoral, non-Christians are recognizing that absolutes *do* exist.

3. **You Christians are a bunch of hypocrites. You have never done anything good for society, just interfered in people's lives!**
   - Tell me, what other religion has done more than Christianity to help people outside their own religion?
   - Christians started many of America's great universities. Many orphanages, hospitals, and charity organizations were begun and operated by Christians. Hundreds of Christian relief organizations exist around the world, and Christians are among the first to respond to natural disasters. Christian ethics eventually destroyed the institution of slavery and promoted women's emancipation. Biblical characters have inspired many of Western civilization's greatest paintings and sculptures. Mostly Christians wrote our Constitution. I could go on and on. Explain to me why you believe Christians are hypocrites and have never done anything good for society.

4. **I think a woman has a right to do what she wants with her own body (i.e. have an abortion)!**
   - If you were pregnant, what would be inside you—a human being or something else?
   - Why do you think an unborn child is not a human being when science demonstrates that life begins at conception?
   - If the fetus is a human being, why shouldn't it be protected by law just like any other person?
   - Why should it be permissible to take the life of another human being just because someone wants to?
   - How can an unborn baby be merely tissue in the case of an abortion and then become a person in a lawsuit, such as when a mother is prosecuted for taking drugs that harm her fetus?

Note: The crux of all abortion arguments is to demonstrate that the fetus is a living person. If life begins at conception, and science clearly demonstrates that it does, the unborn child is entitled to all the rights and protection of any other human being.

5. **All religions are equal; they are just different paths to the same God!**
   - How can all religions be equal when most of them claim to be superior to all other religions?
   - How can all religions be paths to the same God when they have different views on the nature of God, the way to achieve salvation, and virtually every other major doctrine?

6. **You Christians are so intolerant; you think everyone's beliefs are wrong but yours!**
   - If you are tolerant, why do you condemn me for having my beliefs?
   - You think I'm intolerant because I think my view is right, but you think your view is right and you're *not* intolerant. Why isn't this a double standard?

7. **It doesn't matter what I believe as long as it meets my spiritual needs!**
   - What if you're wrong? What if your religious belief leads away from God? Why are you willing to take that risk?
   - What if Jesus really is the only way to God, as the Bible says? Can you explain to me why you are unwilling to check-out Christianity?
   - What do you mean by "spiritual needs?" If the answer is something like, "I feel at peace," or "I experience spiritual fulfillment," or "my heart tells me my beliefs are true," ask the follow-up question: "How does feeling that something is true make it true?" Note: Christians also experience peace and subjective confirmation. However, our faith is based on something objectively tangible—the Bible. We can test our feelings and religious experiences to see if they are from God or from our own emotions. If our sub-

jective feelings are not in harmony with God's Word, they are not from God.

8. **There are no absolute truths!**
   - Are you *absolutely* certain that's true?
   - If there are no absolute truths, why should I believe your statement, "There are no absolute truths"?

9. **Even if truth exists, we can't discover it!**
   - Why should I believe that statement if truth doesn't exist or can't be discovered?
   - Is that a true statement, or are you guessing?

10. **A college professor says in class, "There are no absolute truths!" To humorously illustrate how nonsensical the statement is (we don't want to get on the professor's "bad side"), we raise our hand and ask:**
    - Do you believe what you teach is true?
    - Do you give true and false tests?
    - Does that mean I can give an answer that is wrong to you and it can still be correct because I think it's true?